Communications
in Computer and Information Science   1073

Commenced Publication in 2007
Founding and Former Series Editors:
Phoebe Chen, Alfredo Cuzzocrea, Xiaoyong Du, Orhun Kara, Ting Liu,
Krishna M. Sivalingam, Dominik Ślęzak, Takashi Washio, and Xiaokang Yang

More information about this series at http://www.springer.com/series/7899

Víctor Méndez Muñoz ·
Donald Ferguson · Markus Helfert ·
Claus Pahl (Eds.)

Cloud Computing and Services Science

8th International Conference, CLOSER 2018
Funchal, Madeira, Portugal, March 19–21, 2018
Revised Selected Papers

 Springer

Editors
Víctor Méndez Muñoz
Escola d'Enginyeria
Bellaterra, Barcelona, Spain

Donald Ferguson
Columbia University
New York, USA

Markus Helfert
Dublin City University
Dublin 9, Ireland

Claus Pahl
Free University of Bozen-Bolzano
Bolzano, Bolzano, Italy

ISSN 1865-0929   ISSN 1865-0937 (electronic)
Communications in Computer and Information Science
ISBN 978-3-030-29192-1   ISBN 978-3-030-29193-8 (eBook)
https://doi.org/10.1007/978-3-030-29193-8

This Springer imprint is published by the registered company Springer Nature Switzerland AG
The registered company address is: Gewerbestrasse 11, 6330 Cham, Switzerland

Preface

This book includes extended and revised versions of selected papers from the 8th International Conference on Cloud Computing and Services Science (CLOSER 2018), held in Funchal, Madeira, Portugal, during March 19–21, 2018.

CLOSER 2018 received 94 paper submissions from 33 countries, of which 10% were included in this book. The papers were selected by the event chairs. Their selection is based on a number of criteria that include the classifications and comments provided by the Program Committee members, the session chairs' assessment and also the program chairs' global view of all papers included in the technical program. The authors of selected papers were then invited to submit a revised and extended version of their papers having at least 30% new material.

CLOSER 2018, focused on the emerging area of Cloud Computing, inspired by some of the latest advances that concern the infrastructure, operations, and available services through the global network. Furthermore, the conference considers the link to Service Science as essential, acknowledging the service-orientation in most current IT-driven collaborations. The conference is nevertheless not about the union of these two (already broad) fields, but rather focuses on Cloud Computing. We included the related and emerging topic of Services Science's theory, methods, and techniques to design, analyze, manage, market, and study various aspects of Cloud Computing. Service Science focuses on the intersection between technology and business and helps to understand a range of service systems, as well as how these evolve to create value.

This year's edition includes papers that cover a wide range of topics and challenges, including Measuring Cost in Cloud Migration projects and Cost-efficient Datacentre Consolidation. In order to design and architect cloud system, topics of architecting Microservices, Optimising Quality of Services, and interoperability issues are discussed. Furthermore, papers on service Development on the Cloud and Model-based Generation of Self-Adaptive Cloud Services have been included. Finally emerging and important topics of Malicious Behavior Classification and Energy-Efficient Ge-Distributed Data Centres are discussed.

We would like to thank all the authors for their contributions and also to the reviewers who have help ensure the quality of this publication.

March 2018

Donald Ferguson
Víctor Méndez Muñoz
Markus Helfert
Claus Pahl

Organization

Conference Co-chairs

Markus Helfert   Dublin City University, Ireland
Claus Pahl   Free University of Bozen-Bolzano, Italy

Program Co-chairs

Víctor Méndez Muñoz   IUL, S.A., Universitat Autònoma de Barcelona (UAB), Spain
Donald Ferguson   Columbia University, USA

Program Committee

Alina Andreica   Babes-Bolyai University, Romania
Claudio Ardagna   Universita degli Studi di Milano, Italy
Amelia Badica   Faculty of Economics and Business Administration, University of Craiova, Romania
Marcos Barreto   Federal University of Bahia (UFBA), Brazil
Simona Bernardi   Universidad de Zaragoza, Spain
Nik Bessis   Edge Hill University, UK
Ivona Brandić   Vienna UT, Austria
Iris Braun   Dresden Technical University, Germany
Andrey Brito   Universidade Federal de Campina Grande, Brazil
Ralf Bruns   Hannover University of Applied Sciences and Arts, Germany
Anna Brunstrom   Karlstad University, Sweden
Rebecca Bulander   Pforzheim University of Applied Science, Germany
Tomas Bures   Charles University in Prague, Czech Republic
Manuel Capel-Tuñón   University of Granada, Spain
Eddy Caron   École Normale Supérieure de Lyon, France
John Cartlidge   University of Bristol, UK
Roy Cecil   IBM Portugal, Portugal
Rong Chang   IBM T. J. Watson Research Center, USA
Augusto Ciuffoletti   Università di Pisa, Italy
Daniela Claro   Universidade Federal da Bahia (UFBA), Brazil
Thierry Coupaye   Orange, France
Tommaso Cucinotta   Scuola Superiore Sant'Anna, Italy
Tarcísio da Rocha   Universidade Federal de Sergipe, Brazil
Mohanad Dawoud   Istanbul Technical University, Turkey
Eliezer Dekel   Huawei Technologies, Israel
Frédéric Desprez   Antenne Inria Giant, France

Patrick Dreher	North Carolina State University, USA
Vincent Emeakaroha	Cork Institute of Technology, Ireland
Ruksar Fatima	KBN College of Engineering, India
Tomás Fernández Pena	Universidad Santiago de Compostela, Spain
Mike Fisher	BT, UK
Geoffrey Fox	Indiana University, USA
Somchart Fugkeaw	University of Tokyo, Japan
Fabrizio Gagliardi	Barcelona Supercomputing Centre, Spain
Antonio García Loureiro	University of Santiago de Compostela, Spain
Chirine Ghedira	IAE - University Jean Moulin Lyon 3, France
Lee Gillam	University of Surrey, UK
Katja Gilly	Miguel Hernandez University, Spain
Jose Gonzalez de Mendivil	Universidad Publica de Navarra, Spain
Dirk Habich	Technische Universität Dresden, Germany
Mohamed Hussien	Suez Canal University, Egypt
Ilian Ilkov	IBM Nederland B.V., The Netherlands
Anca Ionita	University Politehnica of Bucharest, Romania
Hiroshi Ishikawa	Tokyo Metropolitan University, Japan
Ivan Ivanov	SUNY Empire State College, USA
Martin Jaatun	University of Stavanger, Norway
Keith Jeffery	Independent Consultant (previously Science and Technology Facilities Council), UK
Yiming Ji	University of South Carolina Beaufort, USA
Ming Jiang	University of Sunderland, UK
Xiaolong Jin	Chinese Academy of Sciences, China
Carlos Juiz	Universitat de les Illes Balears, Spain
Péter Kacsuk	MTA SZTAKI, Hungary
David Kaeli	Northeastern University, USA
Yücel Karabulut	Oracle, USA
Attila Kertesz	University of Szeged, Hungary
Carsten Kleiner	University of Applied Sciences and Arts Hannover, Germany
Ioannis Konstantinou	NTUA, Greece
Nane Kratzke	Lübeck University of Applied Sciences, Germany
Kyriakos Kritikos	ICS-FORTH, Greece
Ulrich Lampe	TU Darmstadt, Germany
Riccardo Lancellotti	University of Modena and Reggio Emilia, Italy
Donghui Lin	Kyoto University, Japan
Shijun Liu	School of Computer Science and Technology, Shandong University, China
Xiaodong Liu	Edinburgh Napier University, UK
Francesco Longo	Università degli Studi di Messina, Italy
Simone Ludwig	North Dakota State University, USA
Glenn Luecke	Iowa State University, USA
Shikharesh Majumdar	Carleton University, Canada
Ioannis Mavridis	University of Macedonia, Greece

Víctor Méndez Muñoz	IUL, S.A., Universitat Autönoma de Barcelona (UAB), Spain
Andre Miede	Hochschule für Technik und Wirtschaft des Saarlandes, Germany
Mohamed Mohamed	IBM Research, Almaden, USA
Hidemoto Nakada	National Institute of Advanced Industrial Science and Technology (AIST), Japan
Philippe Navaux	UFRGS - Federal University of Rio Grande Do Sul, Brazil
Mats Neovius	Äbo Akademi University, Finland
Jean-Marc Nicod	Institut FEMTO-ST, France
Bogdan Nicolae	IBM Research, Ireland
Mara Nikolaidou	Harokopio University of Athens, Greece
Emmanuel Ogunshile	The University of the West of England, UK
Enn Ounapuu	Tallinn University of Technology, Estonia
Tolga Ovatman	Istanbul Technical University, Turkey
Claus Pahl	Free University of Bozen-Bolzano, Italy
Michael Palis	Rutgers University, USA
Mike Papazoglou	Tilburg University, The Netherlands
Nikos Parlavantzas	IRISA, France
David Paul	The University of New England, Australia
Agostino Poggi	University of Parma, Italy
Antonio Puliafito	Universià degli Studi di Messina, Italy
Rajendra Raj	Rochester Institute of Technology, USA
Arcot Rajasekar	University of North Carolina at Chapel Hill, USA
Arkalgud Ramaprasad	University of Illinois at Chicago, USA
Manuel Ramos-Cabrer	University of Vigo, Spain
Christoph Reich	Hochschule Furtwangen University, Germany
Daniel Rodriguez-Silva	Gradiant, Spain
Pedro Rosa	UFU - Federal University of Uberlandia, Brazil
António Miguel Rosado da Cruz	Instituto Politécnico de Viana do Castelo, Portugal
Evangelos Sakkopoulos	University of Piraeus, Greece
Elena Sanchez-Nielsen	Universidad De La Laguna, Spain
Patrizia Scandurra	University of Bergamo, Italy
Erich Schikuta	Universität Wien, Austria
Lutz Schubert	Ulm University, Germany
Stefan Schulte	Technische Universität Darmstadt, Germany
Rami Sellami	CETIC, Belgium
Wael Sellami	Higher Institute of Computer Sciences of Mahdia, Tunisia
Giovanni Semeraro	University of Bari Aldo Moro, Italy
Carlos Serrão	ISCTE - Instituto Universitário de Lisboa, Portugal
Armin Shams	Sharif University of Technology, Iran
Keiichi Shima	IIJ Innovation Institute, Japan
Adenilso Simäo	Universidade de São Paulo, Brazil

Frank Siqueira	Universidade Federal de Santa Catarina, Brazil
Josef Spillner	Zurich University of Applied Sciences, Switzerland
Ralf Steinmetz	Technische Universität Darmstadt, Germany
Yasuyuki Tahara	The University of Electro-Communications, Japan
Cedric Tedeschi	IRISA - University of Rennes 1, France
Gilbert Tekli	Nobatek, France
Joe Tekli	Lebanese American University (LAU), Lebanon
Guy Tel-Zur	Ben-Gurion University of the Negev (BGU), Israel
Rafael Tolosana-Calasanz	University of Zaragoza, Spain
Michele Tomaiuolo	University of Parma, Italy
Orazio Tomarchio	University of Catania, Italy
Slim Trabelsi	SAP, France
Francesco Tusa	University College London, UK
Geoffroy Vallee	Oak Ridge National Laboratory, USA
Robert van Engelen	Florida State University, USA
Bruno Volckaert	Ghent University, Belgium
Mladen Vouk	N.C. State University, USA
Bo Yang	University of Electronic Science and Technology of China, China
George Yee	Carleton University, Canada
Michael Zapf	Georg Simon Ohm University of Applied Sciences, Germany
Wolfgang Ziegler	Fraunhofer Institute SCAI, Germany

Additional Reviewers

Sonja Bergstraesser	TU Darmstadt, Germany
Belen Bermejo	University of the Balearic Islands, Spain
Alexander Froemmgen	TU Darmstadt, Germany
Cedric Hebert	SAP Labs France, France
Alexis Huf	Federal University of Santa Catarina, Brazil
Menelaos Katsantonis	University of Macedonia, Greece
Christian Koch	Technische Universität Darmstadt, Germany
Alfonso Panarello	Universià degli Studi di Messina, Italy
Benedikt Pittl	University of Vienna, Austria
Daniel Presser	Universidade Federal de Santa Catarina, Brazil
Eduardo Roloff	UFRGS, Brazil
Giuseppe Tricomi	Università degli studi di Messina, Italy

Invited Speakers

Mike Papazoglou	Tilburg University, The Netherlands
Tobias Hoellwarth	EuroCloud Europe, Austria
Péter Kacsuk	MTA SZTAKI, Hungary
Lee Gillam	University of Surrey, UK

Contents

CELA: Cost-Efficient, Location-Aware VM and Data Placement in Geo-Distributed DCs

Soha Rawas$^{(\boxtimes)}$, Ahmed Zekri$^{(\boxtimes)}$, and Ali El Zaart$^{(\boxtimes)}$

Department of Mathematics and Computer Science,
Beirut Arab University, Beirut, Lebanon
{srawas,a.zekri,Elzaart}@bau.edu.lb

Abstract. Geo-distributed data centres (DCs) that recently established due to the increasing use of on-demand cloud services have increasingly attracted cloud providers as well as researchers attention. Energy and data transmission cost are two significant problems that degrades the cloud provider net profit. However, increasing awareness about CO2 emissions leads to a greater demand for cleaner products and services. Most of the proposed approaches tackle these problems separately. This paper proposes green approach for joint management of virtual machine (VM) and data placement that results in less energy consumption, less CO2 emission, and less access latency towards large-scale cloud providers operational cost minimization. To advance the performance of the proposed model, a novel machine-learning model was constructed. Extensive simulation using synthetic and real data are conducted using the CloudSim simulator to validate the effectiveness of the proposed model. The promising results approve the efficacy of the CELA model compared to other competing models in reducing network latency, energy consumption, CO2 emission and total cloud provider operational cost.

Keywords: Carbon footprint · Energy-efficient · Latency ·
Geo-distributed data centres

1 Introduction

Cloud computing plays a significant role in today's network computing by delivering virtualized resources as pay-as-you-go services over the Internet. However, the growing demand for cloud computing services has led to the establishment of geo-distributed DCs worldwide with thousands of computing and storage nodes to ensure availability and disaster recovery. Consequently, this led to a radical increase in the DCs' energy consumption, turning it into high operational cost rates, low profits for Cloud providers, and high carbon non-environment friendly emissions [1]. Figure 1 displays the Synapse Energy Economics CO2 price/Ton forecast that will be applied all over the world by the beginning of 2020 [2]. Moreover, increasing awareness about CO2 emissions leads to a greater demand for cleaner products and services. Thus, many companies have started to build "green" DCs, i.e. DCs with on-site renewable power plants to reduce the CO2 emission which leads to operational cost minimization [3].

© Springer Nature Switzerland AG 2019
V. M. Muñoz et al. (Eds.): CLOSER 2018, CCIS 1073, pp. 1–23, 2019.
https://doi.org/10.1007/978-3-030-29193-8_1

An important fact is that the carbon emission rate varies from one DC to another based on the different energy sources used to power-on the cloud DC resources (such as coal, oil, and other renewable and non-renewable resources) [4]. Moreover, the CO2 emission of DC is closely related to electricity cost paid by cloud provider since it depends on the sources used to produce electricity [5]. Therefore, selecting a proper data centre for customer's requests dispatching attract research attention and have become an emergent issue for modern geo-distributed cloud DCs in big data era.

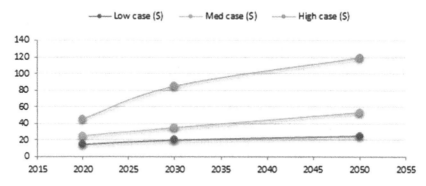

Fig. 1. 2016 CO2 Price/Ton forecast by Synapse extracted from [2].

The modern geo-distributed data centres proposed as a new platform idea are inter-connected with cloud users via the Internet. One of the most challenging problems for this environment is network latency when serving user request. Studies show that minimizing latency leads to less bandwidth consumption [6]. This consequently improves the pro-vider revenue by minimizing the Wide Area Network (WAN) communication cost. Latency, which refers to the time required to transfer the user request from user's end to the DC, is also taken into consideration for Service Level Agreement (SLA) and Quality of Service (QoS) purposes. Bauer et al. [7] show that Amazon Company can undergo 1% sales reduction for a 100-millisecond increase in service latency.

Inspired by the heterogeneity of DCs, carbon emission rate and their modern geographical distribution, this paper studies the virtual machine (VM) placement and the physical machine selections that result in less energy consumption, less CO2 emission, and less access latency while guaranteeing the QoS. The main contributions of this study are as follows:

1- Cost-Efficient, Location-aware VM placement model (CELA) to beneficially affect the cloud user and the cloud service provider.
2- Investigate the initial placement of offline and online user request to enable the tradeoff among the latency, energy consumption of the physical machines, and the CO2 emission rate in geo-distributed cloud DCs.
3- Intelligent machine-learning method to improve the performance of the proposed CELA model.
4- Comprehensive analysis and extensive simulation to study the efficacy of the proposed model using both synthetic and real DCs workload.

The rest of the paper is organized as follows: Sect. 2 studies the related work concerning the VM placement methods in geo-distributed data centres. Section 3 presents the problem statement and the proposed model. Section 4 presents the proposed online and offline VM policies. Section 5 presents the performance metrics that have been used to evaluate the proposed model. Section 6 models the intelligent machine-learning method for normalized weight prediction. Section 7 presents the evaluation method using CloudSim simulation toolkit. Section 8 concludes the paper and presents future work.

2 Related Work

With the increase of distributed systems, the problem of resource allocation attracted researchers from its different views inspired by the heterogeneity of the modern large-scale geo-distributed data centres.

Khosravi et al. [4] propose a VM placement algorithm in distributed DCs by developing the Energy and Carbon-Efficient (ECE) Cloud architecture. This architecture benefits from distributed cloud data centres with different carbon footprint rates, Power Usage Effectiveness (PUE) value, and different physical servers' proportional power by placing VM requests in the best-suited DC site and physical server. However, the ECE placement method does not address the network distance and considers that the distributed DCs are located in the same USA region where the communication latency and cost are negligible. Chen et al. [6] modeled the VM placement method in terms of electricity cost and WAN communication cost incurred between the communicated VMs. Ahvar et al. [8] addressed the problem of DCs selection for inter- communicated VMs to minimize the inter-DCs communication cost. Malekimajd et al. [9] proposed an algorithm to minimize the communication latency in geo-distributed clouds. Jonardi et al. [10] considered the time-of-use (TOU) electricity prices and renewable energy sources when selecting DCs. Fan et al. [5] modeled the VM placement problem using the WAN latency, network, and servers' energy consumption factors.

The proposed model is different from the aforementioned ones since it jointly considers the energy consumption of the servers, CO2 emission rate of DCs, and WAN link access latency and its cost when cloud provider take a decision in DCs selection.

3 System Model

In this section, we describe CELA, a Power and Cost aware Virtual Machine placement model for serving users' request in geo-distributed cloud environment. CELA performs user request by weighting each request's effect on three important metrics that increase the providers as well as the cloud users cost: carbon emission rate, energy consumption, and access latency.

3.1 Motivation and Typical Scenario

With more than 900 K servers, Google has 13 data centres distributed within 13 countries around the world (Google). While Amazon Application Web Services

(AWS) has 42 data centres within 16 geographical regions with more than 1.3 million servers [11]. Consequently, the operating cost has become a predominant factor to the cloud services deployment cost.

The worldwide distribution of DCs provides the fact that different geographical regions mean different energy sources (coal, fuel, wind, solar energy, etc.). DC's CO2 emission rate depends on the used electricity driven by these energy sources to run the physical machines [12]. Additionally, PUE can be considered as an effective parameter to perform the VM placement. It indicates the energy efficiency of the DC [4]. Proportional power of physical machines is another important parameter. Selecting proper physical machines to process user's request has a great impact on energy consumption [1]. Network latency and latency cost (lc) have a great impact on cloud QoS and increases the cloud provider operational cost.

Considering these important parameters, the CELA model aims to select the best suited DC site and physical servers to increase the environmental sustainability and minimize the cloud provider's operating cost.

3.2 Cloud Model Architecture

This section presents the cloud architecture model that captures the relationship between cloud users and geo-distributed cloud environment. Figure 2 encapsulates a simple abstract model representing the relation between the following two main sides: Users side and the Cloud side.

1- User Side: Cloud Users send their Service Request to the Cloud side. The requested services may be an application of any type such as: data transmission (uploading or downloading), web application, data or compute-intensive applications.

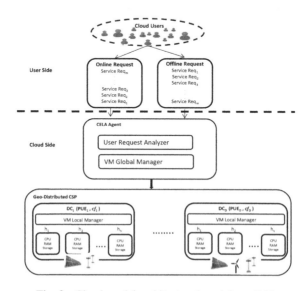

Fig. 2. Cloud model architecture based from [13].

Cloud Users' requests can be Online or Offline Request. The Online Request is an expensive Service Request with high priority. This type of users' request is processed by the Cloud instantaneously. The Offline Request, on the other hand, are handled as batches by the Cloud side.

2- Cloud Side: This side presents the cloud infrastructure and it is made up of the following two main sub components:

a- CELA Agent: The CELA is a cloud service provider's (CSP) broker that acts as an intermediary between the cloud user and the CSP services. The goal of this agent is to redirect the user request to the nearest DC site that process requested services in a greener and minimum operational cost without scarifying cloud QoS. It contains the following sub components:

- User Request Analyzer (URA): its functions are
  - For each user's Service Request (Req_i), it allocates the proper VM (VM_i) to serve the cloud users.
  - Interprets and analyzes the requirements of submitted requested services (in terms of CPU, RAM, Storage, Bandwidth ...) to find the proper VMs that serves the requested services.
  - Finalizes the SLAs with specified prices and penalties depending on user's QoS requirements.
- VM Global Manager: Global cloud resources manager
  - Receives the set of VMs from URA. It interacts with Geo-Distributed CSP VM Local Managers to check each DC PUE, carbon footprint emission rate (cf), and latency cost (lc) to take the best VM placement decision on the DC site selection (lc and cf illustrated in Sect. 3.3).
  - Observes energy consumption caused by VMs placed on physical machines and provides this information to the DC site VM Local Manager to make optimization and energy-efficient management decisions.
  - Provides the VM Local Manager of the selected DC site that should process the cloud user's request with the VM placement decision policy (as proposed in Sect. 4).

b- Geo-Distributed CSP: A service provider has geo-distributed DCs. Each DC has heterogeneous computing and storage resources as well as different utilities and energy sources. Each DC contains an essential node called VM Local Manager. The VM Local Manager applies VM management and resource allocation policies as suggested by the VM Global Manager. Moreover, it calculates energy and carbon emission rate of DC resources to provide this information to the VM Global Manager.

3.3 Problem Formulation

Table 1 summarizes the various notations used in the proposed VM placement problem formulation.

Table 1. Problem formulation notations.

Notation	Description
D	Number of DC sites
H	Number of hosts at each DC
V	Total number of VMs on host h_j
P_{idle}	Server power consumption with no load
P_{full}	Fully utilized server power consumption
U	Amount of CPU utilization
PUE_i	The power usage effectiveness of DC site i
$UnitTransferCost(u_e, dc_i)$	the unit transfer cost of between DC site dc_i and cloud user u_e; \$/GB
$ComCost(flowSize_{d_k}(u_e, dc_i))$	the communication cost for a flow size of data d_k from user u_e served by DC site dc_i
$flowSize_{d_k}(u_e, dc_i)$	flow size of data d_k from user u_e served by DC site dc_i
$Cost_{CO2Emission}$	Total CO2 emission cost; \$
$Cost_{Communication}$	Total communication cost; \$
$UnitEmissionCost_{CO2}$	CO2 emission cost per ton; \$/Ton
CF	Total CO2 emission at a time interval [0, T]; Ton
cf_j	DC site i CO2 emission rate; Ton/MWh
Users	Total number of users requesting cloud services at time t
data	Set of requested user's services data
$p_{d_k}(u_e, dc_i)$	is 1 if data d_k is placed in server hj in DC dc_i; otherwise, it is 0

Preliminaries

To model the VM placement method, a number of factors are considered, these parameters demonstrated as preliminaries before proceeding in complete formulation.

Power Consumption Model

In this paper, the energy consumption and saving predicted as used in [13]. A linear power model verifies that the servers' power consumption is almost linearly with its CPU utilization. This relationship could be illustrated using the following equation:

$$P(u) = P_{idle} + \left(P_{full} - P_{idle}\right) * u \tag{1}$$

where P_{idle} is server power consumption with no load, P_{full} is fully utilized server power consumption, and u is the amount of CPU utilization.

Therefore, the power consumption of a server/host hj holding a number of VMs v on data centre site i during the slot time [0, T] is denoted as $P\left(h_{(i,j)}\right)$. Noting that each host can hold more than one VM: $h_{(i,j)} = \sum_{k=1}^{v} VM_{k,i,j}$ and each VM is executed at only one host such that: $\sum_{i=1}^{D} \sum_{j=1}^{h} VM_{k,i,j} = 1, \forall VM_k$.

Power Usage Effectiveness (PUE)

PUE is the most popular measure of data centre energy efficiency. It was devised by the Green Grid consortium [5]. It is a metric used to compares different DC designs in terms of electricity consumption [4]. The PUE of DC i is calculated as follows:

$$PUE_i = \frac{dc_i TotalPowerConsumption}{dc_i ITDevicesPowerConsumption} \tag{2}$$

where $dc_i TotalPowerConsumption$, is the total amount of energy consumed by DC facilities such the cooling system, the IT equipment, lightning, etc. The $dc_i ITDevicesPowerConsumption$ is the power drawn due to IT devices equipment.

Network Model

Figure 3 shows the network model for the data transmission between the cloud users who are graphically at the same region, and the DC site that is similar to the one presented in [5, 13]. Therefore, we assume that each user ue is connected by a WAN link. These links cost the cloud provider whose bill is based on the actual usage over a billing period [6]. The unit cost of data transfer between the DC site dci and cloud user ue is denoted as UnitTransferCost(ue,dci) in \$/GB. However, the cost of intra-DC communication is ignored since it is very low compared with WAN transfer cost [5]. Therefore, the communication cost for a flow size of data dk (GB) from user ue served by DC site dci is calculated as follows (see Fig. 4):

$$ComCost(flowSize_{d_k}(u_e, dc_i)) = UnitTransferCost(u_e, dc_i) * flowSize(d_k) \tag{3}$$

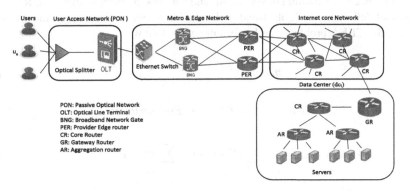

Fig. 3. Users connected to DC through WAN extracted from [5, 13].

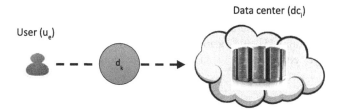

Fig. 4. User (u_e) sends data (d_k) to DC (dc_i) Scheme extracted from [5].

Carbon Footprint Emission Rate (cf)

DC carbon footprint emission rate is measured in g/kW. It depends on the DC energy sources and electricity utilities. Therefore, the carbon footprint emission rate of DC i operated using l number of energy sources (such as, coal, gas, others) is computed as follows [12]:

$$cf_i = \frac{\sum_{k=1}^{l} E_{i,k} * cr_k}{\sum_{k=1}^{l} E_{i,k}} \tag{4}$$

where $E_{i,k}$ is the electricity generated by energy source k (such as coal), and cr_k is the carbon emission rate of the used utility k.

Modeling of the Optimization Problem

The CELA aim to minimize the total cost through minimizing the weighted sum of the two main objectives: carbon emission cost, and network communication cost. Refers to the symbol definitions in Table 1 and preliminaries model as discussed in the previous sections, the CELA problem can be formulated as follows:

$$minimize \left(\begin{matrix} Cost_{CO2Emission} \\ Cost_{Comm} \end{matrix} \right) \tag{5}$$

$$Cost_{CO2Emission} = CF * UnitEmissionCost_{CO2} \tag{6}$$

$$CF = \sum_{i=1}^{D} PUE_i * cf_i * \sum_{j=1}^{h} P(h_{i,j}) \tag{7}$$

$$Cost_{Communication} = \sum_{i=1}^{D} \sum_{e=1}^{users} \sum_{k=1}^{data} ComCost(flowSize_{d_k}(u_e, dc_i)) \tag{8}$$

subject to:

$$\sum_{i=1}^{D} \sum_{j=1}^{h} p_{d_k}(h_j, dc_i) = 1, \forall d_k \tag{9}$$

$$\sum_{i=1}^{D} \sum_{j=1}^{h} v_{(i,j)}^{core} \leq host_{(i,j)}^{core} \tag{10}$$

$$\sum_{i=1}^{D} \sum_{j=1}^{h} v_{(i,j)}^{ram} \leq host_{(i,j)}^{ram} \tag{11}$$

$$\sum_{i=1}^{D} \sum_{j=1}^{h} v_{(i,j)}^{storage} \leq host_{(i,j)}^{storage} \tag{12}$$

$$\sum_{i=1}^{D} \sum_{j=1}^{h} v_{(i,j)}^{bandwidth} \leq host_{(i,j)}^{bandwidth} \tag{13}$$

Equation 5 presents the CELA optimization model. Equation 6 shows that the total CO_2 emission cost is equal to the CO_2 unit emission cost per ton multiplied by the total DCs' CO_2 emission for time interval [0, T]. Equation 7 calculates the total carbon footprint (CF) of cloud provider that depends on a number of factors as illustrated above. Equation 8 represents the communication cost. It depends on users' flow size as well as the unit cost of data transfer from cloud users' location to selected DC's site. Equation 9 mandates that a user request is executed at only one DC. Equations (10, 11, 12, 13) dictates that the resources requirements of the mapped VMs on a physical server cannot exceed the total capacity of the server.

4 CELA Heuristics for VM Placement

We propose different VM placement algorithms for the LECC agent that is aware of energy consumption, *PUE*, CO_2 emission rate (*cf*) and network latency cost (*lc*). More specifically the LECC agent follow the following methodology.

In this section, different VM placement policies for the CELA agent are proposed. More specifically the CELA agent follow the following methodology:

1. Select the DCs location from given set of D available DCs. The main goal of this step is to satisfy the CELA multi-objective optimization functions, i.e. minimize the total cost: carbon emission cost and network communication cost the form the CELA model (Eq. 5). To satisfy this goal, CELA agent should select the DCs with minimum PUE, cf, and lc using Eq. 14.

$$minimum(\alpha_1 * PUE * cf + \alpha_2 * lc) \tag{14}$$

where $\alpha_1 \& \alpha_2$ are constant normalized weights used for weighting the two sub-objectives such that $\alpha_1 + \alpha_2 = 1$ (Sect. 6 demonstrates how these weights are calculated using intelligent machine learning model).

2. Apply energy efficient VM placement policies in the selected DCs based on cloud user's request type.

4.1   Offline MF-CELA

Offline-CELA VM placement: indicates offline VM placement such that the requested services requirements are prior known by the CELA Global Manager.

Assume that D is the total number of DC sites and each DC site has h number of servers, such that h varies between DCs. At a certain time t, CELA agent tries to optimally place the user VMs. For the offline cloud user's requested services, we propose the MF-CELA VM placement algorithm (see Algorithm 1 below). It is a greedy method that selects a DC site with minimum communication latency cost, minimum PUE and minimum CO2 emission rate. In addition, the algorithm tries to minimize the number of selected active servers.

Algorithm 1. Most-Full Power and Cost-aware virtual machine placement (MF-CELA).

<u>Input</u>: DC sites D={$dc_1, dc_2, ..., dc_s$}
HostList at each DC site h={$h_1, h_2, ... h_h$}
Users request vmList V={$vm_1, vm_2, ..., vm_n$},
Network latency cost matrix $lc(u_e, dc_j)$
<u>Output</u>: destination for requested V's
<u>Processing</u>:
1: Get information from DCs VM Local Manager
2: Sort DC sites D in an ascending order of $(\alpha 1 * PUE * cf + \alpha 2 * lc)$
3: Fed selected DC site VM Local Manager to apply
   Most-Full VM placement Policy
4: Sort hostList h in an ascending order to its
   Utilization
5: For each vm in vmList V do
6:   While host h_j has enough capacity to accommodate vm_u
7:       set vm_u at host h_j
8:   End While
9: End For

The URA module in the CELA agent receives the users requests and produces the proper VMs; the VM Global Manager utilizes the information given by the CSPs VM Local Manager to take the best DC site selection that has the minimum ($\alpha 1$ * PUE * cf + $\alpha 2$ * lc) (line 2). Then, it feeds the selected DC site VM Local Manager with Most-Full VM placement policy decision. The VM Local Manager sorts the host lists in an ascending order to its Utilization (line 4). If the selected host hj has enough resources for VM accommodation (line 6–8), hj will be a destination for vmu.

4.2   Online BF-CELA

Online-CELA VM placement: indicates online and continuous VM placement during the run-time of the DCs. The user's requests are coming one by one, such that the CELA Global Manager has no prior information about the requested services requirements.

BF-CELA method is also a greedy algorithm (see Algorithm 2 below) that uses the Best Fit method for VMs placement and servers selections after locating DC sites with minimum communication latency cost, PUE and CO2 emission rate (line 2).

Algorithm 2. Best-Fit Power and Cost-aware virtual machine placement (BF-CELA).

Input: DC sites D={dc_1,dc_2,...,dc_s}
HostList at each DC site h={h_1, h_2, ... h_h}
Users request vmList V={vm_1,vm_2,...,vm_n},
Network latency cost matrix $lc(u_e, dc_j)$
Output: destination for requested V's
Processing:
1: While vmList do
2:    Get information from DCs VM Local Manager
3:    Sort DC sites D in an ascending order of ($\alpha1 * PUE * cf + \alpha2 * lc$)
4: Fed selected DC site VM Local Manager to apply Best-Fit VM placement Policy
5: Sort hostList h in an ascending order to its Availability
6:    For each host in sorted hostList
7:         if host h_j is suitable for vm_u
8:              set vm_u at host h_j
9:    End For
10: End While

We adapted the Best-Fit VM placement strategy so that the VM Local Manager sorts the list of host in an ascending order to its Availability (line 5). If the selected host hj has enough resources for VM accommodation (line 6–9), hj will be a destination for vmu.

4.3   Online BF-SLA-CELA

The aim of the BF-SLA-CELA algorithm is to provide a trade-off between SLA violations and energy saving to minimize the penalties cost for SLA violations per active host.

Algorithm 3. Best-Fit SLA violation, Power and Cost-aware virtual machine placement (BF-SLA-CELA).

Input: DC sites D={dc_1,dc_2,...,dc_s}
HostList at each DC site h={h_1, h_2, ... h_h}
Users request vmList V={vm_1,vm_2,...,vm_n},
Network latency cost matrix $lc(u_e, dc_j)$
Output: destination for requested V's
Processing:
1: While vmList do
2:    Get information from DCs VM Local Manager
3:    Sort DC sites D in an ascending order of ($\alpha1 * PUE * cf + \alpha2 * lc$)
4:   Fed selected DC site VM Local Manager to apply Best-Fit-SLA VM placement Policy
5: Sort hostList h in an ascending order to its Availability
6:    For each host in sorted hostList
7:         if host h_j is suitable for vm_u **with x MIPS margin**
8:              set vm_u at host h_j
9:    End For
10: End While

As Algorithm 3 shows, the main difference between BF-CELA and BF-SLA-CELA is that the algorithm will use a margin of x MIPS (line 7) that minimizes the SLA violation penalties cost and contributes to revenue maximization.

5 Performance Metrics

This section presents the performance parameters that will be used to measure the effectiveness of the proposed CELA model.

Makespan: Makespan indicates the finishing time of the last task requested by cloud customer. It represents the most popular optimization criteria that reflect the cloud QoS.

$$Makespan = maximum_{t \in tasks}\{f_t\} \tag{15}$$

where f_t denotes the finishing time of task t.

Active Servers (AS): Minimizing the number of active servers by utilizing the activated ones is an important criterion for cloud service providers. It leads to maximum profit through serving cloud user's requests with minimum number of resources without degrades the cloud QoS. AS counts the number of active servers that used to complete a bunch of task per time slot.

$$AS = \sum_{i=1}^{D} \sum_{j=1}^{h} (Ah_{ji}) \tag{16}$$

where Ah_{ji} denotes the activated hosts in distributed DC sites D.

SLAH: SLAH is the SLA violation per active host. It is the percentage of time an active host experiences 100% utilization of CPU. The SLAH can be calculated as follows [4]:

$$SLAH = \frac{1}{h} \sum_{j=1}^{h} \frac{ViolationTime\_h_j}{ActiveTime\_h_j} \tag{17}$$

where h, *ViolationTime_h_j*, and *ActiveTime_h_j* is the total number of hosts, the h_j SLA violation time, and active time respectively.

Electricity Cost: The Electricity Cost metric calculates the average amount of electricity cost per day. Equation 18 illustrates the calculation:

$$Cost_{Electricity} = \sum_{i=1}^{D} f_E^i * E_i * PUE_i \tag{18}$$

where f_E^i, E_i, PUE_i is the electricity price, energy consumption and the PUE at DC i respectively.

Revenue: The Revenue metric calculates the average profit per day. The cloud provider Revenue per day calculated using the following equation:

$$Revenue = TotatlIncome - Cost_{Electricity} - Cost_{CO2} - Cost_{Penalties} - Cost_{communication}$$

$$(19)$$

where Total Income is the VMs income. $Cost_{Electricity}$, $Cost_{CO2}$, $Cost_{communication}$ calculated using Eqs. 18, 6, and 8 respectively. The $Cost_{Penalties}$ calculated as follows:

$$Cost_{Penalties} = RF * SLAH \qquad (20)$$

6   Weight Prediction Model

The normalized weights of Eq. 14 are important factors that contribute in finding an optimal solution to the VM placement problem. While deciding among the multiple normalized weights (α_1 & α_2), each one can be in conflict with the other. We applied machine learning (ML) techniques to determine optimal values for the parameters. Figure 5 illustrates the basic schema of the proposed methodology to find the CELA-NWPM model. The following sections describe the process of finding the weights.

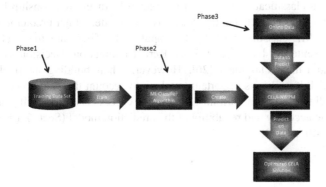

Fig. 5. CELA-NWP model scheme.

6.1   Phase 1

The first phase of the proposed prediction model represents collecting the training data set to build the ML model. The training set extracted according to the probabilistic dependencies among CELA parameters. The structure of the data set parameters are extracted knowledge and simulation results. For forecasting of the input data, we use real DCs cloud management information as represented in Table 2. This information provides key insights to find the important attributes that could affect the normalized weights decision.

Table 2. Machine learning data set specifications extracted from [2, 5, 14–17].

Type	Specifications
Workload	1-Planetlab [14] 2-Random Workload using Uniform Distribution
Workload size (number of tasks/per day)	1000–5000
VMs file size (MB)	0.05–1500
VMs	EC2 (XSmall, Small, Medium, Large)
PMs	HP Proliant G3, G4, and G5 IBM server X3470, 3480, 5670, 5675 [15]
Locations	4 different zones (US, Asia, Australia, Brazil)
Management system	MF-CELA, BF-CELA & BF-SLA-CELA
PUE	1.1–2.1 [16]
CO2 emission rate (Ton/MWh)	0.1–0.7 [17]
CO2 emission cost ($/Ton)	20–120 [2]
WAN communication distance and price ($/GB)	0.09–0.25 [5]

6.2   Phase 2

In this phase, a classification algorithm is used to learn the relationship between the training set attributes collected at the first phase. To model a finer predictor, we need to use a suitable ML classifier with light computations. There are many classification methods represented in literature such as: Kernel Estimation, Decision Trees, Neural Networks and Linear classifiers [26]. However, when building an intelligent ML predictor model, it is always important to take into account the prediction accuracy. In that case, finding the best algorithm to build our CELA- NWPM intelligent predictor depends on the accuracy and reliability of the prediction model (Sect. 7.1 illustrates the used ML classifier type).

6.3   Phase 3

Using the learned CELA-NWPM model, we are able to predict the CELA normalized weights. When VMs request is made, the CELA-NWPM intelligent predictor responsible of providing the normalized weights of the CELA objective function to execute the requested VMs using the cost efficient DCs. It should return the normalized weights that will provide the optimum performance of the proposed CELA model.

7   Performance Evaluation

To validate the effectiveness of the proposed model, we have extended the CloudSim Toolkit to enable CELA VM placement policies testing. CloudSim is an open source development toolkit that supports the development of new management policies to improve the cloud environment from its different levels [18]. To model the CELA VM placement methods, we utilized CloudSim 3.0.3 by modifying the DC broker algorithm that plays the role of mediator between the cloud user and service provider.

7.1 Simulation Setup

We conducted experiments on Intel(R) core(TM) i7 Processor 3.4 GHz, Windows 7 platform using NetBeans IDE 8.0.2 and JDK 1.8. Our simulation has two different scenarios. Scenario1 is a synthetic one that randomly modelled the cloud-computing environment to measure the effectiveness of the CELA model in terms of AS and Makespan. In this scenario, we modelled the offline IaaS environment and applied the offline-CELA approach. Scenario 2 modelled the online SaaS dynamic environment. It applied the online-CELA dynamic approach to measure the efficacy of the proposed model with respect to CO2 emission, Electricity Cost, Revenue and more performance metrics as discussed in Sect. 5.

CO2 Emission Rate and PUR Data
To approximate the DC's CO2 emission rate, we used the information extracted from the U.S. Energy Information website [17]. Its cost is taken as 20$/Ton as suggested by latest study of US Government on CO2 emission economic damage [19]. While the PUE value for distributed DCs is generated randomly in the range of [1.3, 1.8] based on the Amazon and Google latest PUE readings and work studied by Sverdlik [25].

Approximating Latency with Distance
Since there is no general analytical model for the delay in the network, we use geographical distance to approximate the network latency between a user and geo-distributed DCs. Although distance is not an ideal estimator for network latency, it is sufficient to determine the relative rank in latency from end-user to DCs as indicated in [5]. Moreover, we use the WAN Latency Estimator [21] to estimate the network latency in milliseconds.

CELA Normalized Weight Prediction
To model the CELA-NWPM intelligent predictor, we used the open source ML tool Weka [22]. Weka is an advanced tool designed by the University of Waikato to provide data mining and ML tasks. It contains a large number of ML classifiers. We have tested several Weka's embedded ML algorithms to select an accurate predictor model. The accuracy of the results was calculated using the Mean Absolute Error (MAE) formula. MAE is an ML classifier metric that measures the average magnitude of the errors in a set of forecast.

Our training data set consisted of more than 4500 instances. 70% of data used as training set and the rest used as testing set. In this paper, our approach applies the machine learning k-nearest neighbor technique (k-NN) [23] to the workload data set to train the CELA-NWPM model. The k-NN method is a supervised learning algorithm that helps to classify the ML data set in different classes. It provides good prediction using a distance metric.

7.2   Experimental Results

Scenario 1

To evaluate the Offline-CELA policies, we modelled an IaaS cloud environment with 4 DCs sites (in 4 different geographical regions such as USA, Europe, Brazil, and Asia). The aim of this scenario is to strike a trade-off among the latency of data access and the energy consumed by the DCs that is evaluated using the workload Makespan and AS metrics respectively. Therefore, two different tests are conducted: one to measure the effectiveness of CELA model in data placement, while the other to study the overall performance of the CELA model on QoS.

Table 3 shows the relationship between DCs distributed sites PUE, CO2 rate emission, number of servers in each DC, and average distance between the DCs sites and end users based on [17, 19, 21, 24, 25]. To measure effectively the AS metric, two different cloud environments are tested. One considered hosts are homogeneous of Type 1 (as shown in Table 4), and use small VM instance type (as shown in Table 5). The other are considered heterogeneous hosts of types: Type 1 and Type 2 (as shown in Table 4) and four different VM types (as shown in Table 5). The number of hosts for each DC varies within the range [220:440]. We assume that hosts will consume the full system power when the server is on. We use SIGNIANT Flight pricing model as transferring WAN pricing cost [24].

Table 3. Geo-distributed DCs specifications based from [17, 19, 21, 24, 25].

DC	dc1	dc2	dc3	dc4
PUE	1.3	1.7	1.65	1.5
CO2 tons/MWh	0.864	0.350	0.466	0.678
Average distance (miles)	10500	6500	2200	8400
Average latency (milliseconds)	190	120	45	150
WAN transfer cost (S/GB)	0.181	0.08	0.01	0.138

Table 4. Host's type and specifications extracted from [15].

Host's type	Specifications
Type 1	HP ProLiant ML110 G4 (1 x [Xeon 3040 1860 MHz, 2 cores], 16 GB)
Type 2	HP ProLiant ML110 G5 (1 x [Xeon 3075 2660 MHz, 2 cores], 16 GB)

Table 5. Amazon EC2 VM(s) specification extracted from [16].

VM instance type	Cores	MIPS	RAM (MB)	Bandwidth (Mbps)	Storage (GB)	Price/hour (Euro)
Extra small	1	500	613	100	0.633	0.02
Small	1	1000	1740	100	1.7	0.047
Medium	1	1500	1740	100	0.85	0.148
Large	1	2000	870	100	3.75	0.2

Makespan. The algorithm used to compare the Makespan metrics is MF-ECC and MF-Random. MF-ECC, a Most Full Energy and Carbon-aware VM placement method and similar version to MF-CELA without considering network latency for DC site selection. In the other hand, MF-Random select DCs randomly and apply the MF VM placement policy for host selection. The objective of this experiment is to find the effect of using network latency as an important factor when choosing DCs to execute users' request.

Figures 6a and 6b show the workload Makespan improvement achieved by the location aware MF-CELA algorithm over MF-ECC, and MF-Random methods using 3 different numbers of VMs request as shown in Table 6. Taking the transferring cost into consideration, our MF-CELA algorithm significantly outperforms the MF-ECC in achieving high cloud QoS with approximate 25% rate of Makespan enhancement. However, it is clearly reveal the unstable performance of MF-Random method due to the nature of random selection.

Table 6. Cloud resources based from [13].

Simulation type	Number of VMs	Number of cloudlets
Small	500	1000
Medium	1000	2000
Large	1500	3000

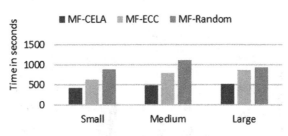

Fig. 6a. Workload Makespan in different number of cloudlets and VMs - homogenous environment.

AS. This experiment compares MF-CELA with Simple-CELA, BF-CELA, LF-CELA, and FF-CELA. All are a similar version to MF-CELA in DCs selections. However, Simple, BF, LF, and FF are VM placement methods that chooses, as the host for a VM, the host with less PEs in use, the best fit host in terms of available MIPS, the least full host in terms of available MIPS, and the first fit host in terms of available MIPS respectively.

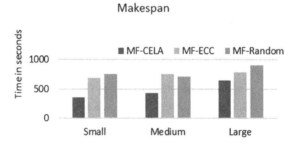

Fig. 6b. Workload Makespan in different number of cloudlets and VMs – heterogeneous environment.

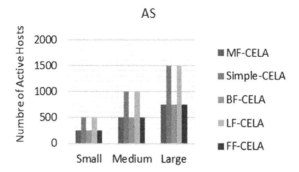

Fig. 7a. AS in different number of cloudlets and VMs – homogenous environment.

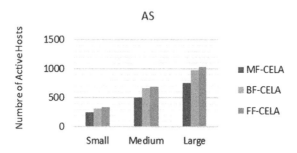

Fig. 7b. AS in different number of cloudlets and VMs – heterogeneous environment.

Figure 7a demonstrates that MF-CELA VM placement method reduces energy consumption with an average of 50% compared to Simple-CELA and LF-CELA algorithms and using 3 different numbers of VMs request as shown in Table 4. Although the result shows that FF-CELA and BF-CELA contribute to energy saving same as MF-CELA, however, this will not be the case when heterogeneous cloud environment is considered as shown in Fig. 7b Note that, in this experiment, the number of activated hosts is taken as a measure for energy consumption.

Scenario 2

This section evaluates the Online-CELA proposed policies. We employed real Planetlab traces to emulate the online SaaS cloud environment. The SaaS cloud environment was modelled with 4 DCs sites. The DCs distributed sites PUE, CO2 rate emission, and average distance between the DCs sites and end users are the same as indicated in Table 3. However, hosts are considered heterogeneous of type Type 1 and Type 2 as indicated in Table 4. According to the linear power model (Eq. 1), and real data from SPECpower benchmark (Standard Performance Evaluation Corporation, 2017), Table 7 presents the hosts power consumption at different load levels.

Four different VM types are used inspired by Amazon EC2. Table 5 displays the characteristics of VM instances and their hourly price. To generate a dynamic workload, Planetlab benchmark workload is employed to emulate the SaaS VM requests. Each VM runs application with different workload traces. Each trace is assigned to a VM instance in order. We choose 3 different workload traces from different days of the Planetlab project. The simulation represents one-day simulation time. The algorithm runs every 300 s.

BF-CELA and BF-SLA-CELA VM placement algorithms are compared to two different competing algorithms FF-CELA and Simple-CELA. Both are a version of CELA model, i.e. they use the same method of CELA to select DC sites. However, the first one applies First Fist algorithm for host selection, and the other applies the Simple policy.

To find the importance of considering the PUE, CF, and network latency factors in DC site selection, BF-LCC and BF-LEC are used. Both are other versions of BF-CELA. However, in DC site selection, the first one (Best Fit Location Carbon and Cost-aware) does not consider the PUE, while the second (Best Fit Location Energy and Cost-aware) ignores the carbon emission rate factor.

Table 7. HP servers host load to energy (Watt) mapping table extracted from [15].

Server type	0%	10%	20%	30%	40%	50%	60%	70%	80%	90%	100%
HP G4	86	89.4	92.6	96	99.5	102	106	108	112	114	117
HP G5	93.7	97	101	105	110	116	121	125	129	133	135

Power Consumption. Figure 8a illustrates the efficiency of the proposed CELA methods in comparison with FF and Simple algorithms using 3 different workload traces and different number of VM requests per day. As results reveal, BF-CELA and BF-SLA-CELA algorithms reduce energy with an average of 20% and 15% respectively.

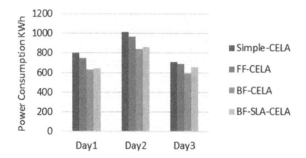

Fig. 8a. VM placement algorithms power consumption extracted from [13].

Electricity Cost. Figure 8b show the effect of energy reduction on electricity cost. Since BF-CELA algorithm has lower power consumption as shown in Fig. 8a, this directly affects the electricity cost. Based on the information extracted from the U.S. Energy Information website [17], we consider energy price in the range of [4, 20] Cent/KWh. To calculate the electricity cost at four different DCs, we use the average (12 Cent/KWh) as an electricity price. It was predictable that CELA algorithms will outperform other placement methods. Figure 8b proves the importance of energy reduction on minimizing the electricity cost. In general, BF-CELA and BF-SLA-CELA improved the cloud provider electricity cost with an average of 17% as shown in Fig. 8b.

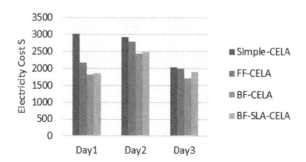

Fig. 8b. VM placement algorithms electricity cost.

Carbon Footprint. Figure 8c studies the importance of using the CF and PUE factors in CELA model in reducing the CO_2 footprint under different number of workload traces. BF-CELA and BF-SLA-CELA compared to BF-LEC (non-carbon efficient), BF-LCC (non-power efficient), FF-CELA and Simple-CELA (carbon and power efficient). Based on Fig. 8c, BF-CELA and BF-SLA-CELA decrease the CO_2 emission with an average of 16% and 29% compared to other competing VM placement algorithms. Considering the algorithms behaviour, we can conclude that the PUE and CF factors play an important role and lead to significant reduction in energy and CO_2 emission.

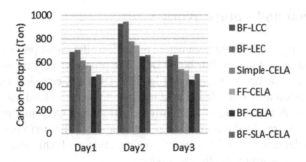

Fig. 8c. VM placement algorithms' carbon footprint.

SLAH. Figure 8d highlights the importance of BF-SLA-CELA in reducing the SLA violation without ignoring energy saving to minimize the penalties cost. The experiments show 54% as an average reduction in SLA violation compared to BF-CELA and FF-CELA algorithms.

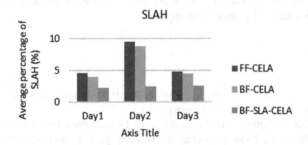

Fig. 8d. Average percentage of SLAH violation.

Revenue. To calculate the net Revenue per day, the penalties for missing VM SLA are taken as 10% refund. Figure 8e illustrates the importance of CELA model on increasing the cloud provider net profit. As Fig. 8e shows, BF-CELA and BF-SLA-CELA algorithms outperform other competing VM placement algorithms.

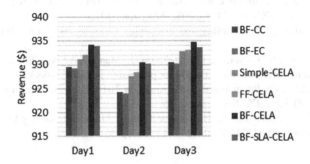

Fig. 8e. VM placement algorithms net revenue.

8   Conclusion and Future Work

This paper investigates different parameters that affects the cloud provider decision in VM and data placement in geo-distributed DCs. The proposed and implemented CELA model strike the trade-off between WAN latency, DC CO2 emission rate, PUE, and energy consumption to find a suitable host machine to process cloud user request. The main aim of CELA model aim is to improve cloud system QoS, minimize its operational cost and assure cloud environmental sustainability. The performance of CELA model that modeled as a multi-objective optimization problem advances using an intelligent machine learning prediction model.

CELA-NWP aim to find the best weighting between the multi-objectives that guides the cloud provider to DC selection. Different VM placement approaches are implemented and evaluated to solve the problem of CELA model. To validate the effectiveness of the proposed mode, extensive simulations are conducted. The experimental results show the importance of CELA model in DCs selection and cloud provider net profit improvement. This is beside its great effect in optimizing DCs energy consumption. As future directions, our aim is to extend the CELA model to handle the cost of moving data inside the modern high-performance network DCs that cause the main source of power consumption.

References

1. Al-Dulaimy, A., Itani, W., Zekri, A., Zantout, R.: Power management in virtualized data centers: state of the art. J. Cloud Comput. 5(1), 6 (2016)
2. Luckow, P., et al.: Spring 2016 National Carbon Dioxide Price Forecast (2016)
3. Rawas, S., Itani, W., Zaart, A., Zekri, A.: Towards greener services in cloud computing: research and future directives. In: 2015 International Conference on Applied Research in Computer Science and Engineering (ICAR), pp. 1–8. IEEE, October 2015
4. Khosravi, A., Andrew, L.L.H., Buyya, R.: Dynamic VM placement method for minimizing energy and carbon cost in geographically distributed cloud data centers. IEEE Trans. Sustain. Comput. 2(2), 183–196 (2017)
5. Fan, Y., Ding, H., Wang, L., Yuan, X.: Green latency-aware data placement in data centers. Comput. Netw. 110, 46–57 (2016)
6. Chen, K.Y., Xu, Y., Xi, K., Chao, H.J.: Intelligent virtual machine placement for cost efficiency in geo-distributed cloud systems. In: 2013 IEEE International Conference on Communications (ICC), pp. 3498–3503. IEEE, June 2013
7. Bauer, E., Adams, R.: Reliability and availability of cloud computing. Wiley, Hoboken (2012)
8. Ahvar, E., Ahvar, S., Crespi, N., Garcia-Alfaro, J., Mann, Z.A.: NACER: a network-aware cost-efficient resource allocation method for processing-intensive tasks in distributed clouds. In: 2015 IEEE 14th International Symposium on Network Computing and Applications (NCA), pp. 90–97. IEEE, September 2015
9. Malekimajd, M., Movaghar, A., Hosseinimotlagh, S.: Minimizing latency in geo-distributed clouds. J. Supercomput. 71(12), 4423–4445 (2015)

10. Jonardi, E., Oxley, M.A., Pasricha, S., Maciejewski, A.A., Siegel, H.J.: Energy cost optimization for geographically distributed heterogeneous data centers. In: 2015 Sixth International Green Computing Conference and Sustainable Computing Conference (IGSC), pp. 1–6. IEEE, December 2015

11. AWS Global Infrastructure (2017). https://aws.amazon.com/about-aws/global-infrastructure/. Accessed Jan 2017

12. Zhou, Z., et al.: Carbon-aware load balancing for geo-distributed cloud services. In: 2013 IEEE 21st International Symposium on Modeling, Analysis & Simulation of Computer and Telecommunication Systems (MASCOTS), pp. 232–241. IEEE, August 2013

13. Rawas, S., Zekri, A., El Zaart, A.: Power and cost-aware virtual machine placement in geo-distributed data centers. In: CLOSER, pp. 112–123 (2018)

14. Planet lab traces. https://www.planet-lab.org. Accessed Jan 2017

15. Standard Performance Evaluation Corporation (2017). http://www.spec.org. Accessed Jan 2017

16. Google Data Centers. Google Inc. (2017). https://www.google.com/about/datacenters/efficiency/internal/. Accessed Mar 2017

17. EIA, US Energy Information Administration (2017). http://www.eia.gov/. Accessed Mar 2017

18. Calheiros, R.N., Ranjan, R., Beloglazov, A., De Rose, C.A., Buyya, R.: CloudSim: a toolkit for modeling and simulation of cloud computing environments and evaluation of resource provisioning algorithms. Softw. Pract. Exp. **41**(1), 23–50 (2011)

19. Thang, K.: Estimated social cost of climate change not accurate, Stanford scientists say (2015). Accessed 5 June 2016

20. Google Inc. https://www.google.com/about/datacenters/inside/locations/index.html. Accessed Jan 2017

21. Wan Latency Estimator. http://wintelguy.com/wanlat.html. Accessed Feb 2017

22. Hall, M., Frank, E., Holmes, G., Pfahringer, B., Reutemann, P., Witten, I.H.: The WEKA data mining software: an update. ACM SIGKDD Explor. Newsl. **11**(1), 10–18 (2009)

23. Weinberger, K.Q., Saul, L.K.: Distance metric learning for large margin nearest neighbor classification. J. Mach. Learn. Res. **10**(Feb), 207–244 (2009)

24. Signiant organization. (2017). http://www.signiant.com/products/flight/pricing/

25. Sverdlik, Y.: Survey: industry average data center pue stays nearly flat over four years. Data Center Knowl. **2**(06) (2014)

26. Pereira, F., Mitchell, T., Botvinick, M.: Machine learning classifiers and fMRI: a tutorial overview. Neuroimage **45**(1), S199–S209 (2009)

Will Cloud Gain an Edge, or, CLOSER, to the Edge

Lee Gillam[✉]

Department of Computer Science, University of Surrey, Guildford, UK
l.gillam@surrey.ac.uk

Abstract. This paper accompanies a keynote speech given at the 8th International Conference on Cloud Computing and Services Science, CLOSER 2018. The keynote offered an overview of 'traditional' and 'new' Cloud Computing, and what we might appreciate of each. In respect to 'traditional', issues of performance and energy efficiency, and the potential conflict between these, were discussed, as well as how these were still relevant to 'new' Cloud. Key to the 'new' Cloud is the advent of so-called function-as-a-service and edge, to which these issues of performance and lessons learned from energy efficiency can be applied. Important to this is to establish what we mean by edge as distinct from other things as may be similarly referred to. The relevance of new Cloud, then, to Connected and Autonomous Vehicles offers for an industry vertical that could exploit such formulations, and attempts to do this will lead to a variety of technical and research questions. Also, with a person in America having been killed by a vehicle acting autonomously near to the timing of this talk, safety concerns should never be far from thinking in addressing such questions.

1 Introduction

The notion of what we may now consider as traditional cloud emerged from utility-based computing following on from work undertaken by Sun with network.com and IBM with compute-on-demand back in 2005 and - since 2006 - is an area in which Amazon has emerged as a market leader. Cloud standards exist, with the principal defining standard from the National Institute of Science and Technology that identified the three service models of software, platform, and infrastructure (abbreviated to SPI, and all 'as a service'), four delivery models, and five key characteristics – the 3-4-5 [1]. The ISO definitions of ISO/IEC 17788 followed later. Cloud, delivered as public, is mostly composed of large, economically efficient, and so easily maintained but still expensive, data centers. Major providers tend to have relatively small numbers of geographical regions in which these things exist, and bringing them together gives the providers a good economic advantage in being able to support large user numbers within large setups at an incrementally small cost. As the likes of Geoffrey Moore would identify, a Big Four exists; variously with Amazon as the biggest of these and made up by the likes of Microsoft, IBM and Google; some might suggest Alibaba as being most ready to displace one of these.

© Springer Nature Switzerland AG 2019
V. M. Muñoz et al. (Eds.): CLOSER 2018, CCIS 1073, pp. 24–39, 2019.
https://doi.org/10.1007/978-3-030-29193-8_2

Each of these has brought similar innovations around service delivery, and so in addition to virtual machines (VMs) each now offers containers - and all support Docker – as well as functions. Docker, of course, leads to a lock-in to a particular kernel, in contrast to the operating system independence achieved with virtualization and the use of virtual machines. However, there is advantage to be had in the size of what results from this, and flexibility remains in container contents. For functions, it is necessary to commit to a programming language that is supported by the system being used (i.e. the vendor) and define broad characteristics of execution such as the maximum usable memory and runtime; multiple approaches, with no emergent or de facto standard, exist across providers. Containers and functions can both be useful components in the delivery of microservices.

As well as SPI, then, some will offer container-as-a-service and function-as-a-service. Largely, these are subtypes of the existing service models. And beyond these, we also now encompass notions of "edge" computing, which may cover a number of possibilities and the location of the edge acts as both a defining characteristic and an implication for the kinds of capabilities offered and to whom.

Edges, along with functions and containers, offers an idea of how computing can be (re-)distributed, with distributed computing approaches resurgent. Where the traditional cloud consolidated systems into big data centers run by large corporate entities, the same kinds of capabilities are now being pushed back out towards where people and the devices that need the computational power are. A Big Four exploiting the opportunities this offers is yet to emerge, although the current Big Four in cloud are all revealing certain edge offerings and time will tell which has traction. However, opportunities would seem to exist for others, and with consideration for certain kinds of edges it may be that telecommunications companies are well placed to be at the forefront.

The keynote, and this accompanying paper, comprises four parts and covers research addressed in relatively recent work [2–10]. First, we further clarify this traditional cloud, in particular with respect to performance variation and implications related to energy efficiency. Second, in new cloud, we look to how some of this influences so-called serverless compute, and how performance becomes important again. With the multiplicity of possible edges, we identify a specific edge of interest, and the potential this offers. Third, in respect to an application area, we consider connected and autonomous vehicles, with reference to an active research project. Finally, we pose a number of technical/research challenges that emerge from these considerations.

2   Traditional Cloud

Traditional cloud provides for the illusion of infinite capacity, and proving – through usage – that it is not could be expensive. In such a cloud, it is possible to provision significant amounts of compute resource to undertake work for a desired period of time, as long as somebody is prepared to pay the bill.

The biggest cloud provider by various measures is Amazon Web Services. In 2014, AWS' scale, at a time when they were offering 11 regions and 28 availability zones, was projected at 2.8 to 5.6 million servers [11]. At the start of 2018, AWS had 18 regions with 54 availability zones, and five more regions coming. At the upper end of Morgan's estimate, this is some ten million servers. By 2012, AWS already boasted storing a trillion objects in S3, with that number doubled by April 2013, implying much greater numbers now. At such scale, significant economies have to exist in managing it in order to deploy and maintain large numbers of servers in those regions, variously spread around the world. Cloud datacentres also have a large physical footprint. According to a report by Greenpeace, [12] Microsoft's Illinois datacentre is some 700,000 square feet – the compares to football club Manchester United's pitch size of 80,000 square feet: multiple football pitches, then, per DC.

With regions at distance from many, one limiting factor on usage is latency. A company called Datapath has several images of latency figures measured from various location to AWS. In one example latency map[1], from a location in the US, latencies range from 37 ms on the east coast to 66 ms on the west, and moving further away from there, to 166 ms somehow on the west coast of Africa. Such times are worth noting when working, as will be addressed later, with edge – these are the latencies to beat.

If latency is an important factor, which it is to a reasonable extent for websites already, likely latencies will limit the regions usable, and potentially the availability zones, to use. Since Cloud pricing tends to be region-specific, latency may also result in a commitment to price. In AWS, it is very typically cheaper to run in the eastern US than in any other location. However, availability of suitable resources within a latency threshold then becomes a factor. The best resources may be further away, with higher latency but, when latency is a dictating factor, architecting an application carries dependencies on the capabilities available within this latency; and available resources at low latencies that are less effective may already cost more. It is necessary, then, to consider latency against cost and capability; the latter relates to availability of the hardware most adept for the application. Table 1 shows regions by date from US East, built first in 2006, through to Asia Pacific, Sydney in 2012, and the availability of CPU models related to a single instance type within those: an instance type may be backed by multiple models at the same price; sometimes, there is a one-to-one correspondence between CPU model and instance type - at least for a time – but not always over time.

Different CPU models will offer for different performance, and different regions will provide different proportions of CPU models backing the instance type. Some regions may not have any servers containing a particular CPU model. If a certain model was best for your workloads, you'd prefer to avoid regions that cannot offer those. But performance is not simply a matter of better or worse. CPU models that provide for better integer performance, for example, may offer worse floating point performance.

Figure 1 shows results from several benchmarks run on CPU models backing such instances. Benchmarks cover integer, floating point, and memory bandwidth – the latter being most visibly impacted by contention. The red box follows performance of the Intel Xeon 5430; the orange box follows performance of the Intel Xeon 2650. If the workload is integer oriented, the 5430 offers better performance, at the same price, than

---

[1] Viewable at: https://cdn-images-1.medium.com/max/1000/1*jBdZHhe_Ow6o5p9ZepVBMw.jpeg.

Table 1. Proportion of CPU models backing a first generation EC2 instance type across multiple regions and availability zones [13], as made available to one user. Note, in particular, the absence of certain models over time.

Region	AZ	E5430	E5-2650	E5645	E5507
US East, N. Virginia, 2006	us-east-1a	31%	0	25%	44%
[year Region started] -	us-east-1b	5%	59%	29%	7%
Cheapest	us-east-1c	0	47%	52%	1%
	us-east-1d	18%	31%	44%	7%
EU West, Dublin, 2007	eu-west-1a	4%	75%	19%	2%
	eu-west-1b	28%	0	44%	28%
	eu-west-1c	4%	0	63%	33%
US West, N. California, 2009	us-west-1b	0	0	13%	87%
	us-west-1c	8%	0	18%	74%
SA, San Paulo, 2011	sa-east-1a	0	81%	19%	0
	sa-east-1b	0	86%	14%	0
US West, Oregon, 2011	us-west-2b	0	73%	27%	0
Asia Pacific, Sydney, 2012	ap-southeast-2a	0	64%	36%	0
	ap-southeast-2b	0	75%	25%	0

the 2650. However, for floating point the 2650 is better at the same price. The workload will dictate the hardware that is better for it, and as a consequence the cost will differ – you pay more for it to run for longer meaning, essentially, you're paying more for worse service.

A given user, then, has a variety of potential trade-offs for cost-efficient work in cloud. Starting from latency, suitable hosting locations are suggested and this offers an initial price range. The amount and type of computational power is then a concern: this is a performance determination related to price for suitable resources. The reverse route would be to consider which availability zones offer suitable resources, and see whether this provides for acceptable latency. The resulting location selection isn't the final issue since potential availability of suitable resources doesn't guarantee availability when needed, nor the ability to specify these; this provides for a kind of instance lottery – knowledge of the prior probability may help, but variation on cost should also be factored in. Since what is available appears also to differ by user, with users apparently mapped to a subset of possible resources, each user has to conduct their own analysis. Each user, then, incurs costs in performance determination ahead of time, and potentially also during live use. And, of course, the composition of the infrastructure changes over time, so it is not possible to assume that doing this once for a user fixes it for all time.

It is important to note, then, that obtaining cost efficient performance in the cloud carries costs and requires some technical exploration, with heterogeneity in hardware a significant factor – and one relatively rarely accounted for in experimental findings: much work on cloud performance tends to assume homogeneity and that variations simply aggregate out. Through suitable investigation, however, a decent amount of cost-efficient performance may be gained.

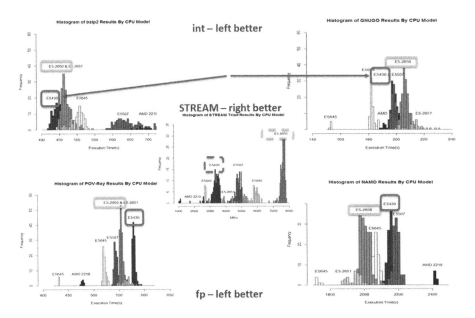

Fig. 1. Variations in performance of 5 benchmarks – two for integer, two floating point, and one memory bandwidth - for a single AWS instance type. Note, specifically, positions of E5430 outlined in red, and E5-2650 outlined in orange, with respect to each other and other CPU models. Figure is modified from [5]. On all but the centre chart, where lines are dashed, the left side of the chart represents better performance (Color figure online)

Furthermore, it is not possible to eliminate resource uncertainty: some instances may simply suffer from severely hampered performance: one instance performed the Povray benchmark in 1379 s, some thirteen standard deviations from the mean. An unwitting user would be paying rather more for such bad performance! On occasion, it may not even be possible to obtain certain CPU models, or even instance types, as may be preferred, if they are all committed to other users – although this at least demonstrates that it is an illusion of infinite resources. Also, one predominating reason for resource uncertainty is contention. When other virtual machines are running or being started alongside your own on a shared host – with smaller virtual machine instance types much more likely to run on such shared resources that much larger - increases in runtimes will happen at certain times with rises for a period and eventually falls back to certain levels - depending on the other workloads that are contending. Sometimes this can appear particularly noisy. Using a dedicated host, and placing competing workloads onto it, such effects are readily demonstrable by measuring runtimes in one instance when loads are run on other instances: as expected, we see rises of a certain size, a return to expected performance when no other loads are run, and some substantially longer runtimes such as an example shift from 75 s to almost 350 s when large amounts of competition exist, as shown in Fig. 2.

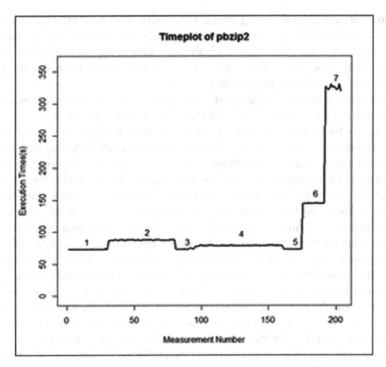

Fig. 2. Effects of running benchmarks in 15 other instances on a dedicated host, evidenced by variations in runtimes in an instance running pbzip2 (16 m4.large instances in total). Baseline performance (periods 1, 3, 5) exists when no benchmarks are run; other times are when others are running pbzip2 (2), sa-learn (4), one STREAM (6) and 2 STREAM (7) processes.

The idea that a cloud service brokerage could reduce some of the difficulties of assuring performance may be appealing. However, exploration of creation of such a broker identified significant profitability issues for such an endeavour, making it difficult to sustain [2]. Such a broker would have to operate with high volume, low profit margin, opportunities. The advent of per-second billing in a number of cloud providers makes such an opportunity small and fast diminishing. This view also tends to contradict research elsewhere on cloud brokerage, but largely since such research has tended to avoid considering broker profitability, the cost of setting up an organization, or the running costs. It also doesn't tend to consider the costs of transactions over an exchange, or the willingness of users to pay for such a service over and above what they're getting from a cloud provider. Various research ideas will appear appealing until tested against operational realities.

2.1 Energy

Computational performance, of course, carries implications to the amount of energy used. Ignoring cost, it may be possible to achieve equivalent performance on two different systems with different amounts of energy, provided that addition of energy relates to additional capability – e.g. higher CPU frequencies or additional cores. Since runtime is variable with hardware due to heterogeneity, it is necessary to determine the amount of power required to deliver a particular runtime on some given hardware, assuming it can be delivered at all. And, at the same time, best performance might not be the most energy efficient performance.

Within a data center, the highest cost for server use tends to be defrayed by the first paid-for work the server is doing, with additional work then at marginal cost. There are various figures for how much energy a server consumes whilst merely switched on - anything from ten to seventy percent of the maximum. And whilst having the server do more work improves the cost justification for the provider, this is potentially to the detriment (in risking contention) of the consumer (user) - the less loaded the server, the lower the runtimes and the less the user pays, and this is also the worst arrangement for the provider. There appears to be an incentive, then, for unscrupulous providers to offer instances with worse performance! Workload consolidation also appears geared towards providing worse performance. Ironically, much research on datacentre efficiency involves consolidation without any consideration for how much this would annoy users due – vitally – to the detrimental impact on performance (i.e. the amount of work done is considered as constant and unaffected, and so the associated price is also considered constant because the effects of contention are not appreciated). Worse still, similar workloads are more likely to create contention, and if there is a 'best' CPU for some work then either seeking for these 'best' or consolidating all such work to the same server(s) through migration, further increases the likelihood of detriment. If you are the owner of those workloads, you then carry a higher risk of becoming your own noisy neighbour and, moreover, being the cause of your own increases in costs. Unconsolidated work, then, should be better for the user. For the provider - with an assumption of contention-free processing - consolidation through migration carries cost in requiring duplicate resource during the period of migration, and produces network traffic. The time required for migration, of course, varies with the amount of data on disk, and in memory pages, that needs to be transferred. Merely to maintain the status quo on energy efficiency, the costs of such additional resource use must first be recouped and this is only achievable if (i) servers without loads are powered down and switched off for a sufficient period, and/or (ii) more work is done using less energy for a sufficient period at the target. Clearly, with contention, (ii) is rather less likely AND the user is less happy. Much research on consolidation also ignores such costs, effects, or both.

If energy being deployed to support migration is unrecoverable, there's little to gain from migrating. Consider, for example, if the workload migrated would have completed quickly, potentially even before migration is complete – cost would have been incurred without any opportunity for benefit. Additionally, if we assume that cloud providers are buying energy in contracts for fixed amounts, there may be little incentive for such actions in the first place. As such, assumptions that providers of cloud systems want to do this may not always be correct. But assuming that there is a motivation for such activity, it would make sense to account first for energy efficiency absent powering down. For a given workload, we can create an ordering of preferred machines, and only offer migration as an option when a preferred machine is the target – so the workload would run for a shorter time, and we carry an assumption that such running is more energy efficient; in reality, this may not be true. Already, though, if we were migrating towards longer runtimes, energy use carries longer durations, and the user is less likely to be happy, so even this assumption is useful. If, additionally, contention is avoidable, and runtimes don't lead to large amounts of redundant migrations, at minimum costs would be recovered. This is the basis of a method we refer to as Consolidation with Migration Cost Recovery (CMCR) [7]. In CMCR, running workloads can only be migrated where greater efficiency is assured (or, at least, assumed). We then look to an offset in time where the cost of migration has been recovered - from which point it is assumed to become more energy efficient. This attends to both costs and (avoidance of) effects of migration, albeit with assumptions regarding inspectability of workloads in contrast to the supposed opaqueness of VMs.

Experimental work for CMCR addressed nine scheduling approaches, multiple mechanisms for scheduling and consolidation, and its omission, and over 12,000 heterogeneous hosts, that being the size of a small data center, for some 25 million virtual machines characterizing tasks from the Google workload trace data, and also five settings on minimum elapsed runtimes to avoid large numbers of migrations for short-lived workloads [5]. Migration rounds were considered every five minutes in an otherwise on-demand setting, and only for hosts that were less than twenty percent utilized. One shortcoming of using Google trace data is that it doesn't contain CPU information. Usefully, however, we were able to infer this through an alignment of workload types to distributions from the aforementioned performance evaluations, so could infer hardware that would map from runtimes to the Google data. With mappings from priorities in workloads to povray, NAMD, and STREAM, we obtained the machine rankings needed. With skewed lognormal distributions for CPU models - mostly good performance but with a long tail of bad performance – it becomes possible simply to read a CPU model for each Google workload, and determine feasibility for migration. Such mapping is certainly imperfect, but useful absent suitable data.

Findings confirmed, as might be expected, that effective VM allocation is initially quite advantageous – again making certain assumptions of inspectability of workloads, in contrast to the opaqueness of VMs. Of course, more consolidation would tend to be indicated when loads are distributed across larger numbers of servers, so VM allocation approaches that produce a narrower distribution already reduce the potential for consolidation, and consideration of longer runtimes then reduces the number of candidates for migration.

Such an approach remain susceptible to the existence of substantial variations in workload over time – without additional information, and even greater inspectability, it will be unclear when an application is running at maximal demand, or whether its requirements will shift – e.g. from integer to floating point performance.

3   New Cloud

Serverless computing is now posed as a means to address much computational work. That which is presented as function-as-a-service is not far removed from what the likes of Google were doing a decade previously with Google App Engine: it's a platform, running some code for a small aspect of work, with limited configurability of underlying resources, and constrained in maximum runtime. Where cloud providers have moved to per-second billing (some with a one minute initial run cost), function billing can be at the hundred milliseconds level (rounded) and priced based on a combination of runtime and memory usage.

An application, then, must be decomposed into sets of individually runnable functions. Functions allied to a persistent storage capability may also be referred to as microservices. The result of such decomposition is that complex relationships will exist between functions with some dependent on others, and with coordination or orchestration of these becoming an issue.

Underlying such offerings, of course, are servers that still carry the same kinds of hardware variability discussed above. AWS Lambda, for example, runs functions in containers, and these containers run inside virtual machines. As such, hardware performance carries directly through to application performance, along with any natural variation. With function invocation times rounded up to the nearest hundred milliseconds, very minor variations will carry no impact. But when the spreads on runtime are much more varied this should offer concerns both to how much it's costing and to how well an application as a whole is performing. If a very frequently used function was inefficiently implemented, or runs on hardware least suitable for it, the effect of this may become amplified. Not only is performance being lost, but increased costs are incurred on every single function invocation, and a complex application may have parts further dependent on this. The need to consider suitable performance should not be overlooked.

If we look under the hood of a function in AWS Lambda, for a Python (2.7) runtime[2], we will see a python runtime launched against something called bootstrap.py.

```
USER         PID  %CPU %MEM    VSZ    RSS TTY       STAT START     TIME
COMMAND
490            1  1.3   0.3 212024  15372 ?          Ss  16:49     0:00
/usr/bin/python2.7 /var/runtime/awslambda/bootstrap.py
490            7  0.0   0.0 117208   2476 ?          R   16:49     0:00 ps
auxw
```

We can also uncover information about the CPU and operating system:

```
model name      : Intel(R) Xeon(R) CPU E5-2666 v3 @ 2.90GHz
cpu MHz         : 2900.066
cache size      : 25600 KB
Linux   ip-10-23-17-3   4.4.35-33.55.amzn1.x86_64   #1   SMP   ...
x86_64 x86_64 x86_64 GNU/Linux
```

Here, we have a dual core system running at 2.9 GHz, and with understanding of the characteristics of performance of c4 benchmarks with respect to workloads it should be possible to infer performance expectations. Others[3] have seen functions being backed by a 2.8 GHz E5-2680, which implies a c3 instance. Different instance

---

[2] Arbitrary applications cannot be 'installed' as root, but pre-built applications can be loaded into and run on the container's file system provided that no further privileges are needed. As such, it is possible to find out more about the working environment.

[3] http://zqsmm.qiniucdn.com/data/20150416152509/index.html.

types and, again, different hardware may be backing functions, and so performance of functions will be determined to some extent by that. In addition, since we can run certain pre-built applications from functions, the STREAM benchmark can tell us how much memory bandwidth is available, as shown in Fig. 3, and hopefully this is coincident with the amount of memory that's requested/allocated to a function.

```
-----------------------------------------------------------------
STREAM version $Revision: 5.10 $
-----------------------------------------------------------------
...
-----------------------------------------------------------------
Function    Best Rate MB/s   Avg time     Min time     Max time
Copy:            1979.3      0.091534     0.080836     0.116964
Scale:           1974.5      0.099291     0.081033     0.117087
Add:             2370.4      0.122582     0.101247     0.157255
Triad:           2362.9      0.126896     0.101569     0.157570
```

Fig. 3. Results for memory bandwidth available to the function according to a run of STREAM.

3.1   Edge

Having considered performance for functions, we turn our attention to edge computing. However, there are multiple possible edges covering:

- the (local) 'network' edge, sometimes considered as coincident with devices that connect some number of sensors, although an example of something similar can be a mobile phone as this offers an aggregation whilst providing local compute capability
- a 'customer' edge or edge router, which is a device at the edge of some customer's network, assuming that such a perimeter is readily identifiable
- a 'provider' edge, at the edge of some provider's network, although where that is may be hard to demonstrate in practice

The edge of interest here is the one that relates an edge data center, with a correlate in content delivery networks – a more local data centre. More specifically, such a data centre offering a few racks of so-called multi-access or mobile edge computing (MEC) [14], making it a more local data center in very close proximity to the radio access network (RAN) enabling connectivity for mobile telecommunications, e.g. alongside a (5G) evolved Node B (eNB).

In principle, work that may have been offloaded to a more distant cloud datacentre can instead be offloaded to this edge, offering potential for much lower response times. According to the specification, a MEC server allows for virtual machines to be run, so should also be able to support containers that could in turn run functions. This, then, provides for similar capabilities to traditional clouds at the edge of the mobile network. Functions at the edge, then, offer for fast execution, and being close to where the work is being done implies additional gains from low latency. However, concerns would exist with respect to capacity – especially in contrast to large cloud datacenters. Of course, edge servers are also still hardware, and so are similarly susceptible to hardware variations as discussed above.

It is important, here, to distinguish such edges from other proximate notions. Firstly, we have to discount the notion of fog due to confusion over what fog means per se, with several possibilities offered up by the Open Fog Consortium. This was previously clear: fog extended cloud to some edge and was additional to cloud; this was reinforced with examples of distributed applications that had both cloud components and fog components: "A has one Cloud component, and two Fog components [..] B has one cloud component, one component in the Core, and a Fog component" [15]. However, various Open Fog documents present fog as *between* clouds and things, *including* cloud or *in* cloud and all of them are potentially equally valid and equally invalid at the same time. Moreover, the Open Fog consortium say that fog is often erroneously called edge computing, so even if we're not sure about how it fits with cloud, it's not supposed to be thought of as a competing notion for edge.

Next, we distinguish it from a notion of cloudlets, from CMU, as between mobile device and cloud[4] –It is certainly relatable, since it is considered as a data-center-in-a-box[5]. This notion doesn't yet seem to expose an integration with telecommunications. Interestingly, however, CMU formed an Open Edge Computing initiative in 2015, and the most tangible development from there to date seems to be OpenStack++, which allows for migrations between OpenStack clusters. Edges need virtual machine management, and some treatment of things moving from one eNB to another: what was important, from the perspective of data or state, needs to be migrated to follow. These are, modulo telecommunications, similar.

Finally, consider that migrations may occur between heterogeneous hardware. Such a migration requires consideration of the impact to performance of this heterogeneity, not least to request a suitable resource to continue work at the same rate. The time required for the migration to happen is also important in offering for handover without a break in service. And these factors become critically important if large numbers of users are moving quickly between edges as they would for our considered application area.

4 New Cloud for Connected and Autonomous Vehicles

Along with the internet of things, as includes the internet of tractors, internet of kettles, and internet of fridges, we can consider the internet of vehicles, and the application area likely to provide substantial challenge in satisfying computational needs exists in respect to Connected and Autonomous Vehicles (CAV).

A number of advantages are suggested for CAV in being able to do something about, for example:

- 8 m accidents every year with 1.3 million fatalities and 7 million injuries
- ninety billion hours in traffic jams
- substantial CO_2/NO_2 emissions plus a variety of particulates

---

[4] This should also be distinguished from the notion of a cloudlet in the CloudSim simulator, where it is a task.

[5] For some, though, the large boxes with data centres in are called 'containers', not to be confused with those used in e.g. Docker - in case the current terminology is at risk of being in any way clear.

In principle, then, offering for CAV would allow us to make the world a better place, or at least improve the environment. Various and numerous companies are investing in this area, which offers for a rich set of research questions, including but not limited to:

- can cars become fully independent?
- what technologies are needed in order to support CAV?
- how will humans and vehicles interact with each other and their environment?

Assistive driving technologies already exist in many vehicles, with anti-lock braking systems a very common example but also with adaptive cruise control. But it is a long way from these to fully autonomous driving. There is also a significant risk if any of such technology goes wrong.

An example CAV is offered by Waymo, which reportedly generates a gigabyte of data every second - two petabytes per car per year assuming just 600 hours use per year. Simply archiving, and paying for storage, of this volume of data over a network offers some a technical challenge, but with an estimate of two billion total vehicles by 2020, the totality of such data could be much more significant and with obvious peak times of such data being generated. And this only from cars. Of course, some data may be processed on board the vehicle and may not be needed elsewhere. Furthermore, data produced and consumed by such vehicles would vary both by time and by road conditions: for example, in traffic jams, with large numbers of static users, more demand would exist in specific locations on information services.

As part of a programme of research in the UK run by the EPSRC and Jaguar Landrover, the University of Surrey is contributing to a five year research project called Cloud Assisted Real time methods for Autonomy (CARMA). CARMA is investigating the advantages of MEC with 5G and cloud, and the challenges of security, performance, and latency that emerge. The three key parts of the architecture are, of course, (i) cloud; (ii) edges, and for that we consider MEC as discussed above; and (iii) vehicles, as shown in Fig. 4.

There is a growing need for computational capability to support CAV. The multiplicity of sensor streams, including RADAR and LIDAR, and interpretation of these for object identification and classification already requires energy be provided for computation. And more compute power means greater levels of energy consumption – a particular challenge, in terms of range maintenance, for electric vehicles. Undertaking some of that processing at edge or in cloud implies power consumption in moving data over the network. And, perhaps, for analytical capabilities that cannot be provided on the vehicle. In addition, some of that analysis will carry tight deadlines on its completion, emphasizing again the importance of low latency (and edge). Where higher latencies can be tolerated, cloud can be used. And, of course, in terms of maintenance it is easier to update computational capability on edges and in cloud than it is to update every vehicle. However, edge largely comes into its own in respect to cooperation amongst vehicles, sharing information that may not otherwise be available to any individual. Low latency is again emphasized as, except when traffic is stationary, information for close-proximity contexts has a limited period of relevance - vehicles may have moved a moderate distance over marginally longer time periods, at which

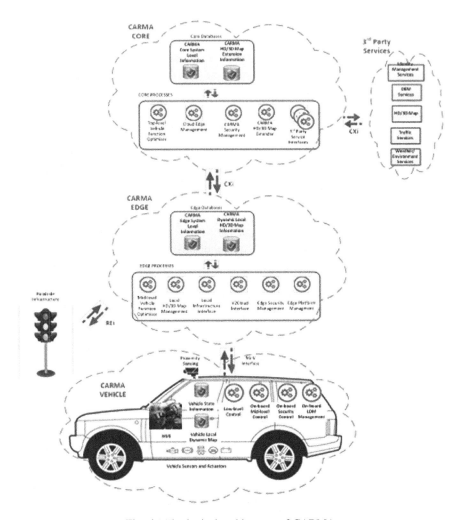

Fig. 4. The logical architecture of CARMA.

point some data regarding highly transient objects may no longer be accurate (e.g. position, speed, direction). Maintenance of such information is variously specified by ETSI as a local dynamic map (LDM), a multi layered data-oriented system where information can be overlaid on a standard 2D road map from a particular provider, with layers of increasingly transient information for such facts as:

- where road infrastructure such as traffic lights are
- locations of roadworks
- locations of accidents
- ambient conditions, such as the existence of fog (not to be confused)
- where (other) vehicles are

- and highly transient information such as the location of people, dogs, cats and other animals that it is important to account for.

With all such information available about a particular geographical area at an edge, it can be broadcast to interested parties. Such information would address things both within and beyond sensor ranges. Appropriately capable systems are required to support this, with decisions needing to be made in real-time about how such capabilities are being run depending on where the available compute power is.

Major cloud providers are already offering (limited numbers of) exemplars for connected vehicles, which are predominantly vehicle-to-cloud (V2C). There are examples for driving behaviour evaluation, geo-fence entry and exit, and sharing of data from sensors for tyres, engine speeds, and a multitude of other characteristics as would relate to diagnostics. But the only examples to date that have added edge are IBM's Edge Analytics, an Edge Agent on a Raspberry Pi and the DGLux tool, and the AWS Connected Vehicle Solution [16] with multiple vehicle services and a hint of inclusion of AWS Greengrass (albeit with minimal description about its purpose or integration). Nevertheless, these will be worth keeping an eye on. The key question for these examples, still, is the anticipated location of the edge. If it is simply on the vehicle, offering simply a little more on-bard compute power and requiring energy from the vehicle, as it appears to be in the AWS example, it remains V2C. The IBM example is indicated as "on premise", suggesting again remaining V2C. However, it doesn't require much to consider locating these edges appropriately and considering them as a proxy for (VMs on) a MEC server. Presently, though, this would emphasise the drawbacks of such examples only providing for limited cloud-like capabilities. Both examples offer for use of MQTT messages, but neither readily provides for pluggable persistence or other services as would be expected in cloud. Of course, the more cloud-like these edges need to be, the more capable the servers have to be, and to go with that the greater the number of vehicles, the greater the need for scale in order to support meaningful quality of service. Large numbers of fast moving mobile users with various demands for low-latency will certainly challenge provision of such supporting infrastructures.

5 Concluding Remarks

In summary, traditional cloud is established and unlikely to disappear any time soon. The need for computation and storage at scale shows no sign of diminishing. However, the purported need to address requirements for latency lower than can be provided by such clouds makes consideration of edge important for certain use cases, allied to function-as-a-service to retain low total execution times for self-contained capabilities. Edge does, though, have to achieve latencies in the low tens of milliseconds, at most, to be beneficial and allow time for computation.

The nature of such an edge is important to establish: here, it is a small datacentre – a few racks of multi-access edge computer (MEC) servers located suitably geographically proximate to a large enough geographical area to be useful by many people, and in very close proximity to the RAN (eNBs), offering cloud-like capabilities. As such. it would be a simple modification to consider MEC as standing for multi-access edge _cloud_. Similar neighboring edges will be needed to account for people moving quickly between them and with state and data shadowing their movements.

We expect such edges, then, to support functions and/or containers along with virtual machines. Functions, being relatively short-lived and doing small pieces of work also bring new complexity in supporting their execution as well as in service coordination and orchestration. However, smaller self-contained capabilities will move more readily in networks, which will be important for moving such capabilities across edges.

Cloud-connected vehicles represents an area of significant and growing interest, although with relatively few concrete exemplars. Numerous challenges exist and are likely to remain valid for some time, some of which likely make for very interesting future research and development activities:

- for providers, what kinds of hardware should be provided, and how can we cope with securing and updating for remote locations?
- which are the optimal locations for such edges?
- how will providers support migration of data, state, and applications?
- how do we cope with heterogeneous hardware, and across telecommunications providers?
- are current approaches to information security sufficient for such formulations?
- what quality of service can be provided for, and will there be performance guarantees?
- how much will the use of such systems cost, and who will pay?
- will end users have access, or will this be reserved for corporate uses?
- how do we cope with variability in capability, including outages?

And finally, and importantly for understanding such a future market: will the resulting Big Four providers be telecommunications companies, cloud companies, or require combination, even integration, of these?

Acknowledgments. The author is grateful to the CLOSER organisers for the invitation to give a keynote, and to the audience for remaining for its duration. The author is additionally grateful to Drs. O'Loughlin and Zakarya for their significant contributions through doctoral research to performance evaluation and energy efficiency, respectively. Work on CARMA is supported by EPSRC and Jaguar Land through grant EP/N01300X/1 as part of the Towards Autonomy: Smart and Connected Control (TASCC) Programme.

References

1. Mell, P., Grance, P.: NIST Definition of Cloud Computing. NIST (2011)
2. O'Loughlin, J., Gillam, L.: A performance brokerage for heterogeneous clouds. Future Gener. Comput. Syst. **87**, 831–845 (2018)
3. O'Loughlin, J., Gillam, L.: Sibling virtual machine co-location confirmation and avoidance tactics for public infrastructure clouds. J. Supercomput. **72**(3), 961–984 (2016)
4. O'Loughlin, J., Gillam, L.: Addressing issues of cloud resilience, security and performance through simple detection of co-locating sibling virtual machine instances. In: 5th International Conference on Cloud Computing and Services Science (CLOSER 2015) (2015)

5. O'Loughlin, J., Gillam, L.: Performance evaluation for cost-efficient public infrastructure cloud use. In: Altmann, J., Vanmechelen, K., Rana, O.F. (eds.) GECON 2014. LNCS, vol. 8914, pp. 133–145. Springer, Cham (2014). https://doi.org/10.1007/978-3-319-14609-6_9

6. Zakarya, M., Gillam, L.: Managing energy, performance and cost in large scale heterogeneous datacenters using migrations. Future Gener. Comput. Syst. **93**, 529–547 (2019)

7. Zakarya, M., Gillam, L.: Energy efficient computing, clusters, grids and clouds: a taxonomy and survey. J. Sustain. Comput. Inf. Syst. **14**, 13–33 (2017)

8. Zakarya, M., Gillam, L.: An energy aware cost recovery approach for virtual machine migration. In: Bañares, J.Á., Tserpes, K., Altmann, J. (eds.) GECON 2016. LNCS, vol. 10382, pp. 175–190. Springer, Cham (2017). https://doi.org/10.1007/978-3-319-61920-0_13

9. Stevens, A., et al.: Cooperative automation through the cloud: the CARMA project. In: Proceedings of 12th ITS European Congress (2017)

10. Gillam, L., Katsaros, K., Dianati, M., Mouzakitis, A.: Exploring edges for connected and autonomous driving. In: IEEE INFOCOM Workshops: CCSNA 2018 (2018)

11. Morgan, T.P.: A rare Peek Intro The Massive Scale of AWS (2014). https://www.enterprisetech.com/2014/11/14/rare-peek-massive-scale-aws/

12. Greenpeace: Make IT Green: Cloud Computing and its Contribution to Climate Change, Greenpeace (2010)

13. O'Loughlin, J., Gillam, L.: Should infrastructure clouds be priced entirely on performance? An EC2 case study. Int. J. Big Data Intell. **1**(4), 215–229 (2014)

14. ETSI. Mobile Edge Computing (MEC). Introductory Technical White Paper, ETSI (2014)

15. Bonomi, F., Milito, R., Zhu, J., Addepalli, S.: Fog computing and its role in the internet of things. In: Proceedings of the First Edition of the MCC Workshop on Mobile Cloud Computing, MCC 2012, New York, USA, pp. 13–16 (2012)

16. Senior, S., Rec, C., Nishar, H., Horton, T.: AWS Connected Vehicle Solution: AWS Implementation Guide (2017). https://s3.amazonaws.com/solutions-reference/connected-vehicle-cloud/latest/connected-vehicle-solution.pdf

Model-Based Generation of Self-adaptive Cloud Services

Stefan Kehrer[✉] and Wolfgang Blochinger

Parallel and Distributed Computing Group, Reutlingen University,
Alteburgstrasse 150, 72762 Reutlingen, Germany
{stefan.kehrer,wolfgang.blochinger}@reutlingen-university.de

Abstract. An important shift in software delivery is the definition of a cloud service as an independently deployable unit by following the microservices architectural style. Container virtualization facilitates development and deployment by ensuring independence from the runtime environment. Thus, cloud services are built as container-based systems - a set of containers that control the lifecycle of software and middleware components. However, using containers leads to a new paradigm for service development and operation: Self-service environments enable software developers to deploy and operate container-based systems on their own - you build it, you run it. Following this approach, more and more operational aspects are transferred towards the responsibility of software developers. In this work, we propose a concept for self-adaptive cloud services based on container virtualization in line with the microservices architectural style and present a model-based approach that assists software developers in building these services. Based on operational models specified by developers, the mechanisms required for self-adaptation are automatically generated. As a result, each container automatically adapts itself in a reactive, decentralized manner. We evaluate a prototype, which leverages the emerging TOSCA standard to specify operational behavior in a portable manner.

Keywords: Microservices · Container · Self-adaptation ·
Model-based deployment · DevOps · TOSCA

1 Introduction

Today's business requires fast software release cycles. To this end, DevOps and continuous delivery have been introduced, which aim at bridging the gap between development and operations by employing automation and self-service tools. Microservices are an evolving architectural style for building and releasing software in line with the DevOps paradigm [1,17]. Microservices are autonomous and independently deployable [12].

However, the autonomous nature of microservices challenges their development: More and more operational aspects have to be ensured by software developers thus leading to a transfer of responsibility - or how Amazon calls it: "you

© Springer Nature Switzerland AG 2019
V. M. Muñoz et al. (Eds.): CLOSER 2018, CCIS 1073, pp. 40–63, 2019.
https://doi.org/10.1007/978-3-030-29193-8_3

build it, you run it" [15]. This is also enabled by technological advances such as container virtualization [9,17]: Cloud services are commonly built as a set of containers, which provide a portable means to deploy services to state of the art container runtime environments such as Marathon[1] on Apache Mesos[2] and Kubernetes[3].

Container-based systems define a context for the software and middleware components required and control their lifecycle: Containers define how to start these components, how to update components at runtime, and how to stop components before termination. Consequently, software developers have to implement container-based systems including operational behavior. Because containers interact with each other, every container has to be configured with specific runtime parameters as well as endpoint information. This configuration of containers might be applied during the deployment of a service. However, in a dynamic environment such as the cloud, runtime parameters have to be adapted dynamically. Furthermore, endpoint information will likely change at runtime, e.g., if a container has to be restarted. Thus, configuration is stored in the environment[4], i.e., configuration stores are used to store required runtime parameters and container registries are used to find other containers. Following this approach, software developers have to wire their implementation with technologies provided by the runtime environment. Besides adding more complexity, this leads to heterogeneous implementations of configuration and lifecycle management. Moreover, technological dependencies on configuration stores and registries provided by the runtime environment decrease the portability benefit inherent to containers.

To cope with the challenges described above, we present a novel model-based approach that eases the development of self-adaptive cloud services. Our approach enables software developers to specify operational behavior of cloud services based on higher-level models and automatically generates the mechanism required for self-adaptation. We transform a supplied cloud service into a self-adaptive one by automatically adding runtime behavior to its containers at a technical level. As a result, each container adapts itself to changes in the container runtime environment in a reactive, decentralized manner. This transformation is provided as a service to developers and thus decouples environment-specific technologies from software development. In particular, we make the following contributions:

- We present a concept for self-adaptive cloud services based on container virtualization in line with the microservices architectural style.
- We introduce a model-based approach to assist software developers in creating these self-adaptive cloud services.
- We provide a transformation method, which describes the steps of generating self-adaptive cloud services at a conceptual level.

---

[1] https://mesosphere.github.io/marathon.

[2] https://mesos.apache.org.

[3] https://kubernetes.io.

[4] https://12factor.net/config.

– We report on an implemented prototype based on the TOSCA standard and state of the art technologies, which automates the transformation method.
– We evaluate our approach by measuring the transformation time as well as the overhead related to an exemplary self-adaptive cloud service.

This work is based on previous research contributions that have been published in the paper AUTOGENIC: *Automated Generation of Self-configuring Microservices* [6], which has been presented at the *8th International Conference on Cloud Computing and Services Science (CLOSER)*. We expand our former work by presenting a concept for self-adaptive cloud services in line with the microservices architectural style and state-of-the-art container runtime environments. Moreover, we discuss our extended model-based approach and show how to implement self-adaptive cloud services.

The paper is structured as follows. In Sects. 2 and 3, we describe the microservices architectural style and a motivating scenario for our work. Section 4 presents our concept for self-adaptive cloud services based on container virtualization. Section 5 gives an overview of the AUTOGENIC approach. In Sect. 6, we discuss a transformation method, which describes the required steps to automate the generation of self-adaptive cloud services. Further, we present and evaluate an implemented prototype in Sects. 7 and 8. Section 9 reviews related work. In Sect. 10, we conclude our work.

2 Microservices

A microservice is built around a business capability and implements the user-interface, storage, and any external collaborations required [10]. Microservices combine concepts from distributed systems and service-oriented architecture leading to several benefits [12]. For instance, microservices can be implemented with different technologies enabling a best-of-breed approach. Thus, new technologies can be adopted and old technologies can be replaced much faster. Composing a system out of many small services also provides benefits for deployment and management: It allows to deploy and scale every microservice independently [11]. Typically, software containers are used to package and deploy microservice components [16]. A topology model or template, which describes the containers a microservice is composed of and their relationships, enables automated deployment [7].

However, the benefits of microservices come with the cost of operational complexity [4]. The autonomous nature inherent to microservices requires application developers to take responsibility for operational aspects such as dynamic configuration [8]. To this end, the *Twelve-Factor App*[5] principles propose to store these information in the runtime environment. Technologies such as configuration stores and registries are used to store configuration values and enable dynamic bindings among containers. Employing technologies like Consul[6], Etcd[7],

---

[5] https://12factor.net.
[6] https://www.consul.io.
[7] https://github.com/coreos/etcd.

or Zookeeper[8] is a common practice for developing microservices [21]. They provide a scalable medium to store configuration information. Thus, microservices are designed as self-adaptive entities, which automatically adapt to changes such as container failures or configuration changes in the environment as well as various management operations.

3 Motivation

In this section, we introduce a cloud service, which is used as a motivating example for our work. The topology of this service is composed of four containers interacting with each other (cf. Fig. 1): The *wordpress* container provides an Apache HTTP server running a WordPress installation. The *mysql* container runs a MySQL database. To answer user requests, the *wordpress* container connects to the *mysql* container and retrieves data stored in the relational database. Frequently requested results are cached by the *memcached* container, which runs a Memcached[9] installation. Memcached is an in-memory object caching system. The *memcached* container is queried by the *wordpress* container before sending a read request to the *mysql* container. Additionally, a separate *backup* container periodically stores backups of the MySQL database by connecting to the corresponding container. This service thus implements the user-interface, storage, and other technical requirements related to a specific business capability in line with the microservices architectural style [10].

For configuration purposes, every container of the formerly described cloud service requires its runtime parameters and endpoint information to interact with other containers in the topology. To access their runtime parameters, containers connect to a configuration store provided by the runtime environment. Similarly, every container connects to a container registry to access endpoint information of other containers (cf. Fig. 1). Whenever a runtime parameter or endpoint information changes in the environment, a container itself is responsible for reacting to this change. Furthermore, containers might exit with failures and have to be replaced by new containers. In this case, containers should automatically detect this new container and resume normally. This kind of self-adaptation ensures self-healing services and thus minimizes downtimes, accordingly.

However, to ensure self-adaptation, software developers have to wire their implementations with operational technologies provided by the runtime environment. We identified several problems with this approach: (1) APIs of the configuration store and the registry have to be used by software developers. Every time the operations personnel decides to choose another technology, software developers have to be instructed and existing implementations have to be modified. (2) The logical name of required containers has to be defined and known by software developers. (3) Storing endpoint information of containers, which are only used internally, in a central registry may lead to conflicts with other deployments and breaks the microservice paradigm, e.g., if another service

---

[8] https://zookeeper.apache.org.
[9] https://memcached.org.

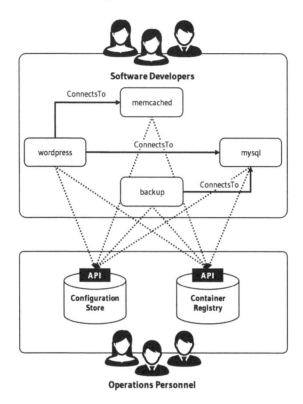

Fig. 1. Cloud services interact with their runtime environment for adapting their runtime behavior in a dynamic and decentralized manner.

requester receives the endpoint information of our MySQL database. This information should be kept private and not exposed to other services. (4) Moreover, portability is limited, i.e., services cannot be deployed to a runtime environment that does not provide the required technologies.

In general, software developers are confronted with environment-specific technologies to enable dynamic adaptation of their services. Technological dependencies on specific configuration stores or registries counteract the portability benefit of using container virtualization.

4 Self-adaptive Cloud Services

We introduce a novel concept for self-adaptive cloud services, which is compatible with state of the art container runtime environments. These container runtime environments provide tools for deploying and managing services or the corresponding containers, respectively. Each service can be composed of one or more containers [3]. Typical management tasks (such as scaling a service) can be easily automated by means of a container runtime environment. For example, new containers are added or existing containers are removed automatically by monitoring the workload of a service. However, to enable these features, containers have to be designed and built including operational behavior. In the following, we present an operational model for services, define the terms management and adaptation in this context, and derive the requirements that have to be fulfilled by self-adaptive cloud services.

Figure 2 shows the operational model that outlines how cloud services are deployed and managed by state of the art container runtime environments. These systems typically provide an interface for software developers to easily deploy a service by means of a *service bundle*. Since services are constructed as independently deployable units, a service bundle contains all the required artifacts to deploy a single service. An important part of the service bundle is the topology model describing the topology of containers and related artifacts (e.g., container images). The topology model contains all information required to automatically deploy a corresponding service to a target runtime environment.

A deployment system processes requests by deploying a set of containers in line with the specification of the service bundle. A monitoring system monitors the load of the running service and provides input to an application controller. Additionally, the runtime environment provides a configuration store and a container registry. Since services store their configuration in the environment (See footnote 4), configuration stores are used to store runtime parameters and registries are used to find other containers. As we can see in Fig. 2, this poses much more requirements on software developers than simply specifying the required containers and their relationships for deployment purposes. Developers also have to consider operational aspects of individual containers such as dynamic configuration and container removal (cf. Sect. 2).

Figure 2 depicts two loops: A *management loop* that ensures container management, which is performed by the application controller, and an *adaptation loop* that ensures the adaptation of software and middleware components operated in containers. Whereas the management loop is ensured by the container runtime environment, containers have to ensure the adaptation of software and middleware components based on environmental changes. As we can see, the management of these services boils down to simply deploying and terminating containers at the right moment. However, adaptation in response to changes initiated by management actions has to be ensured by software developers, who build these containers. Thus, each container has to fulfill the following requirements:

- Start and configure software and middleware components when the container is started.
- Register itself with the container registry to be available for other containers, which are part of the cloud service topology.
- Detect changes of runtime parameters in the configuration store and adapt to these changes.
- Detect changes in the container registry and adapt to these changes.
- Gracefully shutdown software and middleware components before container removal.

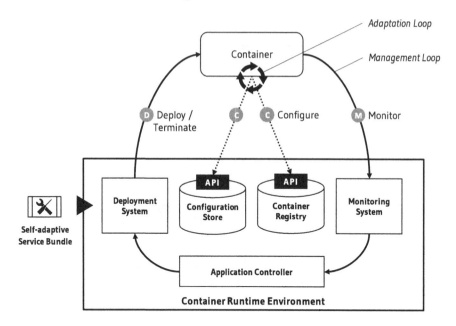

Fig. 2. Operational model of a typical container runtime environment.

Whereas starting and configuring software and middleware components can be defined in a build specification such as a Dockerfile, all other aspects require an environment-specific implementation. We introduce a novel entity per container that addresses these requirements: The so-called *container supervisor*. A container supervisor resides inside a container, controls the lifecycle of provided software and middleware components, and orchestrates their lifecycle according to events in the environment. These events might be changes in the configuration store or container registry as well as signals send by the container runtime environment. At a technical level, a container supervisor is a supervisor process running inside a container. It is started as the root process[10] of the container and controls the lifecycle of all other processes. Further, the root process receives and dispatches signals from the container runtime environment[11].

Figure 3 shows two exemplary container supervisors, which ensure runtime adaptation in an event-based and decentralized manner. We can see two containers namely *wordpress_container* and *mysql_container* (cf. Sect. 3). Both containers are connected to a configuration store and a container registry provided by the container runtime environment (analogously to Fig. 1). In the following, we discuss a series of timely ordered events and the corresponding adaptation mechanisms performed by both container supervisors.

---

[10] A root process is a process with UNIX PID 1.
[11] For example, POSIX signals are an inter-process communication mechanism typically used in Unix-like operating systems and employed by state of the art container runtime environments.

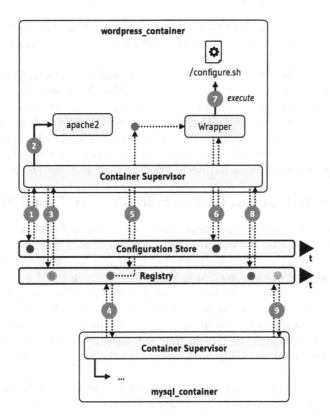

Fig. 3. Exemplary self-adaptation process of WordPress container using a container supervisor.

First, the *wordpress_container* is deployed. Directly after container startup, its container supervisor stores the required configuration values in the configuration store ❶ and starts the Apache HTTP server ❷. When the web server has been started successfully, the container supervisor registers its endpoint information in the container registry ❸. At some point in time, the deployment of the *mysql_container* is processed by the deployment system. In this case, the container supervisor of *mysql_container* executes the local container startup. This includes running the MySQL database. Thereafter, it also registers itself in the container registry ❹. The *wordpress_container* detects this change and triggers a wrapper process, which employs the endpoint information of the *mysql_container* ❺, loads configuration values from the configuration store ❻, and finally executes a configuration script with the required inputs, i.e., endpoint information and configuration values ❼. Steps ❺–❼ are executed whenever the endpoint information of *mysql_container* changes, e.g., due to a container restart. At the end of its lifecycle, a container receives a termination signal from the container runtime environment. In this case, the container supervisor removes its entries from the container registry ❽, ❾ and gracefully stops the running software and middleware components. Note that this kind of event-based self-adaptation is agnostic to the deployment order and thus allows for arbitrary container restarts at runtime.

Reactive self-adaptation as described above enables self-adaptive and self-healing cloud services contributing to service availability. However, to make use of these benefits, software developers have to wire their implementation with technologies provided by the runtime environment. Besides adding more complexity, this leads to heterogeneous implementations of adaptation mechanisms. Moreover, developers are confronted with a bunch of operational technologies to implement the required behavior, which decreases software development times.

5   Automated Generation of Self-adaptive Cloud Services

We propose the *automated generation of self-adaptive cloud services* (AUTOGENIC) to assist software developers in considering operational aspects. We aim at providing a means for software developers to take responsibility for operational aspects of their service in line with the "you build it, you run it" principle. We identified two fundamental design guidelines for such an approach: (1) Software developers have to be enabled to control the lifecycle of their service and its components by simple means. (2) Technological considerations of operational aspects should be hidden from software developers to enable portability and operational flexibility with respect to the runtime environment and tool support.

AUTOGENIC is an approach to decouple service development from environment-specific technologies provided by operations personnel. Our goal is to design a self-service tool for software developers, which supports closer cooperation among developers and operational personnel in the sense of DevOps [5]: Developers are able to consider operational aspects of their services by simple means and operations personnel contributes the technological requirements of the runtime environment, which are automatically added to each service (cf. Fig. 4).

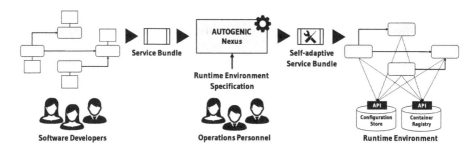

Fig. 4. Overview of the AUTOGENIC approach based on [6].

Our approach follows the microservices architectural style. Microservices are defined as independently deployable units. Thus, we assume some kind of *service bundle*, which describes all service components and specifies their relationships among each other. A topology model describes the topology of software containers and related artifacts. The *service bundle* contains all information required to automatically deploy a corresponding cloud service to a runtime environment.

To model the behavior of a self-adaptive service, we utilize the existing topology model, which is part of every service bundle. We enable developers to annotate each container specified in the topology model with a *lifecycle* and a *configuration model*. Each model contains one or more *operations*. These operations are defined by a name and specify an implementation artifact as well as inputs. The implementation artifact refers to an executable artifact contained in the container (e.g., a script) that must be invoked to execute the operation at a technical level. The inputs can be defined as key-value pairs, which are passed to the implementation artifact upon execution. This leads to two types of operations:

- A **lifecycle operation** is bound to an operational event with predefined semantics. We define three predefined lifecycle operations: create, start, and stop. Create is employed to instantiate a container, start is executed after a container instance has been created, and stop before a container is terminated by the runtime environment.
- A **configuration operation** is an operation without predefined semantics. These operations are specified by software developers. A configuration operation is executed whenever a specified input value changes.

Lifecycle operations specify the artifacts that have to be executed to create, start, or stop a container. The create operation specifies the container image that should be used for deployment purposes, whereas start and stop can be used to specify an application-specific script. Configuration operations can be employed to model any kind of adaptation behavior. In case of our exemplary cloud service, a shell script for connecting to the MySQL database might be specified as implementation artifact of the *configure_db* operation attached to the *wordpress* container (cf. Fig. 5). Additionally, we enable the use of *functions* to specify input values for configuration operations. Functions can be used to reference dynamic attribute values of entities in the topology model, e.g., IP addresses of modeled containers. Referring to our exemplary service, the *configure_db* operation specifies an input named *mysql_ip* with the function *getIPAddress()* that retrieves the IP address of the *mysql* container (cf. Fig. 5).

A core idea of the AUTOGENIC approach is to automatically bind lifecycle and configuration operations modeled by developers to runtime events. Therefore, each container is automatically enhanced with a container supervisor as described in Sect. 4. The container supervisor ensures event dispatching and implements the operations specified in the lifecycle and configuration models as follows. Create and start are triggered during the deployment process. In case of the stop operation, a termination signal sent by the runtime environment is used as trigger. Configuration operations, on the other hand, are executed whenever their input values change. Since these input values are stored in the runtime environment, a corresponding *event-trigger* has to be registered to this change event

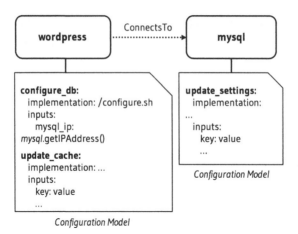

Fig. 5. Service components with configuration models attached based on [6]. Additionally, each component relates to a lifecycle model, which is not shown here but attached in an analogous manner.

in the environment. The callback of this event-trigger is given by the implementation artifact specified for the corresponding configuration operation. A simple example is the configuration of the WordPress container. In this case, reconfiguration is only required if the IP address of the MySQL container changes. This enables reactive configuration and dynamic bindings among containers.

The topology model enhanced with the proposed lifecycle and configuration models, which is part of every service bundle, is passed to a component that we call AUTOGENIC *Nexus* (cf. Fig. 4). AUTOGENIC Nexus takes a developer-supplied service bundle as input and generates a self-adaptive service bundle as output. The transformation applied adds self-adaptation mechanisms to each container at a technical level based on the operations specified in the lifecycle and configuration models. AUTOGENIC *Nexus* is maintained by operations personnel and provided as a self-service tool to software developers. It encapsulates the specifics of the target runtime environment. This might be the access mechanisms of the configuration store and the container registry used in the runtime environment (e.g., APIs) as well as event-dispatching mechanisms to trigger developer-supplied implementation artifacts. The selection of these technologies is an operational decision and thus should be handled transparently to software development. The runtime environment specification has to be considered during the implementation of the AUTOGENIC Nexus (cf. Sect. 7.3).

Implemented once, the AUTOGENIC Nexus provides a self-service tool for developers, which generates self-adaptive service bundles targeted to a specific runtime environment without any knowledge on operational technologies employed. The self-adaptive service bundle contains all required information to deploy a cloud service in an automated manner (cf. Fig. 4). This approach ensures the separation of concerns principle in the DevOps context in line with our design guidelines defined above.

Following our model-based approach, service bundles can be developed independently of the runtime environment. This leads to several benefits compared to service adaptation at the programming level, i.e., directly implementing the API of a configuration store or container registry and wiring POSIX signals: (1) Different technologies can be used to implement the required adaptation behavior depending on the target runtime environment; (2) Developers do not have to build triggers for lifecycle and configuration operations by wiring APIs. Configuration operations are executed whenever their input values change; (3) Logical identifiers of containers are only used in the model and not in the containers themselves leading to higher reusability. Further, these identifiers are private to the topology model of a single service and thus cannot be used by other services. Note that this is an important requirement, e.g., to prevent direct database access from outside the service [15].

6   Transformation Method

The *transformation method* specifies the steps to transform an existing service bundle including its lifecycle and configuration models into a self-adaptive service bundle. This method describes the transformation performed by the AUTO-GENIC Nexus at a conceptual level to guide the runtime-specific implementation by operations personnel. Accordingly, our method describes the transformation independently of (1) the modeling language used for topology, lifecycle, and configuration models, (2) the container format employed for virtualization, (3) operational technologies in the target runtime environment, and (4) the container supervisor and its event-dispatching mechanisms used to build event-triggers. As a result, our method supports the multitude of combinations, which can be found in practice. Figure 6 depicts the transformation method. We describe its steps in the following.

Assumptions: This method requires a service bundle that contains a topology model enhanced with lifecycle and configuration models. Moreover, build specifications for each container are assumed to be part of the service bundle.

Step 1: Scan Topology Model & Build Specifications

We assume that each container specified in the topology model links its lifecycle and configuration model as well as a build specification. Whereas the models describe the desired adaptation behavior, the build specification can be used to derive the current runtime behavior of the container. In this step, lifecycle and configuration models as well as container build specifications are scanned to derive a set of Transformation Requirements (TR). TRs describe the requirements that have to be addressed during the transformation and are provided as input to the next steps. Scanning the lifecycle and configuration models leads to the following TRs:

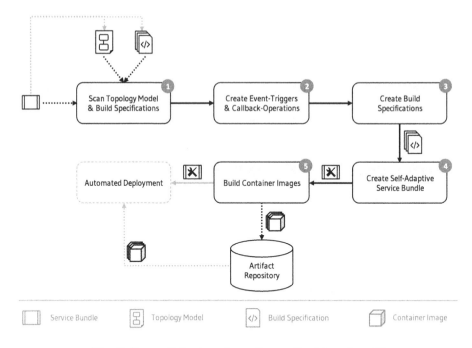

Fig. 6. Steps of the transformation method based on [6]

- A *StartRequirement* is derived from a start operation in the lifecycle model. The implementation artifact defined by the operation has to be executed when a container has been successfully created and initialized.
- A *StoreKeyValueRequirement* describes a key-value pair, which is used as input for a specific configuration operation in the configuration model. This key-value pair has to be stored in the runtime environment during deployment (e.g., by using a configuration store).
- A *KeyWatchRequirement* describes the requirement to watch the value of a specific input key stored in the environment. Whenever the value related to this key changes the corresponding configuration operation, which is specified in the configuration model, has to be executed.
- An *AttributeWatchRequirement* describes the requirement to watch the value of a defined attribute such as the IP address of a specific container. Whenever this value changes the corresponding configuration operation, which is specified in the configuration model, has to be executed.
- A *TerminationRequirement* is derived from a stop operation in the lifecycle model. The implementation artifact defined by the operation has to be executed before a container is forcefully terminated by the runtime environment.

Scanning the build specifications additionally leads to the following TR:

- An *EntryPointRequirement* describes the entrypoint of a container. This is an executable to be run at container startup [22].

TRs allow the automated construction of a new container image (cf. Sect. 6), which fulfills the same functional requirements as the developer-supplied container image, but additionally ensures the modeled self-adaptation mechanisms.

Step 2: Create Event-triggers & Callback-Operations

In this step, the TRs derived have to be addressed. Therefore, implementation artifacts provided by developers have to be bound as callbacks to change events in the environment. Environment-specific event-dispatching mechanisms are employed for this purpose. At the same time, functional aspects of a developer-supplied container should be retained.

StartRequirements can be addressed by simply executing the corresponding implementation artifact at container startup.

StoreKeyValueRequirements are addressed by an initial setup process executed at each container's startup. This setup process stores the required inputs in the environment. After the initial setup process, each container runs the executable captured in its *EntryPointRequirement*.

KeyWatchRequirements as well as *AttributeWatchRequirements* have to be met by installing an event-trigger for the corresponding configuration operation, which executes the implementation artifact specified whenever input values change. The implementation of event-triggers depends on the technologies employed in the target runtime environment. This includes mapping the schema of operational data structures as well as defining access methods and protocols for the configuration store and the container registry.

TerminationRequirements are bound to the termination signal, which is sent by the container runtime environment before termination.

This step results in a set of technological artifacts, which ensure dynamic adaptation of each container with respect to the target runtime environment. The generated technological artifacts automatically trigger the implementation artifacts supplied by the developer either upon operational events (for lifecycle operations) or every time an input value changes in the environment (for configuration operations).

Step 3: Create Build Specifications

To combine the developer-supplied container image with the technological artifacts generated in Step 2, a new build specification is created for each container specified in the topology model. This build specification is built on top of the existing build specification that defines the developer-supplied service. A build specification template may be used, which contains settings required according to the runtime environment specification, e.g., commands to install required software.

Step 4: Create Self-adaptive Service Bundle

Since lifecycle and configuration operations are now managed by the corresponding container itself, these operations are not required in the topology model anymore. Only the create operation is still required and links the newly created container image. In this step, a new service bundle is generated, which provides a portable means to deploy the generated self-adaptive cloud service to the target runtime environment.

Step 5: Build Container Images

Finally, the container images of the newly generated build specifications captured in the self-adaptive service bundle have to be built. Besides creating container images, they have to be pushed to an artifact repository (cf. Fig. 6), which can be accessed during deployment.

Automated Deployment

The generated service bundle provides a means to automatically deploy the generated self-adaptive cloud service to the target runtime environment. Therefore, container images can be retrieved from the artifact repository (cf. Fig. 6) specified in the service bundle.

7   Prototypical Implementation

In this section, we present an AUTOGENIC Nexus prototype. The transformation method describes how to generate a self-adaptive service bundle for the target runtime environment at a conceptual level. Hence, we have to make four decisions with respect to a prototypical implementation: First, we have to specify the modeling language used for topology, lifeclycle, and configuration models. Possible options are any custom modeling language supporting our assumptions, domain-specific languages of container orchestration tools such as Kubernetes and Marathon as well as the TOSCA standard [13]. Secondly, we have to choose a container format such as Docker, Application Container (appc) Specification[12], or the specification of the Open Container Initiative (OCI)[13]. Thirdly, we have to define the operational technologies of the target runtime environment. Typical examples are Consul, Etcd, ZooKeeper, SkyDNS[14], Eureka[15], and Doozer[16]. Finally, a container supervisor is required. A container supervisor can be built from scratch by combining a process supervisor (e.g., Supervisord[17]) with clients of the configuration store/container registry provided by the target runtime environment. Alternatively, ContainerPilot[18] can be used.

In this section, we describe a prototype employing the emerging TOSCA standard as modeling language, which also contains a format for service bundles. We rely on the TOSCA standard because it provides a language to specify topology models of cloud services in a portable manner and concepts to specify dependencies in the model. The TOSCA concept of Lifecycle Operations already

---

[12] https://github.com/appc/spec.
[13] https://www.opencontainers.org.
[14] https://github.com/skynetservices/skydns.
[15] https://github.com/Netflix/eureka.
[16] https://github.com/ha/doozerd.
[17] http://supervisord.org.
[18] https://github.com/joyent/containerpilot.

provides us with compatible modeling constructs to specify lifecycle and configuration operations. Further, we employ Docker[19] as container virtualization technology, Consul as configuration store and container registry, and ContainerPilot (See footnote 18) as container supervisor. We describe TOSCA and a TOSCA-based service bundle of our exemplary cloud service in the following. Moreover, we present an exemplary runtime environment specification. On this basis, we present the implementation of our prototype.

7.1 Topology and Orchestration Specification for Cloud Applications (TOSCA)

The Topology and Orchestration Specification for Cloud Applications (TOSCA) aims at standardizing a modeling language for portable cloud services [13]. Therefore, cloud services are captured as topology graphs modeled in form of a Topology Template. The nodes in the topology are modeled as Node Templates.

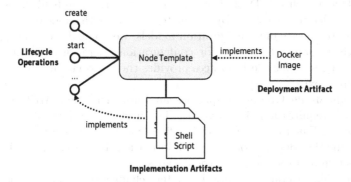

Fig. 7. TOSCA artifacts and lifecycle operations based on [6].

Since a Topology Template is an abstract description of a service topology, Deployment Artifacts such as container images (e.g., Docker Images) are linked to Node Templates as depicted in Fig. 7. Node Templates also define Lifecycle Operations. These Lifecycle Operations are implemented by Implementation Artifacts such as shell scripts (cf. Fig. 7).

Additionally, TOSCA provides a type system that allows the definition of custom types such as Node Types or Artifact Types. These type definitions and the Topology Template are captured in a so-called Service Template. A TOSCA orchestrator processes a Service Template to instantiate nodes. Modeling a TOSCA-based cloud service results in a self-contained, portable service model called Cloud Service ARchive (CSAR) that can be used to deploy service instances in all TOSCA-compliant environments. The CSAR contains the Service Template and related Deployment Artifacts as well as Implementation Artifacts.

---

[19] https://docker.com.

Integrating TOSCA and Containers has been addressed by recent research [2,7]. In the Simple Profile in YAML V1.0 [14], TOSCA provides modeling constructs for containers as well as TOSCA Functions. TOSCA functions allow referencing values of entities in the Topology Template, which have to be resolved at runtime.

7.2   TOSCA-based Service Bundle

In this section, we describe a TOSCA-based service bundle of our exemplary cloud service described in Sect. 3. This service bundle will be used as exemplary input for our prototypical implementation. Note that we only present representative parts of the service bundle.

We use a CSAR as service bundle, which contains a description of the service topology by means of a Topology Template. The Topology Template specifies Node Templates for the containers, namely *wordpress*, *memcached*, *mysql*, and *backup*. Listing 1.1 shows the Node Template of *wordpress*. It specifies its Deployment Artifact, which is a Docker Image (cf. Listing 1.1, line 6–9). This Docker Image is provided to the Create Operation to instantiate the node (cf. Listing 1.1, line 12–13). To specify our configuration models, we append an additional Lifecycle Interface named *Configure* for configuration operations (cf. Listing 1.1, line 14–22). These Lifecycle Interfaces provides the information required by the AUTOGENIC Nexus.

The *configure_db* Operation specifies an Implementation Artifact */config-ure.sh*, which requires four input values. The host of the database is specified with a TOSCA Function (cf. Listing 1.1, line 18). A TOSCA Function specifies an input value that depends on runtime information. In this case, the IP address of *mysql* is required to connect to the database.

Container images only capture file system changes and thus do not provide information on how they have been created. They are constructed of a set of layers each described by a corresponding build specification such as a Dockerfile. However, the TOSCA standard does not allow the definition of build specifications describing the construction of container images. To resolve this issue, we introduced the concept of *Contained Nodes* [7] to model build specifications for each Node Template. Therefore, a *container* Node Template such as *wordpress* links a *contained* Node Template (cf. Listing 1.1, line 3). The *wordpress_build* Node Template specifies the build specification of the corresponding *wordpress-custom* Docker Image (cf. Listing 1.2, line 4–9). Here, the build specification is a Dockerfile.

The containers *memcached*, *mysql*, and *backup* are modeled in an analogous manner and specify their lifecycle and configuration operations as explained above.

```
1   wordpress:
2     ...
3     contains: [wordpress_build]
4     ...
5     artifacts:
6       wp_image:
7         file: wordpress-custom
8         type: tosca.artifacts.Deployment.Image.Container.Docker
9         repository: custom_repository
10    interfaces:
11      Standard:
12        create:
13          implementation: wp_image
14      Configure:
15        configure_db:
16          implementation: /configure.sh
17          inputs:
18            DB_HOST: { get_attribute: [mysql, ip_address] }
19            DB_USER: myuser
20            DB_PASSWORD: pw
21            DB_NAME: mydb
22          ...
```

Listing 1.1: wordpress Node Template in YAML based on [6].

7.3   Runtime Environment Specification

The target runtime environment addressed by our prototype is a TOSCA-based container runtime environment from previous work [7], which can be used to deploy a TOSCA-based service bundle on Apache Mesos (See footnote 2). We selected Consul to store configuration and endpoint information in the environment, which provides both a key-value store to store configuration data and container discovery mechanisms. The Consul ecosystem provides a rich set of tools to access stored data. To enable self-adaptive cloud services, we have to additionally select technologies used to bind configuration operations to events. We chose ContainerPilot, which is an open-source project developed by Joyent. ContainerPilot resembles the UNIX concept of process supervision by providing a supervisor middleware for processes running inside a software container. Besides, it provides integration with service discovery tooling, which we apply to bind event-triggers to configuration operations. ContainerPilot is configured by passing a configuration file, which contains the processes to be run. A Docker Registry[20] is employed as artifact repository, i.e., to push and retrieve container images (cf. Fig. 6).

---

[20] https://hub.docker.com/_/registry.

```
1  wordpress_build:
2    ...
3    artifacts:
4      build_spec:
5        file: artifacts/wordpress/Dockerfile
6        type: cst.artifacts.Deployment.BuildSpec.Docker
7        properties:
8          image_name: wordpress-custom
9          repository: custom_repository
10   interfaces:
11     Standard:
12       create:
13         implementation: build_spec
```

Listing 1.2: wordpress_build Node Template in YAML based on [6].

7.4 Implementation

In this section, we outline how we implemented our prototype in Java. Therefore, we describe the implementation counterparts of step 1–5 defined by the AUTOGENIC method (cf. Sect. 6).

Step 1: Scan Topology Model & Build Specifications. A TOSCA Parser loads the TOSCA-based service bundle and transforms the Service Template into an internal object. Our RequirementScanner derives TRs (also represented as Java objects) from the Topology Template. Moreover, the RequirementScanner scans the Dockerfiles linked in the Service Template to identify EntryPointRequirements.

Step 2: Create Event-Triggers & Callback-Operations. We employ ContainerPilot version 3.1.1 as container supervisor for each container. The key-value pairs described by StoreKeyValueRequirements are stored in Consul with an initial setup process executed on container startup. Implementation artifacts defined by start and stop operations in the lifecycle model are bound to the corresponding operational events. Moreover, the executable captured in an EntryPointRequirement is executed after the initial setup process. KeyWatchRequirements and AttributeWatchRequirements require the installation of event-triggers. This is not supported by ContainerPilot. Technically, we register separate background processes in the ContainerPilot configuration file. These background processes run Consul watches with the Consul command line tool, which can be used to get informed whenever a value changes. We use Consul watches to trigger envconsul[21] whenever an input value of a configuration operation changes in Consul. Envconsul can be used to launch a subprocess with environment variables read from Consul. Here, envconsul executes the implementation artifact

---

[21] https://github.com/hashicorp/envconsul.

of the corresponding configuration operation and provides the inputs as environment variables. The resulting technological artifacts are a ContainerPilot configuration file and scripts for the initial setup process.

Step 3: Create Build Specifications. To create build specifications, we use a file template for each Dockerfile, which installs a Consul client, envconsul, and ContainerPilot. Additionally, we add the artifacts generated in Step 2. The generation of build specifications is implemented based on Apache FreeMarker[22], which is an open-source template engine.

Step 4: Create Self-Adaptive Service Bundle. A new contained Node Template is added to each container Node Template, which is built on top of the developer-supplied contained Node Template and links the generated build specification. Besides, the Deployment Artifacts of the container Node Templates are updated with the name of the new container images. The generated Service Template is added to a newly generated service bundle, which contains all build specifications and technological artifacts required to build the container images.

Step 5: Build Container Images. To build container images, we assume a Docker Engine running on the host that provides the AUTOGENIC Nexus as a service to developers. We connect to the Docker Engine by using the Docker-Client[23] library developed by Spotify. Docker-Client connects to the Docker Engine via the default UNIX domain socket provided to control Docker-specific functionality. We build the required container images described by the generated build specifications and push them to the artifact repository specified in the Topology Template.

8   Evaluation

To evaluate our prototype, we employ the service bundle of our motivating example (cf. Sect. 7.2). We present two experiments with respect to the automated generation of an exemplary self-adaptive cloud service using the prototype and analyze the resulting overhead. In the baseline experiment, we build all developer-supplied container images specified in the service bundle and measure the total generation time. We define the total generation time as the accumulated time, which is required to build these container images and to push the generated container images to the artifact repository. In the transformation experiment, we run the prototype to generate a self-adaptive service bundle and measure the total transformation time. We define the total transformation time as the elapsed time from the start of the prototype to the point, where all steps of the transformation method have been successfully completed. This also includes pushing the generated container images to the corresponding artifact repository.

We executed our experiments on a CentOS 7 virtual machine with 2 vCPUs clocked at 2.6 GHz, 4 GB RAM, and 40 GB disk running in our OpenStack-based cloud environment. The virtual machine provides an OpenJDK Runtime

---

[22] http://freemarker.org.
[23] https://github.com/spotify/docker-client.

Environment 1.8.0 and Docker Engine 1.12.6. For building container images, we rely on the Docker Engine API v1.24. As artifact repository, we run a private Docker Registry v2.6 on localhost. We executed ten independent runs of each experiment and measured the total generation time and the total transformation time, respectively.

In the baseline experiment, we build a single container image for each container. These container images are built based on the build specification specified in the service bundle. However, all container images require base images from the DockerHub. The *wordpress* container requires downloading *php:5.6-apache*[24] with 377.7 MB, *memcached* requires *debian:stretch-slim*[25] with 55.24 MB, *mysql* requires *oraclelinux:7-slim*[26] with 117.6 MB, and *backup* requires *python:2.7.14-jessie*[27] with 679.3 MB. To ensure that we measure the total generation time without caching, we cleared the Docker cache and the Docker Registry before every run. In this context, caching of container images relates to the intermediate layers stored by Docker to speed up future build processes. Based on the measurements, we calculated an average total generation time of 882 ± 38 s.

In the transformation experiment, we ran our prototype to measure the total transformation time. Therefore, all required container images are built and pushed to the artifact repository. This includes the developer-supplied container images as well as container images generated. Again, we cleared the Docker cache and the Docker Registry before every run. Based on the measurements, we calculated an average total transformation time of 1349 ± 16 s.

The transformation adds an average overhead in size of 67.8 MB per container image. This is largely related to ContainerPilot and Consul-specific tooling. Note that the container images built in the baseline experiment are not self-adaptive. Additional manual effort would be required to enable the same features, thus also leading to larger image sizes.

In summary, the transformation applied by our prototype results in an average overhead of 467 s. However, we enable software developers to implement their cloud services independently of operational technologies, which saves time during development. Moreover, our model-based approach leads to several benefits such as portability of service implementations and the separation of concerns for software developers and operations personnel (cf. Sect. 5).

The overhead measured is basically related to building additional container images, which include the required self-adaptation mechanisms. Note that the measurements depend on the size of required and generated container images, the network bandwidth for downloading the required base images, and the location of the artifact repository. Thus, the reported values may be different in a real world scenario. Additionally, we identified several opportunities to speed up the transformation performance such as building container images concurrently and

---

[24] https://hub.docker.com/_/php.

[25] https://hub.docker.com/_/debian.

[26] https://hub.docker.com/_/oraclelinux.

[27] https://hub.docker.com/_/python.

storing required software packages locally. Obviously, caching techniques offer another opportunity for performance tuning.

9 Related Work

The microservices architectural style proposes decentralized management and prefers choreography over orchestration [4,12,18,23]. Our concept of self-adaptive cloud services enables dynamic and decentralized adaptation and does not rely on centralized orchestration. We argue that state of the art container runtime environments provide the required management functionality and complement their operational principles with decentralized, event-based adaptation managed by a container supervisor.

Several approaches exist to build cloud services with decentralized adaptation capabilities. The authors of [20,21] propose an architecture for self-managing cloud-native applications, which enables scalable and resilient self-managing applications in the cloud. They employ distributed in-memory key-value stores as means to communicate changes among components. With respect to the operational principles employed, their approach is similar to ours. However, our model-based approach contributes to the ease of development of self-adaptive cloud services. Thus, developers are relieved of the burden of wiring their implementations with APIs of operational technologies. The authors of [19] present a solution to the service discovery problem based on Serf[28]. Their approach proposes an additional *Serfnode* container, which manages a required container instance. In contrast, we introduce a container supervisor that manages the lifecycle of a single container. Whereas Serfnodes do not require building new container images, they require extra configuration and only solve the service discovery problem. Moreover, the presented solution does not provide the same abstraction level compared to our model-based approach, which uses lifecycle and configuration models to define operational behavior at a higher level.

Microservice chassis[29] such as Spring Cloud[30] might be used at the programming level to implement self-adaptive services. However, microservice chassis are bound to a specific programming language and are limited to supported operational tooling. Netflix Prana[31] provides a side car for services based on the NetflixOSS[32] ecosystem. This enables the use of Java-based NetflixOSS libraries for microservices written in other programming languages. Registrator[33] enables service discovery features for Docker containers by watching the runtime environment. All these technologies provide alternatives to some operational aspects addressed by our approach. However, they are restricted to a specific runtime

---

[28] https://www.serf.io.
[29] http://microservices.io/patterns/microservice-chassis.html.
[30] http://projects.spring.io/spring-cloud.
[31] https://github.com/Netflix/Prana.
[32] https://netflix.github.io.
[33] https://github.com/gliderlabs/registrator.

environment, operational technologies, or a programming language. On the contrary, we address the portability issue (cf. Sect. 3) by proposing a model-based approach.

10   Conclusion and Future Work

In this paper, we present a method to generate self-adaptive cloud services by following a model-based approach. We thus decouple software developers and operations personnel by separating their concerns and contribute to the portability of cloud services. A novel self-service tool for software developers automatically transforms a supplied service bundle to a self-adaptive service bundle, which is specifically suited for the targeted runtime environment, and thus also enables flexibility for operations personnel with respect to technological decisions and changes. Furthermore, the transformation method captures the steps to generate self-adaptive cloud services in a reusable manner and can be employed to guide environment-specific implementations of the AutoGenIc Nexus concept. We validated our approach by implementing a prototype based on the TOSCA standard and state of the art technologies.

In the future, we plan to add user interfaces, which allow developers to reconfigure the runtime parameters of their cloud services. This allows rapid changes if the source code does not have to be refactored. Every change is directly propagated by the configuration store (e.g., Consul) and triggers the defined callback operation in a reactive and decentralized manner in line with the microservices architectural style. Moreover, we plan to investigate how the concepts presented here can be beneficially employed for migrating legacy applications to the cloud.

References

1. Balalaie, A., Heydarnoori, A., Jamshidi, P.: Microservices architecture enables devops: migration to a cloud-native architecture. IEEE Softw. **33**(3), 42–52 (2016)
2. Brogi, A., Rinaldi, L., Soldani, J.: TosKer: a synergy between TOSCA and Docker for orchestrating multicomponent applications. Softw. Pract. Exp. **48**(11), 2061–2079 (2018)
3. Burns, B., Oppenheimer, D.: Design patterns for container-based distributed systems. In: Proceedings of the 8th USENIX Conference on Hot Topics in Cloud Computing (HotCloud), pp. 108–113. USENIX (2016)
4. Fowler, M.: Microservices Resource Guide (2017). https://martinfowler.com/microservices/
5. Hüttermann, M.: DevOps for Developers. Apress (2012)
6. Kehrer, S., Blochinger, W.: Autogenic: automated generation of self-configuring microservices. In: Proceedings of the 8th International Conference on Cloud Computing and Services Science, CLOSER, vol. 1, pp. 35–46. INSTICC, SciTePress (2018). https://doi.org/10.5220/0006659800350046
7. Kehrer, S., Blochinger, W.: TOSCA-based container orchestration on mesos. Comput. Sci. Res. Dev. **33**(3), 305–316 (2018)

8. Kookarinrat, P., Temtanapat, Y.: Design and implementation of a decentralized message bus for microservices. In: 2016 13th International Joint Conference on Computer Science and Software Engineering (JCSSE), pp. 1–6, July 2016
9. Kratzke, N., Quint, P.C.: Understanding cloud-native applications after 10 years of cloud computing - a systematic mapping study. J. Syst. Softw. **126**, 1–16 (2017)
10. Lewis, J., Fowler, M.: Microservices a definition of this new architectural term (2014). https://martinfowler.com/articles/microservices.html
11. Leymann, F., Breitenbücher, U., Wagner, S., Wettinger, J.: Native cloud applications: why monolithic virtualization is not their foundation. In: Helfert, M., Ferguson, D., Méndez Muñoz, V., Cardoso, J. (eds.) CLOSER 2016. CCIS, vol. 740, pp. 16–40. Springer, Cham (2017). https://doi.org/10.1007/978-3-319-62594-2_2
12. Newman, S.: Building Microservices, 1st edn. O'Reilly Media Inc., Sebastopol (2015)
13. OASIS: Topology and orchestration specification for cloud applications (TOSCA) version 1.0, committee specification 01 (2013). http://docs.oasis-open.org/tosca/TOSCA/v1.0/cs01/TOSCA-v1.0-cs01.html
14. OASIS: TOSCA simple profile in YAML version 1.0, committee specification 01 (2016). http://docs.oasis-open.org/tosca/TOSCA-Simple-Profile-YAML/v1.0/cs01/TOSCA-Simple-Profile-YAML-v1.0-cs01.html
15. O'Hanlon, C.: A conversation with werner vogels. Queue **4**(4), 14:14–14:22 (2006)
16. Pahl, C., Brogi, A., Soldani, J., Jamshidi, P.: Cloud container technologies: a state-of-the-art review. IEEE Trans. Cloud Comput. (2017). https://doi.org/10.1109/TCC.2017.2702586
17. Pahl, C., Jamshidi, P.: Microservices: a systematic mapping study. In: Proceedings of the 6th International Conference on Cloud Computing and Services Science, CLOSER 2016, vols. 1 and 2, pp. 137–146. SCITEPRESS - Science and Technology Publications, Lda (2016)
18. Schermann, G., Cito, J., Leitner, P.: All the services large and micro: revisiting industrial practice in services computing. In: Norta, A., Gaaloul, W., Gangadharan, G.R., Dam, H.K. (eds.) ICSOC 2015. LNCS, vol. 9586, pp. 36–47. Springer, Heidelberg (2016). https://doi.org/10.1007/978-3-662-50539-7_4
19. Stubbs, J., Moreira, W., Dooley, R.: Distributed systems of microservices using docker and serfnode. In: 2015 7th International Workshop on Science Gateways, pp. 34–39, June 2015
20. Toffetti, G., Brunner, S., Blöchlinger, M., Dudouet, F., Edmonds, A.: An architecture for self-managing microservices. In: Proceedings of the 1st International Workshop on Automated Incident Management in Cloud, AIMC 2015, pp. 19–24. ACM, New York (2015)
21. Toffetti, G., Brunner, S., Blöchlinger, M., Spillner, J., Bohnert, T.M.: Self-managing cloud-native applications: design, implementation, and experience. Future Gener. Comput. Syst. **72**(Suppl. C), 165–179 (2017)
22. Turnbull, J.: The Docker Book: Containerization is the new virtualization. James Turnbull (2014)
23. Zimmermann, O.: Microservices tenets. Comput. Sci. Res. Dev. **32**(3–4), 301–310 (2017)

A Record/Replay Debugger for Service Development on the Cloud

M. Subhi Sheikh Quroush and Tolga Ovatman$^{(\boxtimes)}$ ⓘD

Department of Computer Engineering, Istanbul Technical University,
Maslak, 34469 Istanbul, Turkey
{sheikhquroush,ovatman}@itu.edu.tr

Abstract. Cloud based software development platforms are continuously becoming more powerful and penetrate towards the daily routines of modern developers. This paper presents a debugging approach that can be used in cloud based service development platforms where developer is working on relatively small sized scripts to be hosted on multitenant cloud platforms. Presented remote debugging approach utilizes record/replay technique to re-execute and record the variable evaluations whenever an exception is thrown during the developed service's run-time. Additionally, an alternative recording scheme is also proposed that involves only recording external data accesses. Memory and run-time overhead of proposed approaches show that remote debugging approach can be useful especially when the minimal recording scheme is applied.

Keywords: Cloud based development ·
Remote service debugging · Record/replay debugging

1 Introduction

Latest improvements in cloud computing paradigm is significantly effecting software development technologies as well. Through the last decade as the on premise services continue to shift towards the cloud systems, substantial effort has been paid to offer the related development tools and technologies as online services as well[1]. Additionally, competent online services offer their users the ability to develop their own scripts to customize the behavior of their services as well[2].

In this paper, we extend the study in the 8th International Conference on Cloud Computing and Services Science [11] and present a debugger based on record/replay approach to be used in during the development of the remote services. Our scope is limited to systems where the service to be developed and the development environment is hosted in separate systems. A typical example that we also use as a test bed is development of application specific services

---

[1] E.g. codeanywhere.com, koding.com, etc.
[2] E.g. force.com.

© Springer Nature Switzerland AG 2019
V. M. Muñoz et al. (Eds.): CLOSER 2018, CCIS 1073, pp. 64–76, 2019.
https://doi.org/10.1007/978-3-030-29193-8_4

where the development environment is presented to the user online over a web browser but the developed service is hosted on the cloud.

Performing debugging during the web service interaction is cumbersome since it requires an interactive tracking session where the developer needs to watch remote but yet interdependent variables and control flows. Record/replay debugging can be of use in such scenarios by letting the developer to be able to record and replay the erroneous flows and variables evaluations that has been triggered by the remote calls to the web service. Without using such an approach, developers dig into the error logs performing a postmortem analysis which becomes a needle in a haystack problem most of the time.

Record/replay debugging has been applied on the domain of web applications in the past; in such a study an interactive user interface is used for capturing and replaying web application executions [5]. In our study we have shifted the focus on the applicability of the approach on web services being used in a cloud based platform.

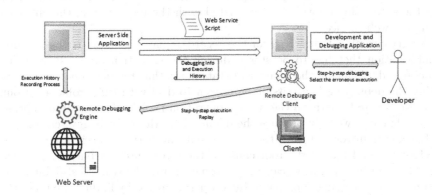

Fig. 1. Architectural representation of the remote debugging approach [11].

An architectural diagram of the developed system is presented in Fig. 1. Throughout this paper, we are going to provide a detailed overview of the remote debugging engine as well as insights on reducing the overhead produced by the approach. For instance, instead of performing a full recording of the variable evaluations, performing a minimized recording it is possible to significantly decrease the overhead of the remote debugging engine. During the minimized recording session only the evaluations of the variables that are affected by external data access like a database query or REST service calls. We also compare the performance gain of minimized recording compared to the full recording arguing on the advantages and disadvantages of adopting such an approach.

The rest of the paper is organized as follows: Sect. 2 discusses the related work in the literature, Sect. 3 presents an outline of remote debugging approach and Sect. 4 examines the implementation details of the remote debugging engine. Section 5 presents the execution time and memory consumption overhead of the approach and Sect. 6 concludes the study and provide future directions.

2   Related Work

This paper presents a remote web service debugging approach by using a record/replay technique on the remote server where web service is being hosted. In a conventional record/replay debugger, debugging information is saved together with the run-time trace of the buggy code. A similar record/replay approach by Brian Burg et al. records the inputs, the variables which are related to the system state and the web calls for the web applications. During the debugging session, a user interface is presented to the developer for the current state of the program using the stored data [5].

Another record/replay based tool TRACR [13], contains live editing features on Javascript code. During the debugging process developer can change debugged code and see the result without repeating web application run. This is also a feature of the remote debugging system that we present in this study.

Another tool to debug web based software is Fiddler [12], which uses the client side to analyze the web services responses. Unlike this approach, our approach uses the server side information associated with the request from the client to debug the web service.

A very prominent drawback of the record/replay technique is the amount of information that has to be stored during the execution of the software to be debugged. Reducing the number of statements that the developer can check during the debugging is a possible approach to deal with this problem. In our study we choose to perform the storage operation lazily, whenever an exception occurs; that way we only produce the debugger overhead for buggy scripts.

Execution history, storing the values that cause the error is used by the developer to understand the root cause of the error during debugging process. History recording operation can be performed using the statistical debugging. In statistical debugging, location of the error is detected by finding the probable error automatically as in the case of the HOLMES framework [6]. Path profiles give the developer extra information about the execution that leads to the error.

Holmes framework do not use extra resources until an error comes floating. In case of an error, Holmes updates the application to detect the error. Our approach is similar to HOLMES to optimize the performance by recording the execution only if the service is throwing an exception. After tan exception is thrown, debugging engine repeats the execution of the service to record all the details.

HOLMES combines static analysis information of the debugged program with the information collected from the bug reports to specify the programs parts that are most probably related to the errors. Such fault localization approaches are not being used by our approach.

In the literature, slicing techniques are also used to selectively debug execution paths. For instance, Cheng Zang et al. separated the slicing operation to offline and online slicing to make the slicing operation faster [14]. In their study a forward slice from root cause and a backward slice from the bug site is extracted, defining the scope to validate a fix. Offline slicing operations involve time consuming techniques like static analysis and the results of the analysis are stored in the database and loaded into the memory when necessary.

We record the erroneous executions the let the developer use the recording data later and to test the scripts without the limitation of waiting the permission from the user to start the remote debugging.

JavaScript's built-in reflection capabilities are used by James Mickens to provide a debugging environment that can work remotely [9]. In Mickens' study user may choose to avoid executing the debugging on the server side. In this situation the debug server sends test scripts to the client to execute and send the result back to the server to get reports about the error.

Proposed remote debugging engine also provides step backwards feature which is called time-travel debugging in the literature. A similar time-traveling debugger is implemented by taking snapshots of the program state at regular intervals and recording all non-deterministic environmental interactions [1,2]. The minimal recording approach in our study uses similar concepts by storing the variable value only when it is related to system state.

There also exists a vast amount of work on using historical execution information and execution traces to debug a program [7,10] but to the best of authors' knowledge the area of using such debuggers in remote debugging is an open area of research.

3   Remote Debugging Approach

The target platform that we design and develop the remote debugging approach is a web based development platform where developers can implement full stack but yet simple business solutions that can be hosted in a multi-tenant cloud environment. Developers can design and express data models, develop scripts to provide services and design web based user interfaces by an online editor provided by the platform[3]. The behavior associated with the web elements and the web services to be hosted by the platform can be defined using MVEL scripting language [4].

MVEL has largely been inspired by the Java syntax, but has some fundamental differences aimed at making it more efficient as an expression language, such as operators that directly support collections, arrays and string matching, as well as regular expressions. MVEL is used to evaluate expressions written using Java syntax.

For a typical development session on the cloud, the developer that uses the cloud platform designs and expresses all the artifacts required by the service development. These artifacts include MVEL scripts that are used to define the operation of the web service or the behavior of the user interface components. Normally, developer tests the written service functionally by executing the service in a test environment provided by the cloud platform. In cases where the testing of web service is unsuccessful because of a defect, the debugging of the

---

[3] Imona Cloud: https://www.imona.com/.

service becomes an issue because the development and the execution is done in different machines. Usually developer relies on logging in order to understand what went wrong on the remote machine which is cumbersome compared to a traditional local debugging process.

At this point, remote debugging comes into action to let the developer execute and debug the MVEL script under development line by line interactively on the server side. A sample development session in the web client using MVEL scripts can be seen in Fig. 3.

A natural objective in providing a remote debugging environment is to be able to let the developer use traditional debugging features such as breakpoints, stepping over, stepping inside a function. However there are some fundamental differences between debugging in local and remote. One of those differences is the possibility of a changes in the state of the server during the debugging session. This situation is an issue in practice because the service is executing in a multi-tenant environment where the external data elements used in the service can be modified between the erroneous execution and the debugging session. To overcome this problem an approach might be to save the state in the server at each state and let the developer decide the level to keep this extra debugging information.

Another important issue in remote debugging arises after the patch for the bug has been applied. Since the state of the server might also change during the patching process developers need a tool to help them to make sure that the issue is solved by the patch. By saving the system state in each service, developer can use the saved input values that causes the error and re-run the program with the saved values and debug the code again to make sure that the code is working after the patch.

The proposed approach is heavyweight for complicated software that might involve thousands lines of code and hundreds of variables but when it comes to more simplistic environments that limit the developer to implement basic services, the outcome of a powerful debugging tool makes it preferable for small scale service development. To decrease the overhead produced by the remote debugger we have developed a reduced level of state information recording, namely 'minimal recording'. As seen in Fig. 2, developer can use minimal recording level to decrease the amount of state information to be saved by the debugging engine.

Currently the remote debugging engine supports only two modes of state recording but it is possible to develop more granular levels to fine tune the overhead of the remote debugging. Next subsections define the two modes of state recording in a more detailed fashion.

3.1 Full Recording

During a full recording session, the remote debugging engine running on the server executes the web service by storing the variable evaluations during all the assignment statements. Variable evaluations will be stored as tuples containing line number of the assignment, the variable name and its value. Hence, at any time, the developer can choose and replay the erroneous execution by selecting it from the list of execution records as seen in Fig. 2.

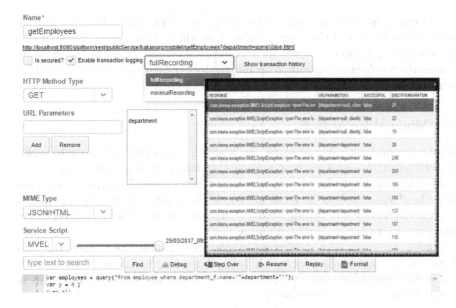

Fig. 2. Selecting the type of recording session and web service to be debugged. Bordered window on the right shows the list of recorded debugging sessions [11].

For each debugging session, the execution engine saves the requests that were sent by the client to the server. The developer may replay the recorded debugging session later by using the remote debugging system. When the developer replays an execution, the platform will get the saved data according to its time and display them in the variable table as seen in Fig. 5.

Fig. 3. MVEL script development window and variable evaluations table (on the right) [11]

At every step of the execution the debugging client will update the variable values in the table and the corresponding line will be highlighted. Even though full recording produces a significant amount of overhead, it might be necessary to store the whole environment to be able to store the data retrieved by database query or a service call during the debugging session.

3.2   Minimal Recording

During minimal recording sessions, the platform saves the variable values only for external data access such as getting the data from a database query or a web service call. By saving the input parameters for the web service, evaluations of the local variables can be recalculated on the client side and do not need to be persisted during a recording session. This way the overhead produced by the debug session recording can be reduced.

During replaying of a debugging session with minimal recording, the lines that contain external data access will be updated by the recorded history. Otherwise the related line will be executed directly and the variable values will be updated from the execution result.

4   Implementation of the Remote Debugging Engine

To be able to provide debugging extensions on top of MVEL scripting language we have used MVEL API to handle compiled MVEL script and develop components that hold debugging information to be annotated to compiled components. To demonstrate the internal structure of the debugging engine better we are going to use a case study web service. Our case study web service (named getEmployees()) will be used to retrieve and process a list of employees that belongs to a company using the services developed on the cloud platform in a multi-tenant way. So the list of employees is retrieved from a shared database where many services have the potential to change the employee list during debugging sessions.

If the web service being executed runs without any exceptions, remote debugger doesn't keep track or persist any information about the run-time variable evaluations but it stores the input parameters provided by the developer (for instance the department name of the employee). If a buggy web service is being executed that causes an exception during run-time, remote debugger is going to use the persisted inputs to re-execute the service using the same set of input parameters and store the recording details line by line from the beginning.

4.1   Internals of the Remote Debugging Engine

MVEL code in Fig. 4 can be used to demonstrate the basic functionality of the remote debugger. Conceptually the code mimics a trivial script that repeatedly obtain a list of employees from the service's database and iterate over the employees. The code example contains different kinds of variable assignments, loops and nested scopes for demonstration purposes.

Remote debugging engine supports the following statements in a typical MVEL script:

```
1    var x = 0;
2    var i = 0;
3    for (i = 0; i < 10; i++) {
4        x = x + 1;
5        y = 1;
6        y = 2;
7        var employees = query("from employee");
8        var employee = null;
9        for (employee: employees) {
10           var y = 0;
11           var name = employee.name;
12           if (employee.name.equals("name2")) {
13               x = 20;
14               y = 25;
15           } else {
16               y = y + 1;
17           }
18           y = y + 1;
19           employee.salary = 200;
20       }
21       z = 1;
22       z = 2 + x;
23       z = 3;
24       y = 3;
25       x = x + 1;
26   }
27
28   y = z / 0;
29
30   return x;
```

Fig. 4. A sample trivial MVEL code.

- Line 1 - `AssignmentNode`: Represents a value assignment to a primitive variable.
- Line 3 - `ForNode`: Represents a for loop, which may include scoped variable assignments.
- Line 8 - `DeclTypedVarNode`: Represents a value assignment to an object. Debugger needs to evaluate and keep track of all property assignments in this case.
- Line 9 - `ForEachNode`: Represents a different type of for loop.
- Line 12 - `IfNode`: Represent a decision node and related alternative decision path nodes (e.g. `else`)

– Line 19 - `DeepAssignmentNode`: Represents a value assignment to an object field.

We'd like to draw attention to some special elements and how we store the related debugging information.

A special case exists for `DeclTypedVarNode` and `DeepAssignmentNode`. Since these kind of assignments change the object altogether, debugging engine needs to persist the whole object (not just the changed property). We store the object in json serialized format in such cases. A sample persisten debugging trace can be seen in Fig. 5.

123 line	ABC variable_name	value	date	123 rest_service_recording
	employees	[{"id":1,"imona_version":93,"dep... [556]	2018-04-29 21:23:19	3,558
2	count	5	2018-04-29 21:23:19	3,558
3	i	0	2018-04-29 21:23:19	3,558
5	employee	{"id":1,"imona_version":93,"depa... [119]	2018-04-29 21:23:19	3,558
6	employeeName	"name1"	2018-04-29 21:23:19	3,558
7	departmentName	"department1"	2018-04-29 21:23:19	3,558
4	result	"1800"	2018-04-29 21:23:19	3,558
5	employee	{"id":2,"imona_version":28,"depa... [119]	2018-04-29 21:23:19	3,558
6	employeeName	"name2"	2018-04-29 21:23:19	3,558
7	departmentName	"department2"	2018-04-29 21:23:19	3,558
4	result	"1800"	2018-04-29 21:23:19	3,558
5	employee	{"id":3,"imona_version":27,"depa... [119]	2018-04-29 21:23:19	3,558
6	employeeName	"name3"	2018-04-29 21:23:19	3,558
7	departmentName	"department3"	2018-04-29 21:23:19	3,558
4	result	"1800"	2018-04-29 21:23:19	3,558
5	employee	{"id":4,"imona_version":2,"depar... [75]	2018-04-29 21:23:19	3,558
6	employeeName	"name4"	2018-04-29 21:23:19	3,558

Fig. 5. The variables values table.

MVEL API [3] provides functionality to compile a script expression by expression and keep the execution status in a context with the function presented in Fig. 6.

```
1    public static Serializable compileExpression(String expression,
2    ParserContext ctx) {
3      return optimizeTree(new ExpressionCompiler(expression)
4      .compile(ctx));
5    }
```

Fig. 6. compileExpression function in MVEL API.

By processing the context of the execution status, debugging engine at the server side is going to inject the variable evaluations to the context and use them at the client side to provide a similar execution flow that resembles the one that caused the exception at the server side.

Another important case is handling nested scopes especially for looping and branching statements. For looping statements, debugger stores the details of the execution in a data structure that contains the iteration count, related scope variables and latest executed statement in the loop. When the debugger enters the loop it will push the iterated object to the execution stack to keep track of the latest iterated object in the looping scope.

For instance in Fig. 4 there exists three nested scopes defined by lines 3, 9 and 12. During the execution, debugger initially pushes the local variables to the stack when the loop in line 3 is hit. Afterwards in line 9, the second nested scope is encountered so a special data structure for the for loop in the current scope is prepared and pushed to stack. Mentioned data structure involves contains current iteration count, related scope variables and latest executed statement. Finally at line 12–15 a branching statement adds another scope, making the debugger push additional data to stack for the loop in line 9. Pushed data contains current `employee` object being iterated as well.

For instance in a plain debugging session, developer may step through all these scopes and end up in line 16 where he reaches the latest statement in the innermost scope. When the developer decides to continue by choosing a conventional 'step' option then the debugger will pull a node from the stack and process it. For this case, the popped statement is going to include the latest executed statement and scope of the for loop in line 9.

When the developer presses on the step back button remote debugger will search in the recorded data for the latest value of the variable in the current line and update it in the right menu (the variables table) and the move the active line to the previous line. This feature works only with the full recording feature.

4.2 Remote Debugging Client

Remote debugging client uses the web services provided by the server side extensions to MVEL executing engine to provide basic debugging functionality to developers. In its current form remote debugger provides step by step execution both in forward and in reverse directions and variable evaluations for the current line being executed.

Another conventional functionality provided by the debugger is inserting and removing breakpoints. Two rest services of the debugging engine can be used to add and remove breakpoints. When the developer presses the continue button in the debugging session the debugger will complete the execution line by line until it reach the breakpoint line.

5 Evaluation

To evaluate the overhead produced by remote debugging, we prepared sample web services to measure the effect of three different metrics:

1. m_1: Execution time overhead with respect to number of database queries/service calls
2. m_2: Execution time overhead with respect to distinct variable assignments

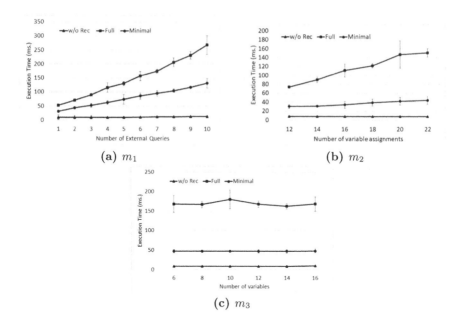

(a) m_1 (b) m_2

(c) m_3

Fig. 7. Execution time overhead of remote debugging.

3. m_3: Execution time overhead with respect to number of variables
4. m_4: Memory consumption overhead with respect to distinct variable assignments
5. m_5: Memory consumption overhead with respect to number of variables

Our experimentation environment consists of a client and a server machine that reside in the same local network to eliminate the latency introduced by network access. Client computer consists of 8 gigabytes of memory and a 4 core 2.20 Ghz processor where server contains 32 GB memory and double 4 core 3.5 Ghz processors. The only application stack hosted by the server is debugged development environment server and a single developer runs the proposed debugging approach at a time. MySQL 5.7 is used in database operations required by the proposed debugging approach and the debugging application is hosted as an add-on to the development platform that is hosted in an Apache Tomcat 7.0.82 application server.

In Fig. 7 we compare the execution time of the sample web service without any recording options towards the overhead presented by the full and minimal recording for the debugging session. To eliminate the effect of environmental factors on the execution we repeat the experiment 20 times and present the error rate as well in the figure.

In Fig. 7(a) it can be seen that with the increasing amount of external data queries, minimal recording method performs better than the full recording as expected. Of course in this experiment an additional work of loops and operations over variables keeping the query results is present causing the grap between the full and minimal recording.

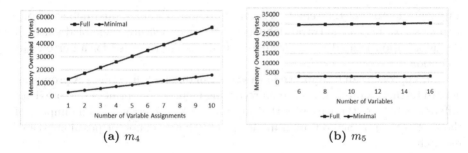

Fig. 8. Memory overhead of remote debugging.

In Fig. 7(b) and (c) we repeated our experiments for m_2 and m_3 using the same experimentation environment. For m_2 the full recording method performance decreases as number of variable assignments increases. Minimal recording performs significantly better in this case. For m_3, changing the number of variables does not affect the performance of the full recording because the platform stores the data for assignments instead of declared variables. The minimal recording is not affected as well.

In Fig. 8 we present the additional memory needed by the remote debugger for full and minimal recording. In (a) we continuously increase the number of distinct variable assignments since assignment produce extra overhead during the service execution recording. For the full recording, extra overhead produced by the approach goes up to 52 KBytes for up to 10 assignments. Overhead is less than 20 KBytes if minimal recording is used.

Please note that the memory overhead is produced only for the programs that throw an exception at run-time, during the recording for the debugging session. In addition, it is possible to fight with this overhead by periodically persisting the recorded data to be sent to client altogether later for the debugging session.

In Fig. 8(b) we see that no additional memory overhead is produced by introducing variables into the script. This is due to the fact that variable evaluations are the main elements that produce debugging data for the recorded session.

6   Conclusion and Future Work

This paper introduces a record/replay debugging approach that can be used in debugging services developed on the cloud. Remote debugging engine is integrated to a cloud based system where developers can implement services on a remote server over web browsers. We also present a minimal recording option where only the variable evaluations affected by external data queries such as web service calls and/or database operations are recorded.

Remote debugger lets the developer debug step by step (either forward or backward) the original interactions that caused the bug present in the service being developed. Lightweight recording sessions produce more scalable debugging sessions in terms of run-time efficiency. Backward stepping option is another important feature of the remote debugger bringing the presented debugger one step closer to be a time-travel debugger. Step back feature is enabled since all the information related with variable evaluations are recorded for an erroneous execution.

Our approach can be improved in a variety of different directions. A promising field to further improve the minimal recording memory footprint is to store delta differences of only the variables that are related to the error [8]. The impact of the proposed approach on programmer productivity is another possible area of research.

References

1. Barr, E.T., Marron, M.: Tardis: affordable time-travel debugging in managed runtimes. In: ACM SIGPLAN Notices, vol. 49, pp. 67–82. ACM (2014)
2. Barr, E.T., Marron, M., Maurer, E., Moseley, D., Seth, G.: Time-travel debugging for Javascript/Node.js. In: Proceedings of the 2016 24th ACM SIGSOFT International Symposium on Foundations of Software Engineering, pp. 1003–1007. ACM (2016)
3. Brock, M., various contributors: MVEL API Javadoc. http://javadox.com/org. mvel/mvel2/2.2.1.Final/org/mvel2/package-summary.html. Accessed 28 July 2018
4. Brock, M., various contributors: MVEL-MVFLEX expression language. https:// github.com/mvel/mvel. Accessed 28 July 2018
5. Burg, B., Bailey, R., Ko, A.J., Ernst, M.D.: Interactive record/replay for web application debugging. In: Proceedings of the 26th Annual ACM Symposium on User Interface Software and Technology, pp. 473–484. ACM (2013)
6. Chilimbi, T.M., Liblit, B., Mehra, K., Nori, A.V., Vaswani, K.: Holmes: effective statistical debugging via efficient path profiling. In: IEEE 31st International Conference on Software Engineering, ICSE 2009, pp. 34–44. IEEE (2009)
7. Engblom, J.: A review of reverse debugging. In: System, Software, SoC and Silicon Debug Conference (S4D), pp. 1–6. IEEE (2012)
8. Hammoudi, M., Burg, B., Bae, G., Rothermel, G.: On the use of delta debugging to reduce recordings and facilitate debugging of web applications. In: Proceedings of the 2015 10th Joint Meeting on Foundations of Software Engineering, pp. 333–344. ACM (2015)
9. Mickens, J.: Rivet: browser-agnostic remote debugging for web applications. In: USENIX Annual Technical Conference, pp. 333–345 (2012)
10. Pothier, G., Tanter, É.: Back to the future: omniscient debugging. IEEE Softw. **26**(6), 78–85 (2009)
11. Quroush, M.S.S., Ovatman, T.: Debugging remote services developed on the cloud. In: Proceedings of the 8th International Conference on Cloud Computing and Services Science, CLOSER 2018, Funchal, Madeira, Portugal, 19–21 March 2018, pp. 426–431 (2018). https://doi.org/10.5220/0006691604260431
12. Telerik: Fiddler web debugging. http://www.telerik.com/fiddler. Accessed 17 Jan 2018
13. Troberg, A., et al.: Improving Javascript development productivity by providing runtime information within the code editor (2015)
14. Zhang, C., Lu, L., Zhou, H., Zhao, J., Zhang, Z.: MoonBox: debugging with online slicing and dryrun. In: Proceedings of the Asia-Pacific Workshop on Systems, p. 12. ACM (2012)

Smart Connected Digital Factories: Unleashing the Power of Industry 4.0

Michael P. Papazoglou[1]([✉]) and Andreas S. Andreou[2]

[1] European Research Institute in Service Science (ERISS), Tilburg University,
5000 LE Tilburg, The Netherlands
mikep@uvt.nl
[2] Department of Electrical Engineering/Computer Engineering and Informatics,
Cyprus University of Technology, P.O. Box 50329, CY3603 Limassol, Cyprus
andreas.andreou@cut.ac.cy

Abstract. Recent initiatives such as the Industrial IoT, or Industry 4.0, as it has been dubbed, are fundamentally reshaping the industrial landscape by promoting connected manufacturing solutions that realize a "digital thread" which connects all aspects of manufacturing including all data and operations involved in the production of goods and services. This paper focuses on Industry 4.0 technologies and how they support the emergence of highly-connected, knowledge-enabled factories, referred to as Smart Manufacturing Networks. Smart Manufacturing Networks comprise an ecosystem of connected factory sites, plants, and self-regulating machines able to customize output, and allocate resources over manufacturing clouds optimally to offer a seamless transition between the physical and digital worlds of product design and production.

Keywords: Manufacturing networks · Industry 4.0 · Industrial internet · Cloud manufacturing · Digital twins · Smart manufacturing networks · Product and manufacturing network lifecycle

1 Introduction

Today, manufacturing is transforming from mass production to an industry characterized by mass customization. Not only must the right products be delivered to the right person for the right price, the process of how products are designed and delivered must be at a new level of sophistication.

Currently, manufacturing is becoming network centric with dynamic, complex interconnected supply and production chains. Traditionally linear supply chains are transformed into highly interconnected, continually changing systems that integrate information seamlessly to advance production and distribution. This implies a focus on core technologies and critical assets with Original Equipment Manufacturers moving toward digitally integrated systems and factories, autonomously running entire production processes, global outsourcing of product component fabrication, and a strategy

This paper is partially funded by the European union's H2020 project Dossier-Cloud – project id #692251.

V. M. Muñoz et al. (Eds.): CLOSER 2018, CCIS 1073, pp. 77–101, 2019.
https://doi.org/10.1007/978-3-030-29193-8_5

that can more readily incorporate ecosystem partners and evolve to a more optimal state over time. We call this interconnected, open ecosystem a Manufacturing Network [1].

A manufacturing network integrates data from diverse sources and locations to drive the physical act of production and distribution. The result can be a "digital-twin" model of the connected 'smart' factory of the future where computer-driven systems create a virtual copy of the physical world and help make decentralized decisions with much higher degree of accuracy [2]. The digital-twin approach enables manufacturers to overlay the virtual, digital product on top of any physical product at any stage of production on the factory floor and analyze its behavior. This approach allows manufacturers to have a complete digital footprint of the entire manufacturing process - spanning product, production, and performance - so that product designers and engineers can make informed choices about materials and processes using visualization tools, e.g., 3D CAD/CAM tools, during the design stages of a digital product and immediately see the impact on a physical version of the product. This capability of digital products can be extended across multiple factories.

In networked manufacturing, we are moving from a push-driven model to a pull-driven model with the consumer becoming much more of a driver in the supply chain and where production systems are more flexible in terms of handling smaller volumes and individualized product portfolios that are part of discrete manufacturing [3].

The digital twin approach in networked manufacturing connects the digital to the physical world allowing visibility in the operations of production systems and manufacturing plants. It focuses more holistically on how end-to-end transparency can provide instant visibility across multiple aspects of the production chain all at once. This provides insights into critical areas by enabling firms to track material flow, synchronize production schedules, balance supply and demand, and production. There is also the increased demand for the individualization of mass production where manufacturers need to meet customer expectations for individualized products and need to collaborate with them and external stakeholders to design and manufacture these individualized products.

Industry 4.0 sets the foundations for completely connected factories that are characterized by the digitization and interconnection of supply chains, production equipment and lines, and the application of the latest advanced digital information technologies to manufacturing activities. Industry 4.0 can be perceived as the rapid transformation of industry, where the virtual world of information technology (IT), the physical world of machines, and the Internet meet, driving access to manufacturing data sources and systems. Paired with powerful tools, such as visualization, scenario analysis, and predictive learning algorithms, this access to data is fundamentally changing how manufacturers operate.

This paper examines the concept of manufacturing in the connected factories of the future and its enabling technologies. It first introduces the concept of Industry 4.0, and overviews standards and recent architectural developments. It then explains how Industry 4.0 technologies have the ability to efficiently extract meaningful data and insights from manufacturing systems and processes, and transform traditional plants into smart collaborative digital factories. This new direction is highly connected to knowledge-enabled factories, referred to as Smart Manufacturing Networks, where devices, production equipment, production services and processes spanning factories and firms are inter-connected - offering decision-making support on the basis of real-time production data – produce on-demand and are continuously monitored, and optimized.

The paper is organized as follows: Sect. 2 discusses the transition to Industry 4.0 by first outlining its basic characteristics and then focusing on the key enablers that facilitate moving to smart manufacturing. Section 3 describes security issues, outlines related standards and their role in support of Industry 4.0 and closes with presenting reference architectures and models. Section 4 makes a brief introduction to smart products and smart machines, while Sect. 5 focuses on Smart Manufacturing Networks analyzing their characteristics, the transformation roadmap, the digital product lifecycle, the knowledge related to product/production processes, and the digital twin lifecycle. Finally, Sect. 5 provides our conclusions.

2 Making the Transition to Industry 4.0

The Fourth Industrial Revolution – also known as Industry 4.0 – represents a paradigm shift to "decentralized" smart manufacturing and production, where intelligent machines, systems and networks are capable of autonomously exchanging and responding to information to manage and coordinate industrial production processes through edge analytics. It is rapidly transforming how companies interact with customers, develop and manufacture new products, and conduct operations by helping integrate systems across production chains.

2.1 Essential Characteristics of Industry 4.0

Currently, there is no consensus regarding the definition of Industry 4.0, rather it has a different meaning for each company depending on the company's production-domain and specific strategy. Moreover, this meaning is highly variable depending on the business process affected - manufacturing, logistics, and the like [2]. Nevertheless, Industry 4.0 in all of its forms and guises is marked by a shift toward a digital-to-physical connection.

Industry 4.0 demands production processes that are much more flexible as well as new machine-to-machine capabilities. It is not enough to have machines that flexibly and easily interconnect with each other; they also have to be geared towards adjusting production dynamically. Industry 4.0 - or Industrial Internet - offers new opportunities to harness manufacturing data so that manufacturers can use knowledge-based and advanced analytics techniques to structure, cross-correlate and gain insights from manufacturing data that originates from multiple systems, equipment, devices, sensors and processes. Subsequently, it automates and guides manufacturing accordingly to optimize planning and scheduling to produce higher quality manufactured products.

The definition of Industry 4.0 in this paper covers six important properties:

1. *Digitization of all physical assets and processes:* The first main characteristic of Industry 4.0 is the digitization of all physical assets and processes. Manufacturers expand their existing range of products with complete digital product descriptions as well as developing the capabilities they need to provide services and solutions

that supplement their traditional product offerings, e.g., embedded systems, sensors, aftercare and product support, etc., ensuring that customer needs are met while boosting the performance of the core product.

2. *Integration of vertical and horizontal value chains:* To enable production, vertical integration of production activities within smart factories, from product design and development and the various shop floor applications, devices, IoT, robot and equipment, is necessary. Furthermore, the increased data being generated throughout the plant floor also need to be accessible within higher-level enterprise systems, placing a new emphasis on seamless vertical network integration. Only by turning this data into meaningful information at the enterprise level can relevant production and business decisions be taken.

   Horizontal integration is combined with vertical integration to offer the prospect of coordination of orders, materials' flow and production data, with all geographically dispersed entities, e.g., customers, distributors and channel partners, materials and sub-product suppliers, contract manufacturers, and technology solution providers, to achieve end-to-end, holistic integration through the entire value chain.

3. *Control and Visibility*: As products move from ideation and development to end of life, the wealth of data produced at every stage of the manufacturing lifecycle can create a product's "digital thread," which denotes the aggregated, product-specific data stream that combines information from a variety of systems and sources. Purpose of the digital thread is to improve design and manufacturing processes by enabling real-time, data-driven actionable insights and decision-making, and control capabilities.

   Visibility denotes the ability to combine business transactional data with manufacturing operational data to gain full visibility and control and improve decision making and action taking. It can include visibility from order entry to inventory to finished product. It also includes real-time tracking and monitoring to prevent raw material, human or machine deviations or failures.

4. *Actionable insights*: The convergence of the IoT, processes and analytics is generating a new world of big data, which is enabling new capabilities such as tailored customer offerings, predictive solutions, streamlining production processes and adaptation to changes. The use of detailed analysis of manufacturing and sensor data from the plants combined with other critical data elements sets the foundation for greater optimization of overall business and control, better manufacturing and operations planning, greater improvement of production processes and product quality, and more efficient maintenance of production assets.

5. *Human-centered automation*: Industry 4.0 will lead to a structural shift towards an integrated digital and human workforce where the focus is on improving the user experience, so that information is presented in the context of manufacturing tasks performed, leading to better decision-making and new possibilities for improvement.

6. *Creation of innovative digital business models and strategic value propositions*: Digitization is eroding traditional barriers to entry in many sectors, creating opportunities for new product types and new value propositions through increased networking with customers and partners.

2.2   Key Enablers

Technologies such as IoT, Cyber-Physical Systems (CPS) and automation, big data and analytics, augmented reality, as well as new user interfaces, sit at the heart of Industry 4.0 and all of them run on the cloud. These technologies enable not just the creation of new value networks, but will also usher in a transition from product-as-a-service to anything-as-a-service models. Their purpose is to move discrete manufacturing activities towards the seamless collaborative and distributed sharing of smart manufacturing. Key enablers for Industry 4.0 include the following technologies:

Big Data Analytics. Industry 4.0 involves data analytics operations as a means of extracting knowledge that drives process optimizations. Gathering plant and supply chain data through a network of sensors and then processing such big data generates new insights, supports decision-making and helps to influence new product designs, streamlines system performance, and maximizes profitability. Some of these operations require advanced analytics that fall in the realm of deep learning and artificial intelligence. This is for example the case with the detection of failure modes in predictive maintenance, where sensors monitoring the operating temperature in mechanical components can track any abnormalities or deviations from an established baseline. This allows manufacturers to proactively address undesired behavior before crippling system failures can develop, which would otherwise lead to plant downtime and lost production revenue.

Augmented/Virtual Reality (AR/VR) and Novel User Interfaces. Product and user experience concepts are typically envisioned and shaped through sketching and CAD modeling and a broad range of options is visualized through virtual means.

AR/VR can change the way engineers design products, test scenarios and designs by using live demos and full immersion before the products are made. AR/VR offer the tools that have the ability to view accurate representations of finished products in real-world scenarios, review and evaluate concepts and alternatives, tweak and adjust and modify designs. AR supported CAD packages allow projection of objects on a real setting viewed for example through the camera of a smart device, as well as rotations in three dimensions, thus enabling the viewing of a designed object from any desired angle, even from the inside looking out on top of a live scenery.

VAR/AR can streamline development, especially when paired with prototyping methods. The result is a reduced technical risk, rapid repetition design cycles and ultimately innovative customized products.

Cyber-Physical Systems. These bring the virtual and physical worlds together using capabilities such as sensing, communication and actuation, to create a networked environment in which intelligent objects communicate and interact with each other. CPSs are transforming the manufacturing industry into its next generation through a closer relationship between the cyber computational space and the physical factory floor, enabling monitoring, synchronization, decision-making and control [4, 5].

Internet of Things. IoT has enabled devices and sensors of all kinds to connect with the Internet and each other to create, share, and analyze information, all without human intervention.

Industry 4.0 has taken IoT even further and applied it on a much grander scale leading to innovations like the smart factory and predictive technology. By outfitting industrial machines with sensors and equipping employees all across the supply and delivery chains with the tools to monitor and respond to the output from these sensors, manufacturers can streamline all production and business operations. Sensors along the production line lead to early detection of potential breakdowns. By relying on predictive maintenance to fix problems before they occur, companies avoid costly downtimes and breaks in production. All these applications improve efficiency, minimize unnecessary expenses, and maximize quality.

The purpose of IoT is "to connect objects", while CPSs aim "to integrate the cyber and physical worlds". Together, they construct a virtual world where sensors, controllers, and other devices are all connected through the network (the IoT-side), and implement this virtual world to the physical world by controlling and coordinating the things connected to this virtual world (the CPS-side).

Cloud-Computing. Cloud-based computing is an essential element of the smart manufacturing revolution. There are two types of possible cloud computing adoptions in the manufacturing sector, (i) Cloud-based manufacturing solutions with direct adoption of some Cloud computing technology, and (ii) Cloud-centered manufacturing - the manufacturing version of cloud computing.

Cloud-based solutions with direct adoption of some cloud computing technology target scalability; operational efficiency; the ability to leverage infinitely scalable computational resources on an on-demand, pay-as-you-go basis; application and partner integration; data storage and management; analytics; and enhanced security. They address isolated problems and fixes and unlike cloud-centered manufacturing they do not offer a more holistic approach.

Cloud-centered (or cloud) manufacturing, extends the concept of virtualization to a shared diversified collection of manufacturing resources e.g., machine tools and factories, offers those resources - primarily in the form of SaaS model - and deploys them at scale to form production lines in response to customer-demand. This manufacturing paradigm allows manufacturing service providers to engage in new, flexible arrangements leading to better utilization of manufacturing capabilities and aims to provide heightened levels of quality and value for consumers of third-party manufacturing services.

Fog Computing. Fog (or edge) computing is heralded by many as the next big thing in the world of Industry 4.0. Fog computing instead of transporting all data over the network and then processing it in the cloud, performs operations on critical data close to the IoT device (endpoint) and application, processing IoT data from a myriad of sensors much faster but also without wasting bandwidth.

"Edge analytics" greatly reduces the amount of raw data that must be stored on servers, either on premises or in the cloud, and reduces the amount of network traffic being generated [6]. Collecting and analyzing data close to the endpoints means that action can take place locally in real or near-real time. In this way, only meaningful information needs to be backhauled to the datacenter or cloud for storage, benchmarking or advanced statistical analysis.

Another important way fog computing will impact modern manufacturing is by facilitating integration - whether of widespread supply chains or of the data streaming – on the basis of IoT-enabled production-equipment on the factory floor [7]. Intelligently integrating data streams from numerous partners, platforms, and devices is challenging enough, but is much more difficult to achieve inside companies' own data centers as opposed to in well-networked data centers operating in the cloud.

Bringing it all Together. The merging of the above technologies, as well as the fusion of business processes and manufacturing processes, are leading the way to the new concept of smart factory [8]. The smart factory will enable highly customized and bespoke products to be produced at acceptable unit costs, using autonomous self-optimizing manufacturing processes and with much lower levels of emissions and environmental impact. The landscape of the smart factory will feature complex and extensive networks linking suppliers, manufacturers and customers.

3 Security, Standards and Reference Models

3.1 The Security Conundrum

Inadequately protected networks, data, processes and operations, and potential manipulation of the plants, pose huge threats to industrial plants and businesses. They are open to a range of attacks and cybercrimes, and threatened by interference, disruption or denial of process controls, theft of intellectual property, the loss of sensitive corporate data, hostile alterations to data, and industrial espionage [9]. Once attackers gain access to a critical application, they can manipulate machines or manufacturing processes remotely. The fact is that most existing industrial facilities were neither designed for connecting to the Internet nor developed with a special focus on IT security.

To assure adequate security, manufacturers must adapt by building in defensive measures to legacy equipment and systems that are now connected. Firms must, for one, ensure the security of the software, infrastructures, application and computer systems used. For another, they must deal with the effects of possible cyber-attacks on the operational safety of devices and plants that are connected to the Internet. This is exacerbated by the fact that firms open up their networks and systems for customers, suppliers and partners [10].

One approach of defense is to insert security measures into application programs, known as "security by design" [10]. Computational intelligence will play an important role by tracking, identifying, and analyzing digital security threats. This can be accomplished by strengthening applications and embedded systems and enabling them to self-protect against tampering, reverse-engineering, and malware insertion. Another solution could be online detection of threats, using machine learning and data analytics techniques for cybersecurity [11]. For instance, we can analyze the normal behavior for privileged users, privileged accounts, privileged access to machines and authentication attempts, and then identify deviations from the normal profile.

An innovative and customized encryption approach to support secure collaborative product development has been recently introduced [12]. Its goal is to maintain the security of the sensitive information in CAD models while sharing other information of the models in the cloud for effective collaboration. In addition, an approach that complements perimeter security by limiting and protecting information flows to internal and subcontracted factory floor devices has been introduced in [13].

Two security frameworks have been recently introduced to combat manufacturing cyber security threats. The NIST Cybersecurity Framework provides organizations with a structure to outline their current state of cybersecurity, considers cybersecurity risks as part of an organization's risk management processes and strengthen their security posture [14]. The Industrial Internet Consortium's 'Industrial Internet of Things, Security Framework' (IISF) identifies and positions security-related architectures, designs and technologies, as well as procedures relevant to trustworthy Industrial Internet of Things systems [15].

3.2   The Role of Standards

The ability of disparate systems to exchange, understand, and exploit product, production, and business data rests critically on standards. The Industry 4.0 developmental stage requires an unprecedented degree of system integration across domain borders, hierarchy borders and lifecycle phases. Today there exist several standards that can be used in the context of Industry 4.0. The standards landscape upon which future smart manufacturing systems can rely comprises integration standards within and across three manufacturing lifecycle dimensions [16]: product, production system, and business.

The standards in support of Industry 4.0 facilitate the delivery and exchange of manufacturing data, connect enterprise operations to plant operations, control systems and actual production and establish repeatable processes with common terminology and understandings of functionality.

Standards that Define Equipment Hierarchy. These standards include the ISA-95 (isa-95.com) standard that was developed to automate the interfaces to connect enterprise application systems with the control systems that operate a manufacturing plant's equipment. The ISO 15746 (www.iso.org/standard/61131.html) standard facilitates the integration and interoperability of process control and optimization capabilities for manufacturing systems that are based on the ISA 95 hierarchy. The IEC 62264 standard (www.iso.org/standard/57308.html) describes the manufacturing operations management domain and its activities, and the interface content and associated transactions within the Manufacturing Operations Management and Business Planning and Logistics view of ISA-95. The emerging IEC 62890 (www.vde-verlag.de/standards/1800343/e-din-en-62890-vde-0810-890-2017-04.html) defines standards for lifecycle management for systems and products used in industrial process measurement, control and automation, and is applicable to hardware and software of automation products and systems.

Standards that Model Manufacturing Processes. The most prominent of these standards is SCOR (www.supply-chain.org), a process reference model that identifies and promotes standardized methods for representing business processes and process interactions and easy communication between manufacturers and their partners.

Product Model and Data Exchange Standards. These include the ISO-1030 and the AutomationML standards. The ISO-10303 standard (www.steptools.com) describes how to represent and exchange digital product information to enable companies to have a proven single definition for all product information related to individual products throughout their lifecycle, independent of changes in process and information technology. And finally, the AutomationML data format (www.automationml.org), standardized in IEC-62714, is an open, neutral, XML-based, data exchange format which enables transfer of engineering data of production systems in a heterogeneous engineering tool landscape.

3.3 Reference Models

A reference architecture provides common and consistent definitions in the system of interest, its decompositions and design patterns, and a common vocabulary to discuss the specification of implementations so that options may be compared. A neutral reference architecture model is essential for further standards work in Industry 4.0 [15]. The two most popular reference smart manufacturing models are summarized below.

Reference Architecture Model for Industry 4.0. RAMI 4.0 [17] provides a common understanding of the relations existing between various individual components for Industry 4.0 by setting a comprehensive framework for the conceptual and structural design of Industry 4.0 systems.

RAMI 4.0 describes a reference architecture model in the form of a three-dimensional coordinate model that describes all the important aspects of Industry 4.0. The three-dimensional coordinate model of RAMI 4.0 includes three dimensions: Layers, Life Cycle and Value Stream, and Hierarchy Levels, as shown in Fig. 1.

The six layers of the vertical axis define the structure of the IT representation of an Industry 4.0 component. This axis represents the business applications, the functional aspects, information handling, communication and integration capability, and ability of the asset to implement Industry 4.0 features.

The *Business Layer* is composed of the business strategy, business environment, and business goals. This layer models the rules which the system has to follow, orchestrates services in the Functional Layer, provides a link between different business processes and receives events for advancing the business processes.

The *Functional Layer* is responsible for production rules, actions, processing, and system control. It also facilitates users as per product features like cloud services (restore/backup functionality). This layer provides a formal description of functions, a platform for horizontal integration of the various functions, and run-time and modelling environment for services which support business processes and applications.

The *Information Layer* structures data in an organized fashion. Its purpose is to provide information about the total number of sales, purchase orders info, suppliers, and location info. It carries information about all products and materials that are manufactured in the industry. It also gives information on the machines and components that are used to build products.

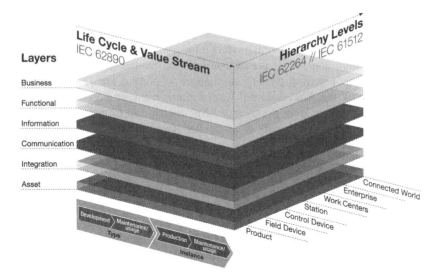

Fig. 1. Reference architecture model for Industry 4.0.

The *Communication Layer* provides standardized communication between the integration and information layers. It also provides services for control of the Integration Layer.

The *Integration Layer* deals with the effective processing of information and can be considered as a link between the physical and digital worlds. Interaction with humans also takes place at this layer, for instance via the use of Human Machine Interfaces.

The *Asset Layer* describes physical components such as motors, machines, documents, software applications, spare parts, system users, customers, suppliers, service providers, or any other physical entity.

The left horizontal axis of RAMI 4.0 represents the *Life Cycle of facilities and products*, based on IEC 62890 for life-cycle management. This axis offers potential for improvement throughout the life cycle of products, machines, factories, software, or even a factory.

The right horizontal axis of RAMI 4.0 represents different functions within factories based on *Hierarchy Levels* from IEC-62264 standards series for enterprise IT and control systems. The hierarchy levels within IEC-62264 are based on the classic ISA-95 standard. In order to represent the Industry 4.0 environment, these functions have been expanded to include workpieces, labelled "Product", "Field & Control Devices", "Enterprises", and the connection to the Internet of Things and Services, labelled "Connected World".

The Industrial Internet Reference Architecture (IIRA). IIRA is an open architecture for industrial internet systems to drive interoperability, to map applicable technologies, and to guide technology and standard development [15]. IIRA is not a standard, rather it provides guidelines on how a safe, secure and resilient architecture can help realize the vision behind the Industrial Internet. The IIRA contains architectural concepts, vocabulary, structures, patterns and a methodology for addressing design concerns. It defines a framework by adapting architectural approaches from the ISO/IEC/IEEE 42010-2011 Systems and Software Engineering - Architecture description standard. The IIRA framework includes viewpoints, lifecycle process, and industrial sectors.

At the core of IIRA are *viewpoints* (See Fig. 2) which identify the relevant stakeholders of Industrial Internet systems, determine the proper framing of concerns and enable architects and engineers to identify and resolve key design issues. These viewpoints provide a kind of checklist that breaks down the system design requirements into four categories, which include business, usage, functional and implementation elements. The *Business Viewpoint* identifies business stakeholders, their business vision, values and objectives. The *Usage Viewpoint* addresses the expected system usage and is represented as sequences of activities involving users that deliver intended functionality. The *Functional Viewpoint* focuses on the functional components in an Industrial Internet system, their structure and interrelation, the interfaces and their interactions, and the relation and interactions of the system with external elements in the environment. Finally, the *Implementation Viewpoint* focuses on technologies for implementing functional components. The IIRA also addresses specific system concerns, such as integration, interoperability and composability, connectivity, analytics and data management.

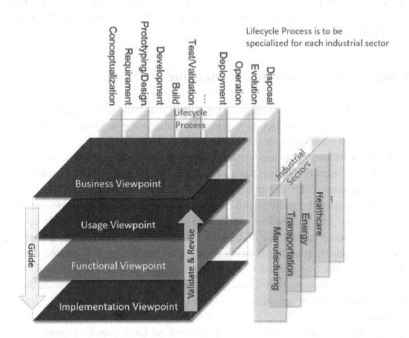

Fig. 2. The Industrial Internet Reference Architecture (IIRA).

As shown in Fig. 2, IIRA through its viewpoints provides guidance to *System Lifecycle Processes* from Industrial Internet system conception, to design, implementation, evolution and disposal. Its viewpoints offer a framework to system designers to think iteratively through important common architectural issues in industrial internet system creation. It also suggests common approaches (concepts and models) as views in each of these viewpoints to aid the identification and resolution of important architectural issues. IIRA is not a description of a system lifecycle process, which varies from one industrial sector to another. Rather, as shown in Fig. 2, this reference architecture is a tool for system conceptualization highlighting important system concerns that may affect the system lifecycle process.

IIRA purposely starts from a generic framework and seeks common architecture patterns to ensure wide applicability to Industrial Internet applications across a variety of *Industrial Sectors* (see Fig. 2). For this reason, the IIRA general framework stays at a high level in its architecture descriptions, and its concepts and models are at a high degree of abstraction. The application of this general architecture framework, as a reference architecture, to real-world usage scenarios transforms and extends the abstract architectural concepts and models into detailed architectures addressing the specificity of the Industrial Internet usage scenarios, e.g., manufacturing, transportation, logistics, etc. In this manner, the IIRA guides the next level of architecture and system design.

The general consensus was that certain aspects of IIRA and RAMI 4.0 intersect with each other, but more work is needed to precisely identify interoperability features between them.

4 Smart Products and Smart Machines

Industry 4.0 is progressively transitioning conventional factories to smart products and services, and networked production machines to enable the holistic digitalization of a supply chain, and an ecosystem of connected digital factories.

Products in Industry 4.0 are 'smart' - with embedded sensors for real-time data collection for measuring product state and environment conditions – connected, and incorporate communication capabilities. Smart products include self-management via the ability to monitor themselves and their environments and can enable remote control, optimization, and processing capabilities. Every smart product holds data about operating conditions, current use and product status. This data provides a virtual copy of each smart product. Such information is collected, updated and evaluated throughout the life of the product as needed, from product design, production to actual customer use and all the way to recycling. Connectivity provides smart products with the ability for machine-to-machine communication, and embedded interfaces enable interaction with human users.

Factory floor machines will evolve their level of intelligence in order to accommodate more knowledge-based processing and predictive planning. The term "smart machine" implies a machine that is better connected and can communicate with other machines and users, is more knowledgeable, flexible, more efficient and safer. The application of smarter control mechanisms to robots and artificial intelligence (AI)-

enabled machines will differentiate Industry 4.0 manufacturing. To date, robots have been restricted to repeatable step-based tasks without autonomy or self-control, or have been deployed in a restricted scope and not on the main assembly line. Industry 4.0 smart robots will work hand-in-hand with humans using human–machine interfaces.

Machine-to-machine communication can be considered the integral technology of the Internet of Things. Through advanced embedded sensor and actuator applications technology, the entire production floor can relay meaningful information, forming the interface between the physical and the virtual worlds. This provides a level of transparency that enables huge improvements in manufacturing performance. Other important aspects of smart machines include their ability to self-monitor and monitor the devices they are connected to, and ability to adapt on-demand. A smart machine is also capable of participating in predictive maintenance practices while minimizing its own environmental footprint and total cost of ownership.

5 The Advent of Smart Manufacturing Networks

Traditionally, manufactures structured their supply chains around siloed functions such as planning, sourcing, manufacturing, or distribution where the manufacturing site is typically not completely integrated. Stakeholders often have little, if any, visibility into other processes, which limits their ability to react or adjust their activities. In addition, many aspects of the production process, including design, manufacturing, and supply, are increasingly outsourced and remain widely fragmented. To succeed, firms need to eliminate these boundaries, by converging plant-level and enterprise networks and creating integrated, end-to-end production networks that are "always-on".

Today, the trend is for networks of smaller, more nimble factories that are better able to customize production for specific regions and customers that will eventually replace large, centralized plants. This gives rise to the concept of Smart Manufacturing Networks (SMNs) [1], which epitomizes smart connected factories. SMNs require reconfiguring supply chains to integrate innovative and disruptive technologies and capabilities that align with overall business strategy. These technologies form the foundation of Industry 4.0 and are coupled with a trend towards highly customizable products that have smarter, dependable, and secure plug and play integration of digital and physical components.

5.1 Smart Manufacturing Network Characteristics

SMNs focus more holistically on how a network that consists of a permanent or temporal coalition of interoperating production systems - belonging to geographically dispersed manufacturing sites and factories - can better achieve joint production objectives. It also focusses on how this coalition can integrate manufacturing data from a variety of diverse sources, locations and manufacturing operations across connected manufacturing sites to drive physical production [1]. In the realm of Industry 4.0, an area of significant focus in SMNs is not only on the product, but on how the SMN capabilities integrate to enable the act of production.

On the technical level, an SMN comprises production systems of geographically dispersed enterprises (supplier networks, external support firms, and outside service organizations) that collaborate in a shared value-chain to design and jointly produce a physical end product. Parts of this product can be manufactured by dispersed sub-contractors running their own production systems in an end-to-end, plug and produce manner. In this way, a specialist factory can fill excess capacity by collaborating with other such like entities, increasing flexibility and reducing costs whilst improving quality of the product for the end consumer.

Production advantages in an SMN are not limited solely to one-off production conditions, but can also be optimized according to a global network of adaptive and self-organizing production units belonging to more than one operator [8]. Digital twins are used in an SMN during the development of a product or when planning production. They make the development process more efficient, improve quality and help to share information between stakeholders. By combining digital twins of a product and the production line, new production processes can be virtually tested and optimized before any physical work can start. In addition, when digital twin information (in the form of abstract knowledge types and structures, see Sect. 5.4) is shared with partners, they are better able to optimize and align their processes.

SMNs couple data and services with a wide range of performance metrics, and can achieve visibility across the extended manufacturing network such that critical manufacturing operations are intercepted, analyzed and executed by applying the best manufacturing practices.

High levels of automation come as standard in an SMN: this is made possible by a flexible network of production systems which, using Industry 4.0 technologies (see Sect. 2.2), can, to a large extent, automatically control and coordinate production processes.

SMNs are increasingly dynamic and complex, and require increasingly more sophisticated information integration. Two important elements of an SMN are vertical and horizontal integration (see Sect. 2.2).

Vertical integration means that demand changes that are recorded in enterprise-level systems can be fed into manufacturing schedules to ensure quantities of products manufactured are more closely aligned with demand for leaner and more efficient manufacturing. Shop-floor machinery is now powered by embedded sensors and control mechanisms that allow via IoT for in-progress production adjustments on the factory floor.

Smart Manufacturing Networks accentuate the shift in horizontal integration towards a flexibly defined extended enterprise thus supporting the evolution into dynamic, global, production networks. Such manufacturing networks enable manufacturers to focus on core competences yet allowing them to offer customized products in any market. A true Smart Manufacturing Network can integrate data from system-wide physical, operational, and human assets to drive manufacturing, maintenance, production planning, scheduling and digitization of operations across the entire manufacturing network.

To achieve their purpose, SMNs rely on domain-specific manufacturing knowledge (see Sect. 5.4). We refer to the collective manufacturing knowledge in an SMN as *manufacturing smartness*. Manufacturing smartness signifies the ability of an SMN to:

1. gain line of sight and provide unobstructed visibility of dispersed production data and coordinated production operations across the entire SMN,
2. optimize use of dispersed data, resources and (human)-expertise,
3. provide help and guidance for making efficient and effective holistic decisions, and
4. plan a coordinated response to individual and collective manufacturing needs.

SMNs aim to improve manufacturing by connecting people to the right information, over the right device at the point of need and cross company boundaries to include suppliers, maintenance partners, and distribution chains. The human role will progress from operators of the machines ("human-in-the-loop") to partners of the machines ("human-in-the-mesh") with the potential for humans and machines to operate more seamlessly and systems to interconnect better than ever before (see Sect. 2.2).

Every SMN could look different due to variations in line layouts, products, automation equipment, and other factors. Despite all potential differences, the components needed to enable a successful SMN are largely universal, and each one is important: data, technology, manufacturing knowledge and processes, security and people engagement.

In the following, we examine first the concept of digital transformation, digital product lifecycle, and then focus on the concept of manufacturing smartness and the process of managing an entire SMN.

5.2 Digital Transformation Roadmap

According to expert reports [18], manufacturing companies expect by the year 2020 to reduce operational costs by 3.6% p.a., while increasing efficiency by 4.1% annually (see Fig. 3). High levels of cost reduction are expected in every industry sector (e.g., aerospace, automotive, industrial manufacturing, metals, etc.).

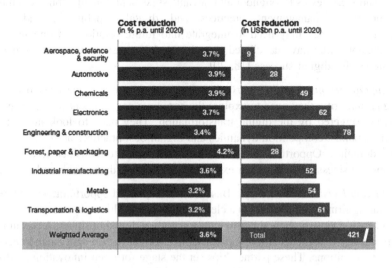

Fig. 3. Industry 4.0 induced reduction of operational per industry sector (source: [18]).

Industry 4.0 will lead us not only to greater industrial productivity, but also to greater commercial creativity by driving digital transformation. Transforming to a digital Industry 4.0 manufacturing model requires a re-estimation of manufacturing sector capacities, processes, operations, policies and frameworks [19].

Digital transformation in the context of Industry 4.0 is the profound transformation of manufacturing and organizational activities, processes, competencies and models to fully leverage the changes and opportunities of a mix of digital technology innovations and their accelerating impact across production and manufacturing, with present and future shifts in mind. Technology innovations - including cloud computing and platform technologies, big data and analytics, mobile solutions, social and collaborative systems, IoT, and AI (see Sect. 2.2), are fueling and accelerating a new era of digital business transformation. Digital transformation in the Industry 4.0 era and the digitization of the enterprise lead to huge leaps in performance and improve digital relationships with customers who contribute to the productivity of the organization.

Many industrial firms have already begun digitizing their business, but often the process has started in organizational silos, rather than following a holistic approach. This will eventually lead to pitfalls. Instead, firms need to take the time to evaluate their maturity level in all areas of Industry 4.0 and develop a digital transformation roadmap. A typical digital transformation roadmap may include the following steps:

Readiness Check and Digital Maturity Assessment: Companies need to determine their current business position and then start their digitalization initiative. They need to conduct a readiness check to determine the following five aspects: viability of business model, human expertise and cultural adoption readiness, technology-levels (the current state or their organization's technology), sophistication levels of data health, and sophistication of processes. This should be followed by undertaking a comprehensive digital maturity assessment in all areas of Industry 4.0 to understand their current strengths and weaknesses throughout all relevant assessment domains (business model, digital practices, management practices and digital capabilities, and which systems/processes they may need to integrate into future solutions). Companies like PWC and CapGemini have developed maturity models to assess how well companies are positioned for digital success [18, 20].

Identifying Opportunities and Threats: Once organizations have a clear perspective on their digital maturity, they need to explore the corporate environment for opportunities and threats triggered by the digital transformation. They need to look into altering customer demands, competition dynamics and digital best practices across all relevant business domains. Opportunities and threats will need to consider five strategic dimensions: business model, human expertise, technology, data health and processes.

Defining Digital Vision and Agenda: Based on the identified opportunities and threats, manufacturing firms need to develop a clear digital vision. This vision needs to provide a comprehensive view on how the firm aims to conduct digital business. A recent trend is for an industry to forge technology partnerships to create a rich ecosystem to achieve their digital ambitions. These partnerships set the stage for open innovation platforms and some manufacturers are already envisioning future as a continuous process of breaking out of traditional molds to spark new ways of producing and moving goods and services, better, faster, and with increasing efficiency.

Prioritization of Transformation Business Segments and Piloting: The next step after defining the digital agenda is to prioritize specific business segments for transformation and select within these pilots based on the perceived business benefits and ease of implementation. Digital transformation introduces complex, systemic challenges, which manufacturers can address by architecting initiatives to connect disparate operations and siloed systems and processes, starting with smaller, focused, department-level pilots and growing them gradually to a unified end-to-end manufacturing ecosystem. The complexity of the implementation will depend on the required level of integration with the existing core business processes and systems. Pilots can help address these issues by targeting a confined scope, but highlighting the end-to-end concept of Industry 4.0.

During this step it is important to pick the right projects. Possible options include vertical integration within one or two manufacturing sites including digital engineering and real-time data integrated manufacturing planning. This can be followed by gradual horizontal integration with selected key suppliers. For instance, enhanced track and trace capabilities and dynamic connections with Enterprise Resource Planning systems at the enterprise-level can make it possible to apply data analytics to optimize supply chain planning end-to-end.

Developing a Digital Transformation Blueprint and Adoption Strategy: Once the transformation domains and pilot initiatives have been selected, prioritized, successfully performed and completed, a digital roadmap has to be created containing transformation details for each of the preceding steps and lessons learned. The digital roadmap provides a comprehensive plan designed to achieve value specific to manufacturing organization outcomes, inclusive of an adoption roadmap, benefit estimate, actions that will deliver those benefits, and monitoring of those benefits. The roadmap will also identify opportunities to improve user experience of the most widely-used manufacturing processes services. The digital transformation journey has to build on a consistent vision shared by all relevant stakeholders. Cultivating a digital environment can only happen with committed leadership. As a result, the digital factory strategy must be placed squarely at the center of the C-suite agenda and become a top priority.

5.3 Digital Product Lifecycle

In discrete manufacturing every manufactured product passes through a standard lifecycle on its path from product concept, through engineering development, to production. The digital product lifecycle in discrete manufacturing usually encompasses the following stages.

Product Ideation/Analysis: This stage includes interaction with customers, and brainstorming, collaboration and 'ideation' of a digital product potential and possibility with product designers and strategists. Objective is to determine and analyze the different product characteristics usually by improving an existing product or design a new product from scratch and variants as part of requests for quote for customized products.

Product Design: covers the techniques, digital tools and expanded mind-set used to design, simulate, and plan a product in an SMN setting. Its objective is to provide a virtual version of a product and all of its variations that can be run through wider ranging tests. The concept of a digital twin is central to product design as it includes design and engineering details describing the product's geometry, materials, components and behavior, individual parts and assemblies that make up the product. A digital twin of a connected product can provide insight into how the product is behaving in the field, helping to steer product design and provide intelligence for successful service calls. During product design engineering teams see not just static mock-ups of a product or system (the traditional 3D digital mock-up driven by CAD), but rather provide insights into its physical behavior, like stress and vibration, as well as behavior associated with software and control systems. A product is first visualized with an engineering design, followed by the creation of a Bill of Materials (BOM). The BOM is a list of parts and materials needed to make a product and shows "what product" to make, not "how" to make it.

Product Planning: During this stage, the design concepts are turned into product requirements and production plans. Planning enables manufacturers to manage manufacturing data, process, resource, and plant data in an integrated product and production environment. Planning bridges the connection between the product centric view of building a product and the plant centric view of building a product in the plant. Planning enables the development of three models critical to manufacturing:

- Manufacturing process model that provides an accurate description as to how the product will be produced.
- Production facility model that provides a full digital representation of the production and assembly lines needed to make the product.
- Production facility automation model that describes how the automation and industrial control systems, such as Supervisory Control and Data acquisition (SCADA) systems, Distributed Control Systems (DCS), and other control system configurations, such as skid-mounted Programmable Logic Controllers (PLC), will support production.

Planning consists of detailed plans explaining the manufacturing process. Within these plans resides in-depth information on the above three models including machinery, plant resources, equipment layout, configurations, tools, and instructions. It also provides a bill of manufacturing processes that contains components and subassemblies and the recipes of operations and resources needed to build the product and stations and cells with the list of operations that can be performed at a particular factory floor station.

Production Execution and Management: Production execution oversees production operations, including functions to control material and product flow between equipment. It includes digitally controlled/sensed equipment, factory floor tools/systems/software, infrastructure systems, and simulations used to optimize production and product quality. It supports production schedule execution and product tracking against scheduled completion times, with adjustments to optimize efficiencies.

Service and Maintenance: Services are seen as an approach to create competitive advantage and market differentiation [21]. The process through which this is achieved is commonly known as servitization. With servitization traditional products can incorporate additional value services, such as maintenance, upgrades in functionality, condition monitoring, remote communications to resolve issues from a distance, consumption monitoring, pushing information to line workers, production outputs, etc. Servitisation is being accelerated by the IoT sensors that can collect huge volumes of data which can be used to improve product quality, reliability, and customer satisfaction.

5.4 Manufacturing Smartness

Currently, manufacturing knowledge is not completely captured in a digital, searchable form in all phases of the manufacturing lifecycle. For example, design drawings, process capability graphs, equipment pictures, manufacturing operation tables, production schedules, statistical-process data interpretations, and engineering change requests are not fully integrated. Furthermore, engineering knowledge is embedded in various stages in the product lifecycle in forms of rules, logical expressions, predictive models, statistics, and information extracted from sensors, such as production, inspection, product use, supplier networks, and maintenance [22]. To circumvent this problem, manufacturing knowledge must be captured, streamlined, structured, interrelated, and curated by means of a formal manufacturing knowledge model.

An SMN can efficiently elicit knowledge from distributed resources and form a coherent body of knowledge that can be analyzed by automated tools to create insights that are used by analysts, engineers and customers alike to optimize product design and production processes. In the following we focus on product, production and quality knowledge related to product/production processes in an SMN setting.

Product structure knowledge should provide a hierarchical classification of the items which form a product. Product knowledge should include all the details about individual parts which compose a product, as well as their attributes and their relations with each other, and is typically released in the form of assemblies, sub-assemblies and components that are organized in a function-oriented structure.

Production knowledge is typically related to the parts in a specific order that can be sourced and combined to manufacture a product. It describes numerous plant level activities and workflows involving equipment (definition, usage, schedule, and maintenance), materials (identification, properties, location, and status), personnel (qualifications, availability, and schedule) and the interaction between them. The production knowledge model is driven by production schedules containing production work orders that are sent to production. These describe the manufacturing operation sequences coupled with manufacturing task time, space, tooling and other resources that include material, equipment, or personnel needed to manufacture the product.

Quality assurance knowledge helps streamline production and ensure that the final products meet the company's quality criteria and ensure customers receive products free from defects and meet their needs. Quality Assurance knowledge includes knowledge about the following aspects of manufacturing:

- *Customer experience and responsiveness*: includes knowledge and metrics about on-time delivery of a completed product on the schedule that was committed to customers.
- *Quality manufacturing*: includes knowledge and metrics about yield, which is the percentage of products that are manufactured correctly, and specifications regarding the manufacturing process and metrics about customer rejects and returns.
- *Production performance*: regards knowledge about the collection of activities that analyze and report performance including production unit cycle times, resource utilization, equipment utilization, equipment performance, procedure efficiencies and production variability. Production performance knowledge typically relies on production throughput, capacity utilization, and production attainment.

In a recent development the authors describe how manufacturing smartness in an SMN is captured in a digital, formal manufacturing knowledge model that classifies it, and encapsulates it in five inter-connected, programmable abstract knowledge types, referred to as manufacturing blueprint images [23]. Manufacturing blueprint images (or simply blueprints) represent and inter-link product data, product and manufacturing process information (both its content and context), product portfolios and product families, manufacturing assets (personnel, plant machinery and facilities, production line equipment), production processing requirements and production workflows. The blueprint images below are programmable abstract knowledge types that classify product and production knowledge achieving separation of production concerns.

Supplier Blueprint: defines a partner firm's business and technical details in an SMN constellation, such as production capabilities, production capacity details, and stakeholder roles.

Product Blueprint: this knowledge type is the "digital record" of a product, which is continuously updated as the product itself passes through its life cycle. The Product Blueprint defines the details of a standard or configurable product, product hierarchy, product parts, materials, and product-related data, such as machine parameters or customer order data, machine and tool data, personnel skills, and all entities necessary to faithfully represent a complete product and ease production work. Such information helps the manufacturer understand how the product behaves in different production environments and provides traceability from inception to retirement.

Services Blueprint: defines and represents all services corresponding to a product (e.g. maintenance, repair, upgrades, spare parts, etc.).

Production Plan Blueprint: defines standard assembly and production solutions, as well as a suitable production plan via a workflow linking the events of discrete activities associated with all aspects of actual production on the factory-floor. It facilitates planning at all levels - plant, region, division and enterprise. It empowers local planners to "own" their production schedules, while allowing line planners to view both individual plant schedules and the aggregate production schedule across all plants.

Quality Assurance Blueprint: ensures process efficiency and asset utilization, process performance, equipment health, and energy consumption levels. It defines process performance and product quality metrics (KPIs) to monitor production operations and solve operation problems across supply and production-chains.

The five manufacturing blueprints described above enable the sharing of a common understanding of manufacturing information among people and software tools; enable the reuse and extension of manufacturing knowledge; make assumptions regarding the manufacturing domain explicit; separate manufacturing from operational knowledge; can be combined in end-to-end constellations describing entire supply chains and process; and can, finally, enable the analysis of manufacturing knowledge leading to improved decision making. The five manufacturing blueprints are generic in nature to ensure wide applicability to Industrial Internet applications across a variety of Industrial Sectors. They can be extended and specialized to address sector-specific requirements. The previous characteristics are necessary to realize Industry 4.0 tenets.

Blueprint images can be stored in a marketplace repository (see Fig. 4), are discoverable, can be queried, compared, interrelated and composed pair-wise into end-to-end constellations defining a composite digital product and its component parts, as well as its associated production plans and schedule.

5.5   Digital Twin Lifecycle

A significant emerging trend in SMNs is the unified, end-to-end digital twin lifecycle that extends from digital product design through production execution, and production monitoring.

To illustrate the SMN digital twin lifecycle process we consider a scenario in which an OEM outsources a portion of its manufacturing operations to either a single or multiple manufacturing partners who manufacture the necessary product parts and then ship them for final processing and assembly at the OEM's facility. In this scenario, we assume that the OEM can obtain a digital representation of components through an industry domain-specific digital marketplace repository (see Fig. 4) and augment them via value-added digital services to meet specific customer needs.

The digital marketplace provides domain-specific manufacturing service offerings rich in diversity and a shared, secure, open-access infrastructure, and functionality to ease service interoperation and composability, and to allow users or a variety of third parties to develop customized solutions.

To effectively deal with heterogeneity manufacturing partners can harmonize their offerings by describing them in a common standardized knowledge model (see Sect. 5.4) and by storing them in the marketplace repository for discovery purposes. The repository provides harmonized digital services that can be combined with other such services to perform a desired task. Production units will then become modules, featuring 'Plug & Produce', enabling fast reconfiguration and optimization of production lines. Figure 4 also shows the SMN digital twin lifecycle stages, which include:

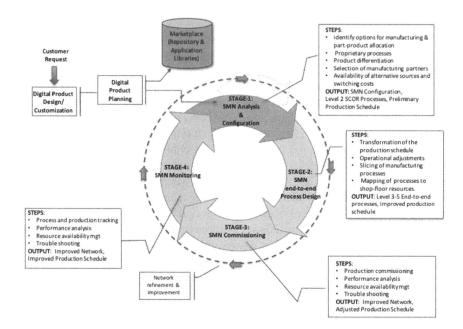

Fig. 4. SMN digital twin lifecycle stages.

SMN Analysis and Configuration: During this stage, the OEM identifies manufacturing options and allocates the production of product parts to potential external partners selected from the marketplace in Fig. 4 that were chosen for outsourcing purposes. By examining entries in the marketplace repository, an OEM determines which product parts can be produced by a third-party supplier. It then assesses the selected partners by examining key indicators, such as manufacturing and engineering capabilities, design and innovation skills, costs, ability to scale, capacity utilization, and the policies of the potential partner. At this stage, the OEM uses simulation and visualization tools to estimate and display alternative network configurations with regards to partners, variants, partner availability, quantities and delivery dates to determine the partners that can jointly contribute to the construction of the final product. In this way, a final set of partners is determined and the SMN is fully configured (see Fig. 4).

SMN Process Design: This stage enables the digitalization of a broad spectrum of production-related functions, including advanced planning and scheduling, quality management and manufacturing intelligence to coordinate processes and systems within and across factories and standardize production across the entire SMN. This stage connects the automation layer with product planning and design, enabling companies to execute according to the plan and schedule. This affords improving the full product and production lifecycle.

Design provides end-to-end visibility into production operations and quality management, connecting the automated operations, equipment, and systems on the shop floor to the decision makers in product development, manufacturing engineering, production and enterprise management. With full visibility into production, decision makers can readily identify areas to be improved within both the product design and associated manufacturing processes, and make the necessary operational adjustments for smoother and more efficient production.

In this stage, it is possible to distribute workloads across multiple suppliers. This phase adopts a vertical slicing (decomposition) of the OEM production process into outsourced parts manufacturer processes, which need to be synchronized and coordinated.

During SMN Design a digital "thread" of local processes and data flows continuously, creating a virtual replica of a manufacturing process that reveals significant insights. Results of this stage are apportioned and stored in the five blueprints described in Sect. 5.4. A detailed example of how this procedure is performed can be found in [23].

SMN Commissioning: is the stage that involves testing the entire production system, including equipment, plant and facility, and handing off the production system for operation. This could be performed on the basis of information contained in the five blueprints in Sect. 5.4.

SMN commissioning covers the digitally enabled tools, technologies, and work concepts that aid in the execution of manufacturing, processing, or assembly of a product. Technologies that influence execution and processing include digitally controlled/sensed equipment, shop floor tools/systems/software, infrastructure systems, and simulations used to optimize production and product quality. SMN commissioning provides up-to-date visibility of all Work in Process (WIP) orders for product lines and production areas.

After commissioning, the production system enters operations and maintenance - a steady state of tactical operations and strategic maintenance activities.

SMN Monitoring: provides real-time visibility, enables traceability of both materials and products throughout their lifecycles, optimizes workflow to ensure lower lead times, facilitates corrective actions for defective products, and optimizes plant operations for effective use of resources and assets. It detects abnormal conditions, machine failures or KPI deviations, e.g., by inspecting end-to-end Quality Assurance and Production Plan blueprints in an SMN, changing consumer demands, laws and regulations (e.g., carbon emission). Its aim is to monitor production processes and either automatically correct them or provide insights to human operators to improve product design and processes, discover deficiencies though analytics and simulation, and provide support to operators for correcting and improving process activities to ensure that the processes supporting a given manufacturing task are performing in accordance with service-level objectives.

During this stage, IoT-based systems distributed throughout the plant floor can capture data along a wide array of dimensions, from behavioral characteristics of the production machinery to characteristics of works in progress (thickness, hardness, torque, and so on) and environmental conditions within the factory itself. By combing performance data from the sensors with predictive analytics simulations, engineers can examine and address performance issues, foresee the need for product maintenance or repair, and ensure that future versions of the product are optimized for day-to-day operating conditions

6 Conclusions

Industry 4.0 is driven by disruptive technologies which promote connected manufacturing solutions that link the supply chain directly to the production line by triggering integrated, automated, autonomous manufacturing processes that make better use of raw materials, and human resources to produce higher-quality products at reduced costs. This is made possible by workpieces and means of production which are digitally networked and are able to communicate. This end-to-end digitization and integration are improving process efficiency, quality management, and productivity, along with real-time insights into the whole manufacturing landscape, building a digital business model that supports data-driven decision-making and integrated platform-based services.

A critical element is the evolution of Industry 4.0 toward a connected, smart, and highly efficient manufacturing network ecosystem that integrates data and processes from many different sources and locations to drive the physical act of production and distribution. This gives rise to the concept of a Smart Manufacturing Network that extends the vertical integration of all corporate functions to the horizontal dimension, knitting together relevant stakeholders - the suppliers of raw materials and parts, external support firms, outside service organizations, the production process itself, and finally the customer - through a network of sensors and digital services managed through an overarching knowledge-driven environment and data analytics engine. The result can be a virtual world, which mirrors and informs the physical world by replicating what is happening on the factory floor.

References

1. Papazoglou, M.P., van den Heuvel, W.-J., Mascolo, J.E.: A reference architecture and knowledge-based structures for smart manufacturing networks. IEEE Softw. **32**(3), 61–69 (2015)
2. i-Scoop: Digital Twins – Rise of the digital twin in industrial IoT and Industry 4.0. https://www.i-scoop.eu/internet-of-things-guide/industrial-internet-things-iiot-saving-costs-innovation/digital-twins/. Accessed 07 Sept 2018
3. Economist Intelligence Unit.: Networked manufacturing: the digital future (2014). https://www.eiuperspectives.economist.com/sites/default/files/EIU%20-%20Siemens%20-%20Networked%20manufacturing%20The%20digital%20future%20WEB.pdf. Accessed 07 Sept 2018
4. Yu, C., Xu, X., Lu, Y.: Computer-integrated manufacturing, cyber-physical system and cloud manufacturing – concepts and relationships. Manuf. Lett. **6**(11), 5–9 (2015)
5. Adamson, G., Wang, L., Moore, P.: Feature-based control and information framework for adaptive and distributed manufacturing in cyber physical systems. J. Manuf. Syst. **43**(2), 305–315 (2017)
6. Peralta, K., et al.: Fog computing based efficient IoT scheme for the Industry 4.0. In: IEEE International Workshop of Electronics, Control, Measurement, Signals & Their Application to Mechatronics, San Sebastian, Spain, pp. 1–6. IEEE (2017)
7. Ezell, S., Swanson, B.: How cloud computing enables modern manufacturing. In: ITIF: Information Technology and Innovation Foundation, American Enterprise Institute (2017)

8. MacDougall, W.: INDUSTRIE 4.0: smart manufacturing for the future. In: Germany Trade and Invest, Gesellschaft für Außenwirtschaft und Standortmarketing mbH, Berlin, July 2014
9. Brandner, M.: Why in Industry 4.0 manufacturing needs to be better prepared for cyber attacks. IoT News, July 2016
10. He, H., et al.: The security challenges in the IOT enabled cyber-physical systems and opportunities for evolutionary computing & other computational intelligence. In: Congress on Evolutionary Computation (CEC), Vancouver, Canada, pp. 1015–1021. IEEE (2016)
11. Thames, L., Schaefer, D. (eds.): Cybersecurity for Industry 4.0: Analysis for Design and Manufacturing. SSAM. Springer, Cham (2017). https://doi.org/10.1007/978-3-319-50660-9
12. Cai, X.T., Wang, S., Lu, X., Li, W.D.: Customized encryption of CAD models for cloud-enabled collaborative product development. In: Thames, L., Schaefer, D. (eds.) Cybersecurity for Industry 4.0. SSAM, pp. 35–57. Springer, Cham (2017). https://doi.org/10.1007/978-3-319-50660-9_2
13. Wegner, A., Graham, J., Ribble, E.: A new approach to cyberphysical security in Industry 4.0. In: Thames, L., Schaefer, D. (eds.) Cybersecurity for Industry 4.0. SSAM, pp. 59–72. Springer, Cham (2017). https://doi.org/10.1007/978-3-319-50660-9_3
14. NIST Smart Manufacturing Workshop, April 2016. https://www.nist.gov/document/nist-sm-workshopappmarketplacepdf. Accessed 07 Sept 2018
15. The Industrial Internet of Things, Reference Architecture V1.80, January 2017. www.iiconsortium.org/IIC_PUB_G1_V1.80_2017-01-31.pdf. Accessed 07 Sept 2018
16. Lu, Y., Morris, K.C., Frechette, S.: Current standards landscape for smart manufacturing systems. NIST Interagency/Internal Report (NISTIR) – 8107, February 2016
17. Hankel, M., Rexroth, B.: The Reference Architectural Model Industrie 4.0 (RAMI 4.0). https://www.zvei.org/en/press-media/publications/the-reference-architectural-model-industrie-40-rami-40/. Accessed 07 Sept 2018
18. PWC: 2016 Global Industry 4.0 Survey, Industry 4.0: Building the Digital Enterprise. https://www.pwc.com/gx/en/industries/industries-4.0/landing-page/industry-4.0-building-your-digital-enterprise-april-2016.pdf. Accessed 07 Sept 2018
19. Salkin, C., Oner, M., Ustundag, A., Cevikcan, E.: A conceptual framework for Industry 4.0. Industry 4.0: Managing the Digital Transformation. SSAM, pp. 3–23. Springer, Cham (2018). https://doi.org/10.1007/978-3-319-57870-5_1
20. Maihöfer, J.: Industry 4.0 Maturity Model – Mirroring today to sprint into the future, CapGemini, February 2018. https://www.capgemini.com/consulting/2018/02/industry-4-0-maturity-model-mirroring-today-to-sprint-into-the-future/. Accessed 07 Sept 2018
21. Raddats, C., et al.: Motivations for servitization: the impact of product complexity. Int. J. Oper. Prod. Manag. 36(5), 572–591 (2016)
22. Feng, S.C., et al.: Towards knowledge management for smart manufacturing. ASME J. Comput. Inf. Sci. Eng. 17(3), 031016 (2017)
23. Papazoglou, M.P., Elgammal, A., Krämer, B.: Collaborative on-demand product-service systems customization lifecycle. CIRP J. Manuf. Sci. Technol. (2018, in press). https://doi.org/10.1016/j.cirpj.2018.08.003

Interoperability Between SaaS and Data Layers: Enhancing the MIDAS Middleware

Elivaldo Lozer Fracalossi Ribeiro[✉], Marcelo Aires Vieira,
Daniela Barreiro Claro, and Nathale Silva

FORMAS (Formalisms and Semantic Applications Research Group),
LaSiD–DCC–IME, Computer Science Graduate Program (PGComp),
Federal University of Bahia, Salvador, Bahia, Brazil
elivaldolozerfr@gmail.com, mairesweb@gmail.com,
dclaro@ufba.br, silva.nathale@gmail.com
http://formas.ufba.br/

Abstract. Nowadays, the volume of digital data grows exponentially. As a result, many organizations store and provide their data in cloud computing services. While Software as a Service (SaaS) is a typical model for application delivery, Data as a Service (DaaS) and Database as a Service (DBaaS) are models to provide data and database management systems on demand, respectively. Heterogeneity of these services makes it difficult to automate communication among them. In these cases, SaaS applications require additional efforts to access those data. Besides that, the lack of standardization from DaaS and DBaaS generates a problem of communication among cloud layers. In this paper, we propose an enhancing version of MIDAS (Middleware for DaaS and SaaS) that provides interoperability between Services (SaaS) and Data layers (DaaS and DBaaS). Our current version of MIDAS is concerned with (i) presenting a Description Logic representation of the middleware and (ii) detailing the Web Crawler. Experiments were carried out to evaluate execution time, overhead, interoperability, and correctness. Results demonstrated our effectiveness on addressing interoperability concerns in cloud computing environments.

Keywords: Cloud computing · Interoperability · Middleware · DaaS · DBaaS

1 Introduction

The advance of the Web has increased the data volume digitally generated and stored, with an estimated total of 40 trillion gigabytes in 2020 [5]. Because these data need to be stored and available both to consumers and to organizations,

---

The authors would like to thank FAPESB (Foundation for Research Support of the State of Bahia) for financial support.

ⓒ Springer Nature Switzerland AG 2019
V. M. Muñoz et al. (Eds.): CLOSER 2018, CCIS 1073, pp. 102–125, 2019.
https://doi.org/10.1007/978-3-030-29193-8_6

data management have been facing some challenges to handle the variety and amount of data. Cloud computing fills some of these requirements, once it provides services with high availability and data distribution, with minimal management effort or service provider interaction [10]. By 2020, nearly 40% of data available will be managed and stored by a cloud computing provider [5].

Cloud computing provides resources as services (e.g., applications, platforms, hardware). These services are organized into levels to be consumed on demand by users in a scheme of pay-per-use [2]. The most common service model is Software as a Service (SaaS), Platform as a Service (PaaS), and Infrastructure as a Service (IaaS) [10]. Besides these, others commonly used are Data as a Service (DaaS), and Database as a Service (DBaaS). SaaS is cloud applications made available to end users via the Internet. DaaS provides data on demand through application programming interfaces (APIs). DBaaS provides database management systems (DBMS) with mechanisms for organizations to store, access and manipulate their databases [6]. Although confusing, DaaS and DBaaS are different concepts [19].

Both social networks and portable devices (e.g., smartphones, and laptops) generate a huge volume and variety of data due to the growth of the Internet of Things [2]. Data are stored in non-structured (e.g., text), semi-structured (e.g., XML, JSON), and structured format (e.g., Relational Database). Governments, institutions, and companies make their data available to users (public or private) on the Internet through DaaS [4].

However, access to different DaaS and DBaaS by SaaS applications needs, in the most of the cases, substantial efforts. This problem occurs because of the lack of interoperability (standardization) between cloud levels [8,15,18]. For instance, if demographic researchers need to make studies about census data provided by governments in different DaaS (and/or DBaaS), they will face the difficult to process these data due to the lack of standards and consequently no interoperability between SaaS and DaaS (and/or DBaaS). To accomplish this interoperability issue, a middleware is presented by [12], called MIDAS (Middleware for DaaS and SaaS).

MIDAS is responsible for mediating the communication between different SaaS, DaaS, and DBaaS [12]. MIDAS makes possible that SaaS applications retrieve data seamlessly from various cloud data sources since MIDAS mediates all communication between SaaS and DaaS/DBaaS. This version guarantees access to DaaS regardless any modification made in the API.

We proposed a new version of MIDAS to provide a transparent interoperability among different cloud layers. MIDAS 1.8 [12] dealt with two important issues: (i) a formal description of our approach and (ii) a join clause to manipulate different data (DaaS and DBaaS) into a single query. Some minor improvements were made in order to adjust MIDAS, such as (i) recognization of different data query structures sent by SaaS, such as SQL and NoSQL queries; (ii) manipulate different DaaS and DBaaS from statements such as join (SQL) and lockup (MongoDB); (iii) manipulate different data models returned by DaaS and DBaaS, such as JSON, XML, CSV, and tables; and (iv) return the result into the required format by SaaS, such as JSON, XML, and CSV.

In this paper, we present some improvements to generating MIDAS 1.9: (i) description of the formal model by Description Logic (DL); and (ii) an in-depth presentation of our Web Crawler.

Some experiments were performed in [12] to evaluate the MIDAS approach, considering four issues: Functional, execution time, overhead, and interoperability. In this paper, we improved our set of experiments to evaluate the novel version of MIDAS and our web crawler. Our results are effective, thus providing a relevant result to the interoperability domain.

The remainder of this paper is organized as follows: Sect. 2 presents the most relevant related works; Sect. 3 describes our current version of MIDAS; Sect. 4 formalizes our middleware; Sect. 5 provides a set of experiments to validate our approach; Sect. 6 presents our results, and Sect. 7 concludes with some envisioning work.

2   Related Works

Some close works have discussed the lack of interoperability. In medical field, authors in [11] propose a solution for heterogeneous DBaaS that share medical data between different institutions. However, this approach handles data that follows the Health Level Seven (HL7) standards, thus minimizing efforts regarding heterogeneity.

Authors in [7] present a framework to solve problems in Big Data systems on oil and gas domain. Their goal was to automate the transfer of information between projects, identifying similarities and differences. Their framework handles only one data source per query, not allowing to merge data from more than one source.

Considering a non-domain-specific interoperability solution, there are two related work [14,17]. These proposals do not deal with different types of NoSQL, nor envision to handle NewSQL approaches. Besides, they manipulate data sources without joining, and they do not work with data provided by DaaS. It is noteworthy that manipulating both DaaS and DBaaS is one of the main advantages of our proposal.

The cloud Interoperability Broker (CIB) is a solution to interoperate different SaaS [1]. This work was evaluated in a dataset through an actual application, but unlike our proposal, they do not consider the interoperability between SaaS and DaaS.

Works in (MIDAS 1.8) [12] has some limitations: (i) The formal model is not standardized; (ii) the Web Crawler architecture is presented without details; and (iii) experiments do not evaluate the Web Crawler.

Thus, to the best of our knowledge, this is the first middleware that interoperates SaaS with DaaS and/or DBaaS in cloud environments.

3   The Current MIDAS

The MIDAS architecture is depicted in Fig. 1. This new approach is composed of seven components (Query Decomposer, Query Builder, Data Mapping, Data

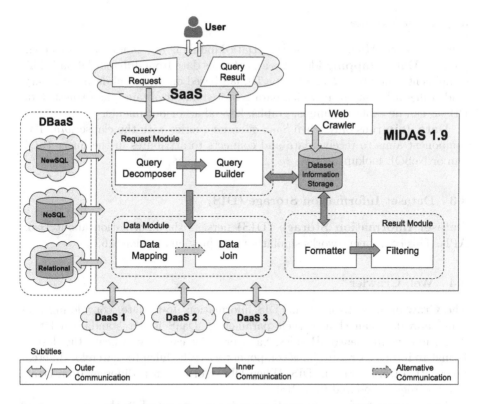

Fig. 1. Current MIDAS architecture.

Join, Dataset Information Storage - DIS -, Web Crawler, Formatter and Filtering), in addition to the SaaS application, and DaaS/DBaaS providers. The following subsections describe those components in details.

3.1   Request Module

Request Module contains two components. **Query Decomposer** receives a query from SaaS (SQL or NoSQL) and maps the query to an internal structure. For instance, SQL structure such as, "SELECT city1, city2 FROM cities" is decomposed by the Query Decomposer into two arrays: One for SELECT clause and the other for FROM clause. The process is analogous to queries with limit, order by, etc. This ensures that Query Builder will create the DaaS/DBaaS request regardless of the API, since MIDAS will create a standardized request.

Query Builder receives the query decomposed and builds a query to DaaS and/or DBaaS. DIS data is required to create the URLs to access the DaaS/DBaaS. After that, the Query Builder sends the query to the DaaS/DBaaS provider. This component accesses multiple DaaS in a single query if the query has a join statement (such as SQL join or MongoDB aggregation).

3.2   Data Module

Unlike previous MIDAS version [12], Data Module is also made up of two components. **Data Mapping** identifies and obtains data from different DBaaS. This component generates a DaaS from a DBaaS based on a manual data dictionary. It identifies a DBaaS from which data is stored and it obtains the request data. DBaaS can be tables, columns, graphs, key-values or documents.

Data Join runs only when SaaS submits queries with the clause *join*. This component aims to receive data and connects to attributes in the query (SQL join or NoSQL lookup).

3.3   Dataset Information Storage (DIS)

Dataset Information Storage (DIS) persists the information about DaaS APIs. This component works similarly to its previous version [16].

3.4   Web Crawler

The **Crawler** aims to maintain DIS information up-to-date, considering that DaaS providers can change their parameters. DaaS is not standardized thus it can modify frequently. Besides, SaaS provider can now indicate the desired format to return its result. This component was scheduled to search for different information from values in DIS. When DIS information is different from DaaS, new recorder is updated into DIS.

Our Crawler performs two actions: (i) It inserts into DIS the parameters of DaaS not yet used by MIDAS; and (ii) it identifies changes in the parameters already used, keeping DIS updated. In other words, even a single DaaS on all DaaS in DIS is updated with the Crawler.

Figure 2 presents the Web Crawler architecture. Initially, spiders are initialized (in Initialize spider) depending on the task: Update information (i) on a single DaaS or (ii) on all DaaS present in DIS. Afterward, data is extracted from the APIs page(s) (in Extract data). The extraction process aims to find the elements, validating them and sending them to the last subprocess (in Format results), which is responsible for formatting data and entering the information into DIS. Any errors during the steps that prevent DIS upgrade are stored in the Crawler log file.

The Crawler has two JSON files: (i) and (ii) configuration. Log file contains the log of each execution of the Crawler, storing when and which DaaS was handled. Errors encountered during execution are also stored, allowing later identification. Configuration file contains elements that guide and navigate the Crawler between web pages, to assist the extraction of data.

A Web Crawler execution script was inserted in MIDAS for control tasks (update on a single DaaS or all DaaS in DIS). This script can be executed by receiving a specific DaaS to be updated. If no DaaS is informed, the Crawler updates the information for all DaaS in DIS (Algorithm 1).

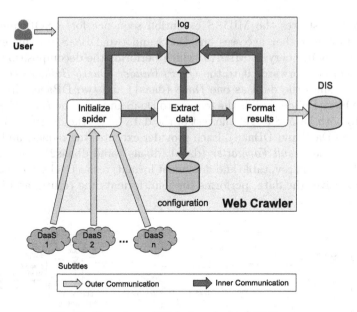

Fig. 2. Overview of Web Crawler architecture.

Algorithm 1. Web Crawler.

1: **procedure** CRAWL(specificDaaS, DIS)
2:     **if** specificDaaS != NULL **then**
3:         URL ← CONFIGURATION(specificDaaS)
4:         A ← ACCESSDAAS(URL)
5:         E ← FINDONEELEMENT(A)
6:         DIS ← E
7:     **else**   ▷ No DaaS passed as parameter
8:         **for all** daas in DIS **do**
9:             CRAWL(daas, DIS)
10:    **return** DIS

In Fig. 1, Web Crawler is positioned at the edge of the MIDAS, since it communicates with components external to the middleware (e.g., DaaS API). With the insertion of the Web Crawler, DIS maintenance has become automated and periodic, since Crawler updates the information when necessary.

3.5   Result Module

After submission of data from DaaS to MIDAS, the previous version of our middleware [12] had only one component: result formatter. In this version, we separate the module into two components to detail the flow of data. **Formatter** and **Filtering** are responsible for formatting, associating, and selecting data before returning to SaaS. Components receives either data from DaaS and DBaaS and performs the merge of such data, regardless the model.

Figure 3 illustrates the MIDAS execution sequence for a SQL query with the join statement that accesses one DaaS and two DBaaS. In this example, SaaS sends a SQL query to MIDAS, which performs the decomposition (*Query Decomposer*) and forwards it to the *Query Builder*. *Query Builder* accesses the DIS and classifies the data as one DaaS (daas1) and two DBaaS (dbaas1 and dbaas2). Query Builder builds the request to DaaS and asks the *Data Mapping* to connect to both DBaaS to get the rest of the data (since the query performs the join between DaaS and DBaaS). Each provider executes the request and returns the result to the *Result Formatter* (daas1, dbaas1, and dbaas2). Each provider returns the result in csv, table and document format, respectively. *Formatter and Filtering* receives the data, performs the join, formats the return, and forwards to the SaaS.

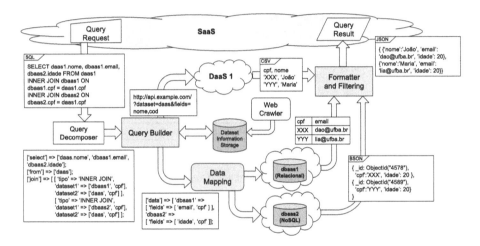

Fig. 3. MIDAS execution sequence among one DaaS and two DBaaS through a join statement [12].

4   Formal Model of MIDAS

The formal model aims to detail the communication among middleware modules, facilitating future improvements. The formalization is based on canonical models [13], sets of keys/values and Description Logic (DL). Firstly, we perform a "general description" of the middleware and then, we described it by DL.

MIDAS can be described in three macro components: mDIS, mSaaS, and mDaaS. The mDIS component is a canonical representation for DaaS in DIS. The mSaaS component is responsible for mapping the query submitted by SaaS into a set of URLs (where each URL performs the query on a DaaS). Finally, mDaaS aims to map the DaaS returns on results to be sent to SaaS. Thus, we can summarize that MIDAS internal model (MIDASql) is given by MIDASql = (mDIS, mSaaS, mDaaS).

4.1   General Description

Each component is formed by a set of elements, to organize the internal structure. Figure 4 depicts a general view of MIDAS. In addition, it is observable now how each element is composed. Each cardinality between sets (represented in capital letter) and individuals (represented in lower case).

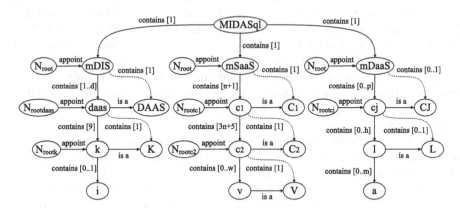

Fig. 4. General view of MIDAS.

For each DaaS, DIS stores 9 data in key-value format: domain, search_path, query, sort, limit, dataset, records, fields, and format, in which not all are mandatory. A set of k (K) maps a specific DaaS (called daas), since each k maps a key, and i maps the value of k. For instance, we can have a DaaS that returns data only in csv format. In this case, $k =$ format; and $i =$ csv. As DIS stores 9 data (in key-value format) for each DaaS, we always have daas (specific DaaS) with 9 k, where K represent information about access and manipulation of daas.

We emphasize that: (i) N_{root} names mDIS, in order to identify the element; (ii) mDIS is formed by several daas (in which DAAS is the set of all daas); (iii) a daas (individual) is formed by a set of keys k (where K is a set of k); and (iv) as some k are optional, each key k contains 0 (k optional) or 1 (k mandatory) value i. The cardinality of each element is described: (i) mDIS contains between 1 and d daas; (ii) each daas contains exactly 9 k (domain, search_path, query, etc.); and (iii) each k contains 0 or 1 i (where i maps the value of k). Finally, just as mDIS has a name that identifies it, the other elements also have ($N_{rootdaas}$ and N_{rootk} name DAAS and K, respectively).

The mSaaS model converts the query (sent by SaaS) into a set with n ($n \geq 1$) URLs to be submitted to DaaS, where n indicates the number of related tables in the query. The first level clauses c_1 identify (i) the related tables individually and (ii) operations common to all tables (e.g., limit). The second level clauses c_2 contain the attributes of c_1: for each query (individual per related table) and common operations. Level v stores information about each c_2.

Assuming a query with join of n tables, mSaaS generates n elements in level c_1 (q_1, q_2, ..., q_n, param) where, in level c_2 the element 'q_i' gather information about the i-th relation and 'param' stores information about the clauses join, order by and limit. Each 'q_i' has exactly 3 elements (Projection, Selection, and Dataset), while 'param' has exactly 5 elements (OrderBy, Limit, Typejoin, CondJoin, and Return).

Thus: (i) N_{root} identify the mSaaS model; (ii) mSaaS contains n+1 (q_1, q_2, ..., q_n, param) first level clauses c_1 (where C_1 is a set of c_1); (iii) each c_1 contains 3n+5 ('Projection', 'Selection', and 'Dataset' for each relation q_i + 'OrderBy', 'Limit', 'TypeJoin', 'CondJoin', and 'Return' for param, i.e., 3n+5) second level clauses c_2 (where C_2 is a set of c_2); and (iv) each c_2 contains between 0 and w values v (where v is an information about some of the related tables or some operation, depends on c_2). Finally, just as mSaaS has a name that identifies it, the other elements also have (N_{rootc1} and N_{rootc2} name levels C_1 and C_2, respectively).

Finally, the mDaaS maps the DaaS returns to SaaS. For this, mDaaS generates a return for each previously generated URL by mSaaS. If there is no join clause in the query, that is, n = 1, then mDaaS only converts the DaaS return to the desired SaaS format. If there is a join (n>1), then the joins are mapped into pairs. In the latter case, the number of elements depends on the return of the DaaS and the information stored in mSaaS (e.g., limit). Thus: (i) N_{root} names mDaaS, to identify the element; (ii) mDaaS contains the number of association conditions (cj) between 0 and p, where CJ is a set of cj; (iii) each cj contains the number of lists (l) between 0 to h lists, where l is a list with all the attributes that contain cj and L is a set of l; and (iv) each list l contains between 0 and m values a, where a is a attribute of the same tuple in which cj is part. Finally, just as mSaaS has a name that identifies it, the other elements also have (N_{rootcj} and N_{rootl}). As stated, cj is a value that the join condition assumes in the specific relation, in order to generate the return.

One of the limitations of the canonical model is the static view presented, since the model represents concepts and not the relationship between them. For this, we modeled the MIDAS with Description Logic.

4.2   MIDAS in Description Logic

Description Logics (DL) is a knowledge representation language to formalize knowledge bases. DL models concepts, individuals, and their relationships. The classification (of a specific language) is based on their expressiveness. For instance, $\mathcal{LA}$ is a DL that allows atomic negation, intersection, universal restrictions, and existential quantification [3].

MIDAS was modeled with $\mathcal{SHOIN}^{(\mathcal{D})}$ since this DL offers all the necessary operators: Concept, rule, universal ($\top$), empty ($\bot$), negation ($\neg$), intersection ($\sqcap$), union ($\sqcup$), universal restriction ($\forall$), existential restriction ($\exists$), hierarchy ($\sqsubseteq$ and $\equiv$), collection of individuals ($\{a_1, \ldots, a_n\}$), inverse properties, cardinality restrictions ($\leq$ and $\geq$), data type, and transitivity [9].

A knowledge base contains information for a specific domain. DL divides the knowledge into intentional and extensional to better structure the modeling. Intentional knowledge (known as TBox) represents the general characteristics of the concepts. On the other hand, extensional knowledge (known as ABox) represents a specific knowledge about each individual that is part of the domain. An example of TBox is "man $\equiv$ person $\sqcap \neg$ woman"[1], while an example of ABox is "man(John)"[2] [3,9].

Definition 1 (MIDAS internal structure). *MIDAS internal structure (MIDASql) is defined as "MIDASql $\equiv$ mDIS $\sqcap$ mSaaS $\sqcap$ mDaaS", where: mDIS is the canonical model of DaaS presented in DIS; mSaaS is the canonical model that maps the query (sent by SaaS); and mDaaS is the canonical model that maps DaaS return(s). An individual belongs to only one canonical model "mDIS $\sqcap$ mSaaS $\sqcap$ mDaaS $\sqsubseteq \bot$".*

In the following subsections, each canonical model (mDIS, mSaas, and mDaaS) is detailed in DL.

Definition 2 (mDIS). *The canonical model that stores DIS information (mDIS) is a tuple "mDIS $\equiv \exists NAME.String \sqcap DAAS$", where: a literal name (NAME) must exist for the canonical model; and DAAS is a set of daas models.*

Definition 3 (daas). *Daas is an element in DAAS ("daas $\sqsubseteq$ DAAS") and it stores information about a specific DaaS. It is defined as "daas $\equiv \exists NAME.String \sqcap K$", where: a literal name (NAME) must exist for each daas; and K is a set of 9 parameters (k) present in DIS for each DaaS (this is, "$=9k \sqsubseteq daas$"). Since DIS is formed by at least one DaaS (that is, there must be at least one daas in DAAS), we define "$\geq 1daas \sqsubseteq mDIS$".*

Definition 4 (k). *A key k ("k $\sqsubseteq$ K") stores one specific information about a specific DaaS. This item can be described as "k $\equiv \exists NAME.String \sqcap i$", where: a literal name (NAME) must exist for each key k; and i is the value of each k. Since the value i about k can be empty or atomic, we define "$\geq 0i \sqcap \leq 1i \sqsubseteq k$".*

Considering a hypothetical DIS with two DaaS (NYC and v8), part of the canonical model $mDIS$ can be seen in Fig. 5: The main node stores the beginning of subtrees, where each subtree stores the information about a particular DaaS. Each node of level i stores information on the k level, immediately above.

Definition 5 (mSaaS). *The canonical model of mSaaS converts a query (submitted by SaaS) in a set with n URLs, where n is the number of related tables in the query. mSaaS can be defined as "mSaaS $\equiv \exists NAME.String \sqcap C_1$", where: a literal name (NAME) must exist for the mSaaS model; and C_1 is a set of first-level clauses (c_1) to map queries and operations.*

---

[1] That is, a man is a person who is not a woman.

[2] That is, John is a man.

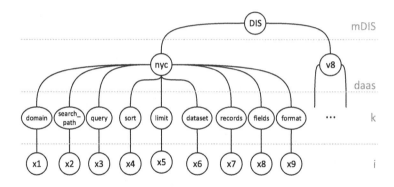

Fig. 5. Example of mDIS for two DaaS [12].

Definition 6 (c_1). *A first-level clause c_1 ("$c_1 \sqsubseteq C_1$") is a information about related tables or operations common to all tables. This item can be described as "$c_1 \equiv \exists NAME.String \sqcap C_2$", where: a literal name (NAME) must exist for each clause c_1; and C_2 is a set of second-level clause to store information about a specific query or a specific operation. We consider "NAME $\equiv \{q_1, q_2, ..., q_n, param\}$", where q_i is an i-th related table and param is a node for storing data about join, order by and limit.*

Definition 7 (c_2). *A second-level clause c_2 ("$c_2 \sqsubseteq C_2$") contain informations about c_1. This item can be described as "$c_2 \equiv \exists NAME.String \sqcap V$", where: a literal name (NAME) must exist for each clause c_2; and V is a set of values (v) for each c_2. We consider that: (i) if c_1 represents a query q_i, then NAME indicates the attributes of q_i, where "NAME $\equiv \{Projection, Selection, Dataset\}$"; however (ii) if c_1 represents param, then "NAME $\equiv \{OrderBy, Limit, TypeJoin, CondJoin, Return\}$".*

Definition 8 (v). *A value v ("$v \sqsubseteq V$") is an element representing information about c_2, with V being empty, atomic, or multivalued. Thus, we define "$V \equiv \{v_1,$*

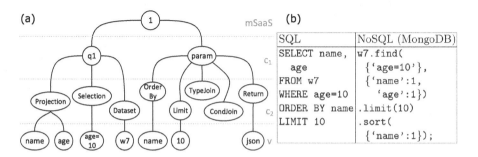

Fig. 6. Example of mSaaS (a); for query without join/aggregation in SQL/NoSQL (b) [12].

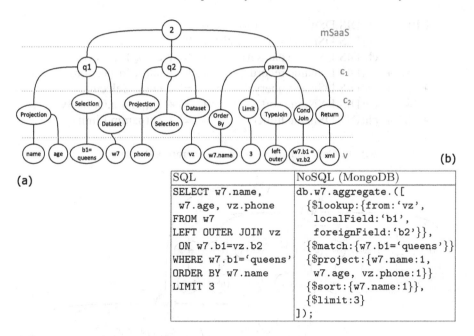

Fig. 7. Example of mSaaS (a); for query with join/aggregation in SQL/NoSQL (b) [12].

$\ldots, v_w\}$", where v_i is the i-th value about c_2, and w is the number of values v in the set V.

For instance, mSaaS presented in Fig. 6(a) is the mapping of queries presented in Fig. 6(b); while mSaaS presented in Fig. 7(a) is the mapping of queries presented in Fig. 7(b).

It is necessary to transform both canonical models into a set of URLs to submit to DaaS. Data from DaaS is received through a URL, MIDASql provides a mechanism to convert mDIS and mSaaS into a set of URLs, the function "generateURLs()". Our function has the following prototype: "URLs generateURLs(mDIS, mSaaS)". This means that, given a *mDIS* and a mSaaS, generateURLs() must returns a set of URLs, where: each URL is a concatenation sequence of mDIS and mSaaS elements; and the number of URLs is equal to the number of query relations (n, n ≥ 1), i.e., each q_i (in mSaaS) generates URL_i. For this, we assume that: "+" is an operator that concatenates two strings (literals or variables); and ch(p) is a function that returns the contents of the child(ren) of p node.

Thus, considering DSname = ch(q_i.dataset), the URL_i is generated according to Fig. 8.

Some observations are important within the function generateURLs(),: (i) when ch(p) does not return any element, the corresponding line p in URL_i must be disregarded; (ii) multivalued result of ch(p) is separated by commas;

$$
\begin{aligned}
\text{URL}_i = \ & \text{ch(DIS.DSname.domain)} && + \\
& \text{ch(DIS.DSname.search\_path)} && + \text{`?'} + \\
& \text{ch(DIS.DSname.dataset)} && + \text{`='} + \text{ch}(q_i.\text{Dataset}) \\
+\ \text{`\&'} + & \text{ch(DIS.DSname.records)} && + \text{`='} + \text{ch}(q_i.\text{Projection}) \\
+\ \text{`\&'} + & \text{ch(DIS.DSname.query)} && + \text{`='} + \text{ch}(q_i.\text{Selection}) \\
+\ \text{`\&'} + & \text{ch(DIS.DSName.sort)} && + \text{`='} + \text{ch(param.OrderBy)} \\
+\ \text{`\&'} + & \text{ch(DIS.DSname.limit)} && + \text{`='} + \text{ch(param.Limit)}
\end{aligned}
$$

Fig. 8. Concatenations from to generate URL$_i$ [12].

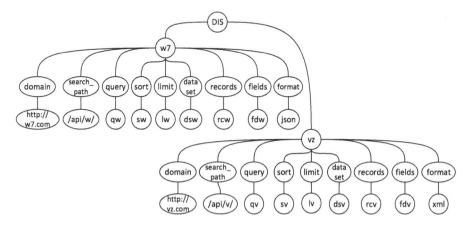

Fig. 9. Example of mDIS for query in Fig. 7(b) [12].

(iii) the last two lines occur only for n = 1 (1 dataset); and (iv) for n ≥ 2 (more than 1 dataset), ch(q_i.Projection) must initially include the corresponding ch(param.CondJoin) if the join criterion is not part of the projection attribute set (e.g., if ch(param.CondJoin) ∉ ch(q_i.Projection)).

Given the mDIS of Fig. 9 and the mSaaS shown in Fig. 6(a), the generateURLs() generates the following URL: URL$_1$ = <http://w7.com/api/w/?dsw= w7&rcw=name,age& q=age=10&sort=name&rows=10>.

On the other hand, given the same mDIS from the previous example (Fig. 9) and the mSaaS shown in Fig. 7(a), the generateURLs() generates the following URLs: URL$_1$ = <http://w7.com/api/w/?dsw=x7&rcw=b1,name,age&qw=b1 ='queens'>; and URL$_2$ = <http://vz.com/api/v/?dsv=vz&rcv=b2,phone>.

For each generated URL, the corresponding DaaS returns the request dataset. Before sending the results to SaaS, MIDAS performs some operations to format the data, such as join, order by, and limit, if applicable. This treatment is carried out employing the canonical model *mDaaS*.

Definition 9 (mDaaS). *The canonical model of mDaaS maps the return(s) of DaaS. The mDaaS can be defined as "mDaaS ≡ ∃NAME.String ⊓ CJ", where: a literal name (NAME) must exist for the mDaaS model; and CJ is a set of distinct values of CondJoin (cj) in the corresponding relation.*

Definition 10 (cj). *An information cj ("cj ⊑ CJ") is a value that the condition of the join (CondJoin) assumes in a specific relation. This item can be defined as "cj ≡ ∃NAME.String ⊓ L", where: a literal name (NAME) must exist for each cj; and L is a set of lists (l) with all attributes that contain cj. Since not every query has clause join, we make cj optional by doing "≥0cj ⊑ mDaaS".*

Definition 11 (l). *Finally, a list l ("l ⊑ L") stores all elements of the same tuple in which cj is part, in the same order of occurrence of the relation (considering from left to right). We define "l ≡ {a_1, ..., a_m}", where a_i is the i-th value to each l, and m is the number of values a in l. Since not every query has clause join, we make l optional by doing "≥0l ⊑ cj".*

Considering that the query in Fig. 7(b) (with join) returns the two sets of data presented in Fig. 10(b), the canonical models (mDaaS) are shown in Fig. 10(a).

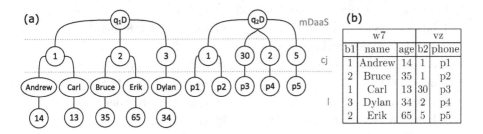

Fig. 10. Example of mDaaS (a); for DaaS returns (b) [12].

Once the *mDaaS* has been generated, the join can be done. The next step depends on the value of ch(param.TypeJoin). For this, in addition to the functions already mentioned, we assume that: lch(p) is a function that returns the last child of a p node; and con(p_1, p_2) is a function that connects the node p_1 to node p_2.

If ch(param.TypeJoin) = 'left outer', the join is performed as follows:

(a) $\forall cj_1 \in ch(q_1D)$ e $\forall cj_2 \in ch(q_2D)$, con(lch($q_1D.cj_1$), ch($q_2D.cj_2$)), $\forall cj_1 = cj_2$;
(b) case $cj_1 \notin ch(q_1.Projection)$, then (i) con($q_1D$, ch($q_1D.cj_1$)) is performed and (ii) cj_1 is removed;
(c) if there is ch(*param.OrderBy*), this node is sorted;
(d) if there is ch(*param.Limit*), this must be the total of ch(q_1D); and finally
(e) q_1D is converted to ch(*param.Return*) and it is sent to SaaS.

Considering the mDaaS of Fig. 10(a), the execution is described in Fig. 11.

Therefore, in order to map and describe MIDAS formally, we have the expressions for the TBox in Table 1.

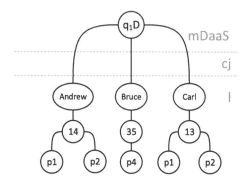

Fig. 11. Example of the execution of mDaaS after left outer join [12].

Table 1. Table with DL expressions of TBox.

1. MIDASql $\equiv$ mDIS $\sqcap$ mSaaS $\sqcap$ mDaaS	13. $c_1 \sqsubseteq C_1$
2. mDIS $\sqcap$ mSaaS $\sqcap$ mDaaS $\sqsubseteq \bot$	14. $c_2 \equiv \exists$NAME.String $\sqcap$ V
3. mDIS $\equiv \exists$NAME.String $\sqcap$ DAAS	15. $c_2 \sqsubseteq C_2$
4. daas $\equiv \exists$ NAME.String $\sqcap$ K	16. V $\equiv \{v_1, \ldots, v_w\}$
5. daas $\sqsubseteq$ DAAS	17. mDaaS $\equiv \exists$NAME.String $\sqcap$ CJ
6. $=9k \sqsubseteq$ daas	18. cj $\equiv \exists$NAME.String $\sqcap$ L
7. k $\equiv \exists$NAME.String $\sqcap$ i	19. cj $\sqsubseteq$ CJ
8. k $\sqsubseteq$ K	20. l $\equiv \{a_1, \ldots, a_m\}$
9. $\geq$1daas $\sqsubseteq$ mDIS	21. l $\sqsubseteq$ L
10. $\geq$0i $\sqcap \leq$1i $\sqsubseteq$ k	22. $\geq$0cj $\sqsubseteq$ mDaaS
11. mSaaS $\equiv \exists$NAME.String $\sqcap$ C_1	23. $\geq$0l $\sqsubseteq$ cj
12. $c_1 \equiv \exists$NAME.String $\sqcap$ C_2	

5   Evaluation

We performed a set of five experiments to evaluate MIDAS. These experiments delimit the relationship between SaaS and DaaS/DBaaS.

Firstly, we evaluate the overhead of our middleware (E_1). We submitted 100 queries directly to both DaaS and DBaaS and, we compared the results with MIDAS access. Queries were performed to return 100, 1000, and 10000 records. Secondly, we evaluate whether the query language (SQL and NoSQL) influences the access time to different data sources (DaaS and DBaaS) (E_2). Through MIDAS, we have submitted 100 queries: (i) With MongoDB to DaaS; (ii) SQL to DaaS; (iii) MongoDB to DBaaS; and (iv) SQL to DBaaS. Thirdly, we evaluate the interoperability of our proposal (E_3). In this experiment, we submit 100 queries to more than one data source: (i) 2 DBaaS; (ii) 2 DaaS; and (iii) 1 DaaS and 1 DBaaS. Fourthly, we evaluated the correctness of the data obtained from the Crawler (E_4). Finally, the Crawler execution time was explored during the data extraction process (E_5) with the same DIS of E_4.

5.1 Our Case Study

Our current MIDAS is based on open source technologies that are found in any cloud with PHP support. It was developed in Heroku cloud[3] because it is an open cloud with sufficient storage space and a complete Platform as a Service (PaaS) for our project. To simulate a SaaS provider, we develop a Demographic Statistics by NY Hospital's web application based on PHP. This web application is hosted in Heroku SaaS instance, and it can be accessed at <https://midas-middleware.herokuapp.com/>.

Regarding DaaS service level, three different DaaS providers are carried to perform experiments E_1, E_2, and E_3:

- P_1: Transportation Sites: 18 attributes and 13600 instances;
- P_2: Hospital General Information: 29 attributes and 4812 instances, and
- P_3: Demographic Statistics By Zip Code: 46 attributes and 236 instances.

Experiments E_4 and E_5 uses a DIS with the following DaaS:

- P_1: Times Square Hotels: 15 attributes and 41 instances;
- P_2: Health and Hospitals Corporation Facilities (HHC): 18 attributes and 78 instances;
- P_3: Borough Enrollment Offices: 15 attributes and 13 instances;
- P_4: Directory Of Homebase Locations: 15 attributes and 28 instances;
- P_5: For Hire Vehicles (Active Drivers): 7 attributes and 183000 instances;
- P_6: Medallion Drivers (Active): 6 attributes and 183000 instances;
- P_7: NYC Wi-Fi Hotspot Locations: 29 attributes and 3179 instances;
- P_8: For Hire Vehicles (Active and Inactive Vehicles): 23 attributes and 111000 instances;
- P_9: Integrated Property Information System: 38 attributes and 15900 instances; and
- P_{10}: Demographic Statistics By Zip Code: 46 attributes and 236 instances.

The same dataset provided by DaaS were persisted into two DBaaS: P_1 in JawsDB[4] and P_2 in mLab[5]. DBaaS are based on MySQL and MongoDB, respectively. The choice for MySQL and MongoDB was motivated by being free databases and by being the most widely used Relational and NoSQL, respectively[6]. Our application (simulating SaaS) performs a join between P_2 and P_3.

---

[3] https://www.heroku.com/.
[4] https://www.jawsdb.com/.
[5] https://www.mlab.com/.
[6] According to ranking https://db-engines.com/en/ranking.

5.2   Experiments

In the first experiment, we submitted 100 queries to both data sources (DaaS and DBaaS) with and without MIDAS. We vary the number of records returned (100, 1000, and 10000). This allows evaluating the influence of MIDAS on the communication between SaaS and DaaS/DBaaS. For this, in the first experiment we submit:

- 100 queries directly to DaaS provider;
- 100 queries to DaaS provider through MIDAS;
- 100 queries directly to DBaaS provider; and
- 100 queries to DBaaS provider through MIDAS.

As stated, we evaluated whether the query language influences the access time depending on the data source.

In the second experiment we submit:

- 100 MongoDB queries to the DaaS provider through MIDAS;
- 100 SQL queries to the DaaS provider through MIDAS;
- 100 MongoDB queries to the DBaaS provider through MIDAS; and
- 100 SQL queries to the DBaaS provider through MIDAS.

Our third experiment evaluates the interoperability of MIDAS. We estimate the average execution time required for MIDAS to relate data from different sources, through the join (or aggregation) statement. The association of the data was made through a zip code field. having in dataset P_1 the attribute as *Zip* and in the dataset P_2 the attribute as *Zip Code*. For this, we submit:

- 100 queries with join statement to two DaaS providers through MIDAS;
- 100 queries with join statement to two DBaaS providers through MIDAS; and
- 100 queries with join statement to one DaaS and one DBaaS providers through MIDAS.

In the fourth experiment, we create a DIS with 10 DaaS and we run the Algorithm 1 for each DaaS. It was checked whether the results were compatible with the data exposed in DaaS API. The recall was calculated by the ratio between the retrieved information (RetInf) and the relevant information (RelInf), i.e. $recall = \frac{RetInf}{RelInf}$.

Finally, in the fifth experiment, the Crawler updated each of the 10 DaaS individually. For each DaaS, the test was performed sequentially six times, with the assurance that the information in the DIS (for each DaaS) was current. After collection, the mean time of each DaaS was calculated disregarding the first execution, since it was an execution with time differing from the others.

6   Results

In this section, we present the results of our experiments, and we discuss them.

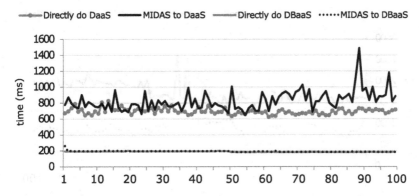

Fig. 12. Return time (y-axis) for each of the 100 queries submitted (x-axis) with a limit of 100 records.

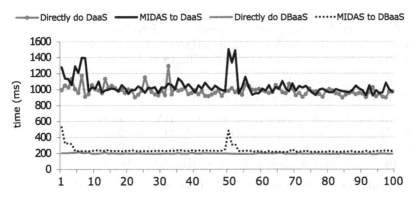

Fig. 13. Return time (y-axis) for each of the 100 queries submitted (x-axis) with a limit of 1000 records.

6.1   Results from Experiment 1

The results obtained from experiment 1 were classified based on the value assigned to the query limit. This value defines the number of records returned and it was restricted up to 100, 1000 and 10000 data records.

Firstly, we submitted 100 queries to return 100 data records. In this case, Fig. 12 shows the average of the execution time:

- 694.88 ± 36.86 ms for queries without MIDAS to DaaS;
- 827.14 ± 121.78 ms for queries through MIDAS to DaaS;
- 186.78 ± 5.98 ms for queries without MIDAS to DBaaS; and
- 190.05 ± 9.28 ms for queries through MIDAS to DBaaS.

Secondly, we submitted 100 queries to return 1000 data records. In this case, Fig. 13 shows the average of execution time:

- 981.09 ± 61.03 ms for queries without MIDAS to DaaS;

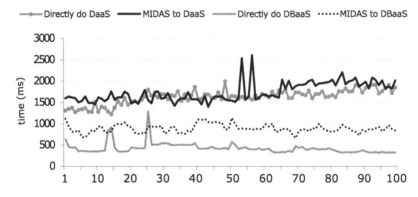

Fig. 14. Return time (y-axis) for each of the 100 queries submitted (x-axis) with a limit of 10000 records.

- 1037.75 ± 109.85 ms for queries through MIDAS to DaaS;
- 196.62 ± 5.31 ms for queries without MIDAS to DBaaS; and
- 236.56 ± 43.99 ms for queries through MIDAS to DBaaS.

Finally, we submitted 100 queries to return 10000 data records. In this case, Fig. 14 shows the average of execution time:

- 1628.34 ± 165.79 ms for queries without MIDAS to DaaS;
- 1739.71 ± 225.21 ms for queries through MIDAS to DaaS;
- 426.29 ± 128.76 ms for queries without MIDAS to DBaaS; and
- 888.16 ± 95.24 ms for queries through MIDAS to DBaaS.

Regarding the overhead caused by MIDAS, we can observe that the average differences of direct queries to DaaS and DBaaS, respectively, when compared to the access through MIDAS were: (i) 19.03% and 1.75%, for 100 data records; (ii) 5.77% and 20.31%, for 1000 data records; and (iii) 6.84% and 108.35%, for 10000 records. Time values are affected by (i) data traffic on the Internet and (ii) MIDAS infrastructure. Some adjustments are been provided to enhace this algorithm.

6.2 Results from Experiment 2

In this experiment, we combine two query languages (SQL and NoSQL) with both sources (DaaS and DBaaS).

As Fig. 15 shows, the following averages of execution time were obtained:

- 1665.78 ± 165.50 ms for MongoDB queries through MIDAS to DaaS;
- 1878.23 ± 230.59 ms for SQL queries through MIDAS to DaaS;
- 938.92 ± 63.05 ms for MongoDB queries through MIDAS to DBaaS; and
- 955.36 ± 87.81 ms for SQL queries through MIDAS to DBaaS.

We can observe that: (i) For access to DaaS, SQL queries were 12.75% slower; while (ii) for DBaaS access, SQL queries were 1.75% slower. The time difference between the two types of queries is minimal. Consequently, no losses associated with choosing the query language.

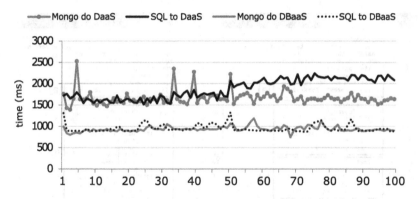

Fig. 15. Return time (y-axis) for each of the 100 queries submitted (x-axis) from different languages to different data sources.

6.3   Results from Experiment 3

In this experiment, we performed a query with join statements that access two different DaaS, two different DBaaS and one DaaS with one DBaaS.

Figure 16 depicts the average of the execution time.

- 106037.99 ± 7053.01 ms for two DaaS providers;
- 30919.58 ± 6837.21 ms for two DBaaS providers; and
- 30899.90 ± 7108.21 ms for one DaaS and one DBaaS

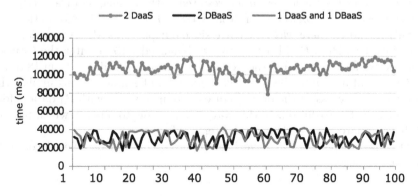

Fig. 16. Return time (y-axis) for each of the 100 queries (x-axis) with join (or aggregation) statement.

In this experiment, we can observe that (i) the average query time to 2 DBaaS is 0.06% slower than 1 DaaS and 1 DBaaS queries; and (ii) the average query time to 2 DaaS is 242.95% slower than 2 DBaaS queries and 243.17% slower than 1 DaaS and 1 DBaaS queries, respectively. When using DaaS, the time values are greater than those presented by DBaaS. This is because DBaaS have mechanisms/structures (such as relational databases) to optimize data handling, different from DaaS.

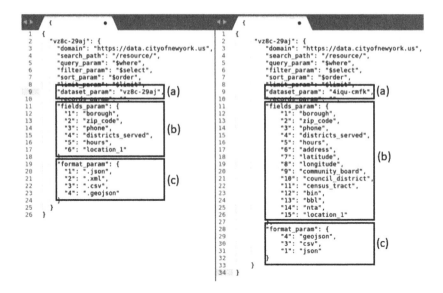

Fig. 17. Information about P_3 before (left) and after (right) of Crawler execution. Featured for the three modified sections.

6.4   Results from Experiment 4

In this experiment, Crawler execution resulted in the change of 3 DaaS (P_1, P_2, and P_3): precisely the DaaS present from MIDAS 1.8. Since this information was manually included, there was no change since our previous MIDAS version.

For instance, P_1 with 14 attributes was changed into 26 after the Crawler execution. Besides that, in P_2, the extraction increased attributes from 18 to 27.

The P_3 had attributes been added, updated and removed. This implies the maintenance of access to the data. Figure 17 compares DIS with P_3 data before and after Crawler execution. In this way, it is possible to observe which parameters have updated (a), added (b) and removed (c).

Note that all parameters have been entered, changed or deleted correctly from our Crawler.

6.5   Results from Experiment 5

In the experiment 5, Fig. 18 shows the execution time for each of the 10 DaaS present in DIS.

The averages obtained vary between 25.6 and 29.6 s. The data extraction process has little variation times (standard deviation of 1.29 s), because the data scraping process occurs with little variation between distinct DaaS (some elements are extracted from Ajax requests, without the need to manipulate elements HTML).

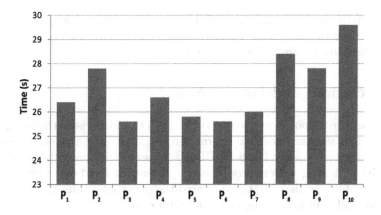

Fig. 18. Average Crawler execution time in the 10 DaaS.

6.6   Discussions

Our case study evaluates MIDAS through its overhead and different languages and data sources.

Despite the fact that the execution time was proportional to the submitted query, in the first experiment the results show that MIDAS inputs an extra overhead regarding direct queries. This depreciation was expected because of the new layer introduced between SaaS and DaaS. It is noteworthy that network bandwidth, cloud providers, and latency might also influence those results.

Considering DBaaS, we observed that the result from a direct access is more rapid than through MIDAS. In fact, MIDAS deals with DBaaS as a DaaS, through the Data Mapping component.

The second experiment states that the query language (e.g., SQL, NoSQL) does not influence the query performance or the return time with both data (e.g., DaaS, DBaaS).

The third experiment, the join clause has a complexity $O(n^2)$ (where 2 is the number of data sources). All the same, we can state that the benefits of our approach to interoperate different data sources outperforms the time spent on gathering the results.

In relation to experiment 4 and 5, the variation of the average execution time is observed. This is because the amount of data manipulated varies according to DaaS. There is also the scenario where the Crawler detects that there are no changes once the data is up to date. With an average time of 26 s for each DaaS, an excessively populated DIS is indicative of how the effectiveness of the Crawler can be improved.

The sequential execution of a given DaaS tends to have a decreasing average time since some data is cached during successive executions. However, external interferences during Crawler execution (such as broadband connection noise) tend to influence time. Additionally, changing HTML layout of pages would make the data extraction process difficult, as some markup elements are used during the process.

All data sources were public and open.

7   Conclusions and Future Work

In this paper, we propose a new version of MIDAS to address issues little explored in the previous version, such as the formal model, and Web Crawler. SaaS applications continue to query DaaS or DBaaS datasets transparently despite the complexity of dealing with interoperability problem in cloud environments.

Our results show that MIDAS delivered the expected results in both scenarios, despite different query languages and data sources.

As a future work, we intend to continue improving MIDAS by adding new characteristics, such as (i) recognization of SPARQL queries and other types of NoSQL; (ii) automate the Crawler for searching novel DaaS and disambiguate data from heterogeneous data sources, and (iii) provide the ABox and evaluate the formalization of MIDAS.

References

1. Ali, H., Moawad, R., Hosni, A.A.F.: A cloud interoperability broker (CIB) for data migration in SaaS. In: 2016 IEEE International Conference on Cloud Computing and Big Data Analysis (ICCCBDA), pp. 250–256, July 2016. https://doi.org/10.1109/ICCCBDA.2016.7529566
2. Armbrust, M., et al.: A view of cloud computing. Commun. ACM **53**(4), 50–58 (2010). https://doi.org/10.1145/1721654.1721672
3. Baader, F.: A new description logic with set constraints and cardinality constraints on role successors. In: Dixon, C., Finger, M. (eds.) FroCoS 2017. LNCS (LNAI), vol. 10483, pp. 43–59. Springer, Cham (2017). https://doi.org/10.1007/978-3-319-66167-4_3
4. Barouti, S., Alhadidi, D., Debbabi, M.: Symmetrically-private database search in cloud computing. In: 2013 IEEE 5th International Conference on Cloud Computing Technology and Science (CloudCom), vol. 1, pp. 671–678. IEEE (2013)
5. Gantz, J., Reinsel, D.: The digital universe in 2020: big data, bigger digital shadows, and biggest growth in the far east. IDC iView - IDC Analyze the Future, pp. 1–16 (2012)
6. Hacigumus, H., Iyer, B., Mehrotra, S.: Providing database as a service. In: Proceedings of the 18th International Conference on Data Engineering, pp. 29–38. IEEE (2002)
7. Igamberdiev, M., Grossmann, G., Selway, M., Stumptner, M.: An integrated multi-level modeling approach for industrial-scale data interoperability. Softw. Syst. Model. **17**, 1–26 (2016)
8. Loutas, N., Kamateri, E., Bosi, F., Tarabanis, K.: Cloud computing interoperability: the state of play. In: 2011 IEEE International Conference on Cloud Computing Technology and Science (CloudCom), pp. 752–757. IEEE (2011)
9. Lutz, C., Wolter, F.: The data complexity of description logic ontologies. Log. Methods Comput. Sci. **13**(4) (2017). https://doi.org/10.23638/LMCS-13(4:7)2017

10. Mell, P., Grance, T., et al.: The NIST definition of cloud computing. Computer Security Division, Information Technology Laboratory, National Institute of Standards and Technology Gaithersburg (2011)
11. Park, H.K., Moon, S.J.: DBaaS using HL7 based on XMDR-DAI for medical information sharing in cloud. Int. J. Multimedia Ubiquit. Eng. **10**(9), 111–120 (2015)
12. Ribeiro, E.L.F., Vieira, M.A., Claro, D.B., Silva, N.: Transparent interoperability middleware between data and service cloud layers. In: Proceedings of the 8th International Conference on Cloud Computing and Services Science (CLOSER 2018), pp. 148–157. INSTICC, SciTePress (2018). https://doi.org/10.5220/0006704101480157
13. Schreiner, G.A., Duarte, D., Mello, R.D.S.: SQLtoKeyNoSQL: a layer for relational to key-based NoSQL database mapping. In: Proceedings of the 17th International Conference on Information Integration and Web-based Applications & Services, p. 74. ACM (2015)
14. Sellami, R., Bhiri, S., Defude, B.: ODBAPI: a unified REST API for relational and NoSQL data stores. In: 2014 IEEE International Congress on Big Data (BigData Congress), pp. 653–660. IEEE (2014)
15. Silva, G.C., Rose, L.M., Calinescu, R.: A systematic review of cloud lock-in solutions. In: 2013 IEEE 5th International Conference on Cloud Computing Technology and Science (CloudCom), vol. 2, pp. 363–368. IEEE (2013)
16. Vieira, M., et al.: Enhancing MIDAS towards a transparent interoperability between SaaS and DaaS. In: Anais do XIII Simpósio Brasileiro de Sistemas de Informação, Lavras, pp. 348–355. SBC, Porto Alegre (2017). https://sol.sbc.org.br/index.php/sbsi/article/view/6062
17. Xu, J., Shi, M., Chen, C., Zhang, Z., Fu, J., Liu, C.H.: ZQL: a unified middleware bridging both relational and NoSQL databases. In: 2016 IEEE 14th International Conference on Dependable, Autonomic and Secure Computing, 14th International Conference on Pervasive Intelligence and Computing, 2nd International Conference on Big Data Intelligence and Computing and Cyber Science and Technology Congress (DASC/PiCom/DataCom/CyberSciTech), pp. 730–737. IEEE (2016)
18. Zeidler, C., Asghar, M.R.: Towards a framework for privacy-preserving data sharing in portable clouds. In: Helfert, M., Ferguson, D., Méndez Muñoz, V., Cardoso, J. (eds.) CLOSER 2016. CCIS, vol. 740, pp. 273–293. Springer, Cham (2017). https://doi.org/10.1007/978-3-319-62594-2_14
19. Zheng, Z., Zhu, J., Lyu, M.R.: Service-generated big data and big data-as-a-service: an overview. In: 2013 IEEE International Congress on Big Data, pp. 403–410, June 2013. https://doi.org/10.1109/BigData.Congress.2013.60

Continuous Architecting
with Microservices and DevOps:
A Systematic Mapping Study

Davide Taibi[1](✉)(iD), Valentina Lenarduzzi[1](✉)(iD), and Claus Pahl[2](✉)(iD)

[1] Tampere University, Tampere, Finland
{davide.taibi,valentina.lenarduzzi}@tut.fi
[2] Free University of Bozen-Bolzano, Bolzano, Italy
claus.pahl@unibz.it

Abstract. Context: Several companies are migrating their information systems into the Cloud. Microservices and DevOps are two of the most common adopted technologies. However, there is still a lack of understanding how to adopt a microservice-based architectural style and which tools and technique to use in a continuous architecting pipeline.

Objective: We aim at characterizing the different microservice architectural style principles and patterns in order to map existing tools and techniques adopted in the context of DevOps.

Methodology: We conducted a Systematic Mapping Study identifying the goal and the research questions, the bibliographic sources, the search strings, and the selection criteria to retrieve the most relevant papers.

Results: We identified several agreed microservice architectural principles and patterns widely adopted and reported in 23 case studies, together with a summary of the advantages, disadvantages, and lessons learned for each pattern from the case studies. Finally, we mapped the existing microservices-specific techniques in order to understand how to continuously deliver value in a DevOps pipeline. We depicted the current research, reporting gaps and trends.

Conclusion: Different patterns emerge for different migration, orchestration, storage and deployment settings. The results also show the lack of empirical work on microservices-specific techniques, especially for the release phase in DevOps.

Keywords: Cloud-native · Microservice · DevOps · Migration · Orchestration

1 Introduction

Software is becoming more complex and development processes are evolving to cope with the current fast-changing requirements imposed by the market, with short time-to-market and quickly evolving technologies. Continuous software engineering, and in particular DevOps, tries to address these aspects, supporting developers with a set of continuous delivery practices and tools to continuously deliver value, increasing delivery efficiency and reducing the time intervals

© Springer Nature Switzerland AG 2019
V. M. Muñoz et al. (Eds.): CLOSER 2018, CCIS 1073, pp. 126–151, 2019.
https://doi.org/10.1007/978-3-030-29193-8_7

between releases [3]. However, traditional monolithic architectures are not easily applicable to this environment and new architectural styles need to be considered. In order to adopt DevOps, the architectural style adopted must be designed with an agile focus; for this purpose, the Microservices [10] architectural style is suitable for this continuous architecture setting.

Microservices are relatively small and autonomous services deployed independently, with a single and clearly defined purpose [10]. Because of their independent deployability, they have a lot of advantages for continuous delivery. They can be developed in different programming languages, they can scale independently from other services, and they can be deployed on the hardware that best suits their needs. Moreover, because of their size, they are easier to maintain and more fault-tolerant since the failure of one service will not break the whole system, which could happen in a monolithic system [12].

DevOps (Development and Operations) is a set of continuous delivery practices aimed at decrease the delivery time, increasing the delivery efficiency and reducing time among releases while maintaining software quality. It combines software development, quality assurance, and operations [3]. DevOps includes a set of steps of the development process (plan, create, verify, package) and of the operational process (release, configure, monitor), combining the activities commonly performed by the development teams, quality assurance and operations teams. In order to adopt the DevOps practices, the architectural style of the system must be design with an agile focus and the microservice architectural style is one of the most suitable architectural style to cope with them [2].

Despite both the microservice architectural style and DevOps being widely used in industry, there are still some challenges in understanding how to develop such kinds of architectures in a continuous software engineering process [2]. In this work, we extend our previous mapping study on architectural patterns for microservices [16].

The goal of this work is two-fold: First we aim to characterize the different microservice architectural styles reported in the literature both as proposals and case studies on implementations. Then we aim to map the reported microservices-based techniques that can be applied to the DevOps pipeline in order to identify existing gaps. Therefore, we designed this work as a Systematic Mapping Study [13,19]. A previous systematic mapping has been published by Pahl and Jamshidi [11] aimed at classifying and comparing the existing research body on microservices mainly considering non peer-reviewed content from web blogs. Our study differs in the following ways:

- *Focus*: We focus on suggested architectural style definitions, emerging patterns and mapping microservices development to the DevOps pipeline, while [11] focused on initially characterizing the available body of research and [16] focused only on architectural styles.
- *Comprehensiveness*: We included results from eight bibliographic sources and papers from the citations of the retrieved papers [19] to increase the paper base. Moreover, we included papers published up to 2016;

- *Systematic approach*: We conducted a Systematic Mapping Study implementing the protocol defined in [13], followed by a systematic snowballing process using all references found in the papers [19];
- *Quality Assessment*: Although this is not a Systematic Literature Review [8], we include only peer-reviewed contributions or non peer-reviewed papers only in case the number of their citations in peer-reviewed ones is higher than the average citations.

The contribution of our study can be summarise as follows:

- Classification of the existing microservice architectural styles and patterns;
- Analysis of advantages and disadvantages of different architectural style principles and patterns based on their implementations reported in the literature;
- Classification of microservice techniques for DevOps;
- Identification of research gaps and trends.

The paper is structured as follows. In Sect. 2 we describe the methodology used. Section 3 shows the results obtained. In Sect. 4 we discuss the results. Section 5 identifies threats to validity. Section 6 end with some conclusions.

2   Methodology

We used the protocol defined by Petersen [13] in combination with the systematic snowballing process [19].

2.1   Goals and Research Questions

We define our research goals as follows:

Goal 1: *Analyze* the architectural style proposals
  for the purpose of comparing them and related implementations
  with respect to their advantages and disadvantages
  in the context of cloud-native software implementation.
Goal 2: *Characterize* microservices-specific techniques
  for the purpose of mapping them to the DevOps process
  with respect to identifying and comparing different techniques for different stages
  in the context of cloud-native software implementation. Regarding G1, we derived the following research questions:
    - RQ1: Which are the different microservices-based architectural styles?
    - RQ2: What are the differences among the existing architectural styles?
    - RQ3: Which advantages and disadvantages have been highlighted in implementations described in the literature for the identified architectural styles?
  Regarding G2, we derived the last research question:
    - RQ4: What are the different DevOps-related techniques applied in the microservices context?

2.2   Search Strategy

Bibliographic Sources and Search Strings. We identified the relevant works in eight bibliographic sources as suggested in [9]: ACM Digital Library, IEEE Xplore Digital Library, Science Direct, Scopus, Google Scholar, Citeeser library, Inspec and Springer Link. We defined the search strings based on the PICO terms of our questions [9] using only the terms Population and Intervention. We did not use the Outcome and Comparison terms so as not to reduce research efficiency of the selected search strings (Table 1). We applied the following queries adapting the syntax to each bibliographic source:

RQ1-3: (microservice* OR micro-service*) AND (architect* OR migrat* OR modern* OR reengineer* OR re-engineer* OR refactor* OR re-factor* OR rearchitect* OR re-architect* OR evol*).

RQ4: (microservice* OR micro-service*) AND (DevOps OR Develop* OR Creat* OR Cod* OR verif* OR test* OR inspect* OR pack* OR compil* OR archiv*; releas* OR configur* OR deploy* OR monitor* OR performance* OR benchmark*).

The symbol * allows to capture possible variations in search terms such as plural and verb conjugation.

Table 1. Search strings - PICO structure [16].

Population	Intervention - terms
P: microservice	microservice*; micro-service*
I: DevOps; architecture; migration	architect*; migrat*; modern*; evol*; reengineer*; re-engineer*; refactor*; re-factor*; rearchitect*; re-architect*; DevOps; Develop*; Creat*; Cod*; verif*; test*; inspect*; pack*; compil*; archiv*; releas*; configur*; deploy*; monitor*; performance*; benchmark;

Inclusion and Exclusion Criteria. We defined the selection criteria based on our RQs considering the following inclusion criteria:

General Criteria: We only included papers written in English. Moreover, we excluded papers that were not peer-reviewed. However, we also considered non peer-reviewed contributions if the number of citations in peer-reviewed papers was higher than average. The number of unique citations was extracted from the eight bibliographic sources removing non peer-reviewed ones. The selected works cover a maximum of two years and we can therefore not expect a high number of citations. For this reason, works with a high number of citations can be considered very relevant even if they are not peer-reviewed.

Selection by Title and Abstract: We removed all papers that do not contain any references to microservices or that use the term microservices for different purposes or in different domains (i.e. electronics, social science...);

Selection by Full Papers: We excluded papers that do not present any evidence related to our research questions or papers using microservices without any clear reference to the adopted architectural style, and microservices-based implementations that do not report any advantages and disadvantages of using microservices. For the first three RQs, we considered proposals of microservices-based architectural styles, implementations of microservices-based cloud systems, migrations of monolithic systems into cloud-native microservices-based systems, papers reporting advantages and disadvantages of microservices-based architectural styles. For RQ4, we considered papers on DevOps techniques applied in the context of microservices-based systems, and papers on *project planning, coding, testing, release, deployment, operation* and *monitoring* techniques applied in the context of microservices-based systems.

Search and Selection Process. The search was conducted in October 2017 including all the publications available until this period. Applying the searching terms we retrieved 2754 unique papers.

Testing Inclusion and Exclusion Criteria Applicability: Before applying the inclusion and exclusion criteria, we tested their applicability [9] to a subset of 30 papers (10 papers per author) randomly selected from the retrieved ones. For 8 of the 30 selected papers, two authors disagreed and a third author was involved in the discussion to clear the disagreements.

Applying Inclusion and Exclusion Criteria to Title and Abstract: We applied the refined criteria to remaining papers. Each paper was read by two authors and in case of disagreed and a third author was involved in the discussion to clear the disagreements. For seven papers we involved the third author. Out of 2754 initial papers, we included 85 by title and abstract.

Backward and Forward Snowballing: We performed the backward and forward snowballing [19], considering all the references presented in the 85 papers (858 references) and evaluating all the papers that reference the retrieved ones resulting in one additional relevant paper. We applied the same process as for the retrieved papers. The new selected studies were included in the aforementioned 12 papers, in order to compose the final set of publication.

Fulfill Reading: After the full reading of the 97 papers performed by two of the authors, the paper identification process resulted in 40 peer-reviewed papers and 2 non peer-reviewed ones. The two works ([S1] and [S2]) added from the gray literature have a dramatically high number of citations compared to the remaining works, with 18 and 25 citations, resp. (average number of citations = 4.21). The related citations are reported together with the full references in the Appendix.

In case of [S2], we also attributed to the same work the citations obtained for [14], since this website was published with the same information two months later.

Table 2. The papers selection process [16].

Selection process	#considered papers	#rejected papers	Validation
Paper extracted from the bibliographic sources	2754		10 random papers independently classified by three researchers
Sift based on title and abstract		2669	Good inter-rater agreement on first sift (K-statistic test)
Primary papers identified	85		
Secondary papers inclusion	858	855	Systematic snowballing [19] including all the citations reported in the 85 primary papers and sifting them based on title and abstract
Full papers considered for review	88		Each paper has been read completely by two researchers and 858 secondary papers were identified from references
Sift based on full reading		46	Papers rejected based on inclusion and exclusion criteria
Relevant papers included	**42**		

The selection process resulted in 42 accepted papers published from 2014 to 2016. Although the term microservice was introduced in 2011, no publications were found from 2011 to 2013. More than 65% of these papers were published at conferences, while another 23% were accepted at workshops. Only 7% of the papers were published as journal articles, and nearly 5% are non peer-reviewed websites (gray literature) (Table 2).

3   Results

We now summarize the pros and cons of microservice-based solutions based on their importance, considering the concerns mentioned most frequently in the papers as being important. We analyze the most common architectural style principles and patterns that emerged from the papers, also including their reported advantages and disadvantages. Moreover, we report on DevOps-related techniques applied. We first report on the principles of microservices architectural styles, as reflected by the literature, and then we extract and categorize the patterns defined in the surveyed literature.

We consider an *architectural style* as a set of *principles* and coarse-grained *patterns* that provide an abstract framework for a family of systems. An architectural style consists of a set of architectural principles and patterns that are aligned with each other to make designs recognizable and design activities repeatable: principles express architectural design intent; patterns adhere to the principles and are commonly occurring (proven) in practice.

3.1 General Advantages and Disadvantages of Microservices and Principles of the Architectural Style

The most common advantages of microservice architectures that are highlighted in the selected works are the following:

- *Increased Maintainability.* All the paper reported microservices-based implementations as the most important considered characteristic.
- *Write Code in Different Languages.* Underlines benefits of using different languages, inconsistent with monolithic applications [S13], [S34], [S11].
- *Flexibility.* Every team can select their own technology based on their needs [S30], [S14], [S38]
- *Reuse.* The creation of a component with shared features increase reusability by reducing maintenance effort since the shared component will be updated only once and the maintenance of the shared microservices, including all the related changes will be reflected by any connected microservices [S34], [S12].
- *Ease of Deployment.* The independent deployment ease the whole development and deployment processes since each microservice can be deployed separately. Therefore, developers of one microservice do not need to recompile and re-deploy the whole system [S30]
- *Physical Isolation.* This is the key for scaling, provided by microservices architectural style [S3] and [S38].
- *Self-Healing.* Previous safe microservice versions can replace failing services [S7], [S30].
- *Application Complexity.* Components application are commonly less complex and easier to manage thanks to the application decomposition into several components [S29]. Process mining could be highly beneficial in this context [18]
- *Unlimited Application Size.* Microservices has theoretically no size limitation that affect monolithic applications [S13].

These can be considered to form the *principles of the architectural style* as they are agreed advantages. On the other hand, several papers identified a set of issues and potential **disadvantages** to be consider during the development of a microservices-based application:

- *Testing Complexity.* More components and patterns of collaborations among them increase the testing complexity [S21], [S24], [S26], [S31], [S37], [S28].
- *Implementation Effort.* Paired with development complexity, implementing microservices requires more effort than implementing monolithic applications [S28], [S30], [S38].
- *Network issues.* Endpoints are connected via a network. Therefore, the network must be reliable [S41], [S14].
  - *Latency.* Network latency can increase the communication time between microservices [S14], [S11], [S9].
  - *Bandwidth.* Communication often depends on the network, implementations must consider bandwidth for normal and high peak operation.

- *User Authorization.* The API exposed by the microservices need to be protected with a shared user-authentication mechanism, which is often much more complex to implement than monolithic solutions [S14].
- *Time on the Market.* Monolithic solutions are easier and faster to develop. In the case of small applications, with a small number of users (hundreds or thousands), the monolith could be a faster and cheaper initial approach. A microservices-based solution could be considered in a second time once performance or other requirements grows [S11].
- *Continuously Deploy Small Incremental Changes.* The simplified deployment allows changing one issue at time and immediately deploy the system [S37].
- *Independent Monitoring.* A microservices architecture helps independently visualize the "health status" of every microservice in the system simplifying the identification of problems and speeding-up the resolution time [S37].
- *Automation Requirement.* A full DevOps stack is fundamental to manage the whole system and automate the whole process. Without the adoption of DevOps the system development would be much slower with microservices than with monolithic systems [S37].
- *High Independence.* Maintaining microservices as highly decoupled is critical to preserve independence and independent deployability.
- *Development Complexity.* Microservices require experienced developers and architects that design the system architecture and coordinate teams. Learning microservices require much longer than monolithic systems [S30].
- *Increased memory consumption.* If each service runs in its own virtual machine, as is the case at Netflix, then there is the overhead of M times as many virtual machine instances are created [S2].

3.2   Microservice-Based Architectural Patterns

In this section, we aim to answer RQ1, RQ2, and RQ3. From the selected works, three commonly used architectural patterns emerge. In this classification, we attribute to the different patterns the papers reporting the usage of a specific style and those where the patterns can be clearly deduced from the description.

We report the results in three Sections that classify the architectural patterns emerging from this review: In the next sub-sections, we identify and describe orchestration and coordination-oriented architectural patterns, patterns reflecting deployment strategies and storage options.

The API-Gateway Pattern

Concept: Microservices can provide their functions in the form of APIs, and other services can make use of them by directly accessing them through an API. However, the creation of end-user applications based on the composition of different microservices requests a server-side aggregation mechanism. In the selected papers, the API-Gateway resulted as a common approach (Fig. 1).

Origin: The API-Gateway is an orchestration style that resembles more SOA principles than REST ones without including the Enterprise Service Bus (ESB).

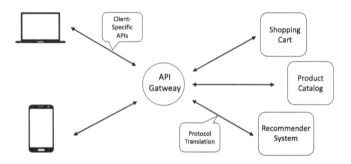

Fig. 1. The API-Gateway architectural pattern [16].

Goal: The main goal is to improve system performance and simplify interactions, therefore decreasing the number of requests per client. It acts as an entry point for the clients, carrying out their requests to the connected services, connecting the required contents, and serving them to the clients [S2].

Properties: The API-Gateway does not provide support for publishing, promoting, or administering services at any significant level. However, it is responsible for the generation of customized APIs for each platform and for optimizing communications between the clients and the application, encapsulating the microservices details. It allows microservices to evolve without influencing the clients. As an example, merging or partitioning two or more microservices only requires updating the API-Gateway to reflect the changes to any connected client. In the example depicted in Fig. 1, the API-Gateway is responsible for communicating with the different front-ends, creating a custom API for each client so that the clients can see only the features they need, which simplifies the creation of end-user applications without adding the complexity of exposing and parsing useless information.

Evolution and Reported Usage: The API-Gateway was named by Richardson [S2]. Ten works implemented different cloud applications based on this pattern reporting several API-Gateway specific **advantages** [S3], [S2], [S12], [S11], [S14], [S31], [S21], [S34], [S39], and [S37]:

- *Ease of Extension.* Implementing new features is easier compared to other architectures since API-Gateway can be used to provide custom APIs to the connected services. Therefore, if a services changes, only the API-Gateway needs to be updated and the connected services to the API-gateway will continue to work seamlessly [S14], [S3]
- *Market-centric Architecture.* Services can be easily modified, based on market needs, without the need to modify the whole system. [S14]
- *Backward Compatibility.* The gateway guarantees that existing clients are not hampered by interface endpoint changes on service version changes [S34].

However, **disadvantages** have also been observed for this architectural pattern:

- *Potential Bottleneck.* The API-Gateway layer is the single entry point for all requests. If it is not designed correctly, it could be the main bottleneck of the system [S14], [S39].
- *Implementation complexity.* The API-Gateway layer increases the complexity of the implementation since it requires implementation of several interfaces for each service [S14], [S34].
- API reused must be considered carefully. Since each client can have a custom API, we must keep track of cases where different types of clients use the same API and modify both of them accordingly in case of changes to the API interface [S34].
- *Scalability.* When the number of microservices in a system explodes, a more efficient and scalable routing mechanism to route the traffic through the services APIs, and better configuration management to dynamically configurate and apply changes to the system will be needed [S37].

The Service Registry Pattern

Concept: The communication among multiple instances of the same microservice running in different containers must be dynamically defined and the clients must be able to efficiently communicate to the appropriate instance of the microservice. Therefore, in order to connect to an existing service, a service-discovery mechanism is needed [S2].

Origin: Richardson also proposed differentiating between "Client-Side" and "Server-Side" patterns [S2]. With client-side patterns, clients query the Service Registry, select an available instance, and make a request. With server-side patterns, clients make requests via a router, which queries the Service Registry and forwards the request to an available instance. However, in the selected works, no implementations reported its usage.

Goal: Unlike the API-Gateway pattern, this pattern allows clients and microservices to talk to each other directly. It relies on a Service Registry, as depicted in Fig. 2, acting in a similar manner as a DNS server.

Properties: The Service Registry knows the dynamic location of each microservice instance. When a client requests access to a specific service, it first asks the registry for the service location; the registry contacts the microservice to ensure its availability and forwards the location (usually the IP address or the DNS name and the port) to the calling client. Finally, unlike in the API-Gateway approach, the clients communicate directly with the required services and access all the available APIs exposed by the service, without any filter or service interface translation provided by the API-Gateway.

Evolution and Reported Usage: A total of eleven papers implemented this pattern. Ten of the selected work make a complete usage of the Service Registry style [S13], [S25], [S10], [S9], [S24], [S26], [S30], [S16], and [S38] while [S23]

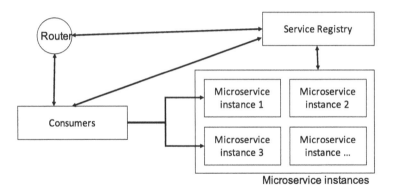

Fig. 2. The service registry architectural pattern.

proposes a small variant, implementing the Service Registry by means of an NoSQL database. O'Connor et al. [S36] report on a case study of a partial migration where a legacy SOA system provided some services in connection with new microservices. In this case, the legacy system was accessed like any other microservice. The Service Registry contained the addresses of all microservices and all services provided by the legacy system.

This architectural pattern has several **advantages**:

- *Increased Maintainability.* All the papers reported an increased maintainability of the systems.
- *Ease of Communication.* Services can communicate with each others directly, without interpretation [S25], [S36].
- *Health Management.* Resilient and scalable mechanisms provide health management and out-scaling functions for atomic and composed services [S7].
- *Failure Safety.* In the case of failure, microservices can be easily restarted, due to their stateless properties [S7].
- *Software Understandability.* Services are relatively small and easy to understand [S1], [S2]
- *Ease of Development.* Smaller services are easier to develop [S1], [S2]
- *Ease of Migration.* Existing services can be re-implemented with microservices, replacing the legacy service by changing its location in the Service Registry that will start to dynamically serve all microservices instances instead of statically pointing to the legacy system [S36].

Several papers also identified **disadvantages** for this pattern:

- *Interface design must be fixed.* During maintenance, individual services may change internally but there could be a need to also update the interface, requiring adaptation of all connected services. They recommend keeping the interface definition as stable as possible in order to minimize the influence in case of interface changes [S38].
- *Service Registry Complexity.* The registry layer increases implementation complexity as it requires several interfaces per service [S16].

- *Reuse.* If not designed correctly, the service registry could be the main bottleneck of the system [S25].
- *Distributed System Complexity.* Direct communication among services increases several aspects: *Communication among Services* [S2], *Distributed Transaction Complexity* [S2], *Testing* of distributed systems, including shared services among different teams can be tricky [S2].

The Hybrid Pattern

Concept and Origin: This pattern combines the power of the Service Registry pattern with that of the API-Gateway pattern, replacing the API-Gateway component with a message bus.

Goal and Properties: Clients communicate with the message bus, which acts as a Service Registry, routing the requests to the requested microservices. Microservices communicate with each other through a message bus, in a manner similar to the Enterprise Service Bus used in SOA architectures.

Evolution and Reported Usage: Six works implemented this pattern [S27], [S33], [S32], [S35], [S4] and [S3] reporting the following **advantages**:

- *Easy of Migration.* This pattern ease the migration of existing SOA based applications, since the ESB can be used a communication layer for the microservices that gradually replace the legacy services.
- *Learning Curve.* Developers familiar with SOA can easily implement this pattern with a very little training.

and a **disadvantage**:

- *SOA Issues.* The pattern does benefit from the IDEAL properties of microservices and from the possibility to independently develop different services with different teams, but has the same ESB-related issues as in SOA.

3.3   Deployment Strategies/Patterns

As part of the architectural patterns, we now describe the different deployment strategies (also referred to as deployment patterns) that emerged from our mapping study. Please note that here we only report on microservices-specific deployment strategies not directly related to DevOps, while DevOps automated deployment approaches are reported in Section III.D.

The Multiple Service per Host Pattern

Principle: In this strategy, multiple services and multiple services run on the same host.

Reported Usage: Four of the selected works implemented this approach [S19], [S33], [S30], and [S7] without specifying whether they deployed the services into containers or VMs. Fifteen works adopted the same pattern by deploying each service into a container [S10], [S25], [S35], [S9], [S8], [S11], [S34], [S32], [S36], [S38], [S37], [S40], [S16], [S41], and [S22]. Richardson refers to this sub-pattern as "Service instance per container pattern" [S2]. Two works implemented this pattern deploying each microservice into a dedicated virtual machine [S27] and [S31]. This pattern is also called "Service instance per virtual machine" [S2].

Despite reporting on the adoption of these patterns, only a few papers discuss their **advantages** such as:

– *Scalability.* Easy scalability to deploy multiple instances at the same host.
– *Performance.* Multiple containers allow rapid deployment of new services compared to VMs [S40], [S34], [S10].

The Single Service per Host Pattern

Principle and Properties: In this pattern [S2], every service is deployed in its own host. The main benefit of this approach is the complete isolation of services, reducing the possibility of conflicting resources. However, this dramatically reduces performance and scalability.

Reported Usage: This pattern has not been implemented or referenced in the selected works.

3.4   Data Storage Patterns

Like any service, microservices need to store data. Sixteen implementations reported on the data storage pattern that they adopted. Among these papers, we identified three different data storage patterns that are also described by [S1], [S24], and [S3]. Although it is recommended to adopt Object Relational Mapping approaches with NoSQL databases [S1], the patterns identified are also applicable for relational databases.

The Database per Service Pattern

Principle and Properties: In this pattern, each microservice accesses its private database. This is the easiest approach for implementing microservices-based systems, and is often used to migrate existing monoliths with existing databases.

Reported Usage: In the selected works, six adopted this pattern [S23], [S12], [S36], [S24], [S11], and [S26]. This pattern has several **advantages**:

– *Scalability.* The database can be easily scaled in a database cluster whithin a second moment [S24], in case the service need to be scaled.
– *Independent Development.* Separate teams can work independently on each service, without affecting other teams in case of changes to the DB schema.
– *Security Mechanism.* Access to other microservices or corruption of data not needed is avoided since only one microservice can access a schema.

The Database Cluster Pattern

Principle and Properties: The second storage pattern proposes storing data on a database cluster. This approach improves the scalability of the system, allowing to move the databases to dedicated hardware. In order to preserve data consistency, microservices have a sub-set of database tables that can be accessed only from a single microservice; in other cases, each microservice may have a private database schema. This pattern was described by Richardson [S2].

Reported Usage: The pattern was implemented by [S27], [S6], and [S15] by using a separated DB schema for each service. [S15] also proposed it for replicating the data across the DBs of each service.

This pattern has the **advantage** of improving data scalability. It is recommended for implementations with huge data traffic while it could be useless in the case of a limited number of users and data traffic. **Disadvantages**:

- *Increased Complexity* through the cluster architecture.
- *Risk of Failure* increases because of the introduction of another component and the distributed mechanism.

Shared Database Server

Principle and Properties: This pattern is similar to the Database Cluster Pattern, but, instead of using a database cluster, all microservices access a single shared database.

Reported Usage: Six implementations adopted this pattern [S13], [S39], [S25], [S18], [S30], and [S16]. All these implementations access to the data concurrently, without any data isolation approach.

The main **advantage** reported is the simplicity of the migration from monolithic applications since existing schemas can be reused without any changes. Moreover, the existing code base can be migrated without the need to make important changes (e.g., the data access layer remains identical).

3.5   DevOps and Microservices

Now, we change focus from microservices as an architectural style with principles and patterns to the relevance of the style as a continuous architecting solution.

In this section, we answer RQ4, reporting the main DevOps related to techniques proposed and applied in conjunction with microservices, summarizing their advantages and disadvantages. The section is structured as follows: After a description of the papers reporting on the application of microservices-based implementations *applying the DevOps pipeline* (partially or completely), we describe the techniques related to each DevOps step: *planning, coding, testing, release, deployment, operation, monitoring.*

DevOps and Microservices. Chen et al. [S8] propose a set of tactics for adopting DevOps with microservices-based implementations. Adopting a set of tools enables (1) continuous integration, (2) test automation, (3) rapid deployment and robust operations, (4) synchronized and flexible environment. Their proposal is to keep four quality characteristics under control (availability, modifiability, performance, and testability) by means of a set of tactics. As an example, they propose checking availability by monitoring the system by detecting exceptions, reconfiguring clusters automatically in case of failures or lack of resources, creating active redundancy (by means of Zookeeper [1]) and rolling back deployed services in case of failure.

Planning and Coding Techniques. This section includes all techniques and tools for code development, including requirement elicitation, software architectures, and coding techniques. As for the architectural styles, we refer to the discussion about the previously described patterns reported in Sects. 3.2 and 3.3. In order to cope with continuously changing requirements whilst ensuring complexity and keeping product evolution under control, Versteden et al. [S16] propose a semantic approach combining microservices and the semantic web. The approach is based on the sharing of a set of ontologies among developers so that they can develop microservices that talk about the same content in the same way. Moreover, this also supports the semantics discoverability of microservices.

Considering the coding activities, Xu et al. [S40] propose "CAOPLE", a new programming language for microservices based on an agent-oriented conceptual model of software systems. This programming language allows defining high-level microservices with the aim of easily developing large connected systems with microservices running in parallel, thus reducing communication overhead among microservices and supporting flexible development.

Testing Techniques. (1) Testing is one of the most challenging issues when building a microservice architecture. A microservice architectural style introduces several new components into the applications, and more components mean more chances for failure to occur. Automated testing, as one of the main steps of DevOps, has advanced significantly and new tools and techniques continue to be introduced to the market. Therefore, testing a microservices-based application is more complicated because of several issues:

- Because of the language independence of microservices, the testing tools need to be agnostic to any service language or runtime [S42].
- Testing must focus on failure-recovery logic and not on business logic, due to the rapidly evolving code [S42].
- Existing SOA testing methods are commonly not suitable for microservices, since they do not address the two issues aforementioned [S42].

Of the selected papers, seven propose new testing techniques for microservices. However, no implementations report the usage of these techniques.

Testing can be divided into several levels, including unit tests, integration tests, system tests and acceptance tests. As for acceptance tests and system level tests, Rahman et al. [S18] and [S17] propose automating acceptance tests for microservices based on the Behavior-Driven Development (BDD). Since integration, system, and acceptance tests usually need access to the production file system, the network, and the databases, they propose running the tests in the developer's local environment by means of a subset of replicated Docker containers replicating the whole system, including all microservices running in the production environment. They propose running the large test suites in parallel with multiple docker containers deployed on the local development machine so as to allow developers to (1) continue testing on the latest data used in production (2) continuously run the complete test suites. Unfortunately, they report that running the entire test suite is time consuming and becomes infeasible when the test suite grows. Despite the approach working perfectly for small projects, in big projects the developers' workstations have very high hardware requirements to run the whole system with all microservices and the development environment, making this approach inapplicable in a real development environment.

Savchenko and Radchenko [S22] propose a model of validation of microservices that can be executed on local developer machines and in a test environment, before deploy the microservice in production. The model is compliant with the ISO/IEC 29119 [5] and it is based on five steps:

1. Define the interface of every microservice
2. Write unit-tests for each microservice
3. If the unit tests are passed successfully, the microservice can be packed into a container and a set of container self-tests can be executed to ensure that all interfaces defined in the first step are working.
4. If the self-test is passed, then the microservice can be deployed in a test environment and functional integration tests, load integration tests, and security integration tests can be performed.
5. If all tests in the previous step are passed, the microservice can be deployed in the production environment.

Meinke and Nycander [S20] propose a learning-based testing technique based on a Support Vector Machine (SVM). Thy propose to monitor the inputs of each microservice and to validate the output with a model checker and learn how to interpret the results by means of a SVM based on a stochastic equivalence checker. This model is applicable to high-load systems where statistically significant results can be used as training data. It is claimed to be more robust than manual checks since it can test more conditions. However, non-deterministic conditions cannot be verified with this approach, even though they are very rare.

Heorhiadi et al. [S42] propose a network-oriented resiliency testing method to continuously test high-level requirements. They propose a two-level testing platform composed of two layers. The first layer composed by network proxies, used to control the communication among microservices, logging any data and reporting communications. The second layer responsible to check the results based on the execution graph, to run the test cases, and, in case of failure, to deploy a new microservice through a "Failure orchestrator". This allows creating and testing long and complex chains of assertions, and validating complex processes. However, the system graph must be provided continuously updated.

Only [S42] has been validated internally by the authors on small sample projects, while the other approaches are only proposals not supported by empirical validations. The applicability of the proposed testing techniques to existing large-scale systems therefore needs to be validated.

In conclusion, we can claim that, based on the analysis of the reported testing techniques of microservices-based systems, there are no common validation models that support continuous integration of microservices.

Release Techniques. No release techniques have been proposed or reported in the selected works.

Deployment Techniques. In the selected works, only one work [S31] proposes a technique and a tool for automatic deployment of microservices, assuming the use of reconfigurable microservices. Their tool is based on three main components: (1) An automatic configuration of distributed systems in OpenStack [4] which, starting from a partial and static description of the target architecture, produces a schema for distributing microservices to different machines and containers; (2) A distributed framework for starting, stopping, and removing services; and (3) A reconfiguration cordinator which is in charge of interacting the automatic configuration system to produce optimized deployment planning.

Operation and Monitoring Techniques. Monitoring cloud services is difficult due to the complexity and distributed nature of the systems. Anwar et al. [S5] highlight the complexity of monitoring task, in particular with microservices-based implementations monitored with OpenStack, reporting that 80% of the commonly collected data are useless, thus collecting only 20% of the actual data would allow analyzing smaller datasets, which are often easier to analyze.

Monitoring is a very important operation at runtime, especially for detecting faults in existing services and taking appropriate actions. In this direction, Rajagopalan et al. [S19] propose an autonomous healing mechanism to replace faulty microservices during runtime, in the production environment. They propose comparing the dependency graphs of previous versions of microservices and, in case of failures, replacing the existing microservice by re-deploying the previous version. Despite reducing performance, this approach increases the probability of returning the correct result.

Bak et al. [S21] describe a microservices-based implementation of a distributed IoT case study where they defined an approach for detecting operational anomalies in the system based on the context. They propose an algorithm for detecting records not conformant to the expected or normal behavior of the data, continuously monitoring the various devices and sensors, and dynamically building models of typical measurements according to the time of the day. Their anomaly detection approach is based on the analysis of performances and supposed malfunctions. As for failure detection, they also defined a root cause algorithm to understand if some devices crash when located in specific geographic areas because of errors in the data collected from sensors, or crash when connecting to certain devices.

Toffetti et al. [S7] also adopt a self-healing technique in their implementation, simply restarting faulty microservices that return unexpected values or that raise any exceptions, in order to provide the most reliable result.

4   Discussion

Most of the implementations reported in the papers are related to research prototypes, with the goal of validating the proposed approaches (Table 4). Only six papers report on implementations in industrial context. Regarding the size of the systems implemented, all the implementations are related to small-sized applications, except [S38] that reports on the migration of a large scale system. Only four implementations report on the development language used ([S11], [S32] Java/NodeJS, [S34] php/NodeJS/Python, [S13] php).

4.1   Architecture and Deployment Pattern Applications

Several patterns for microservice-based systems emerged from existing implementations (Table 3). We can associate some patterns with specific application settings such as a monolith-to-microservice or SOA-to-microservice migration.

Migration: Several implementations report the usage of hybrid systems, aimed at migrating existing SOA-based applications to microservices. Maintenance, and specially independent deployment and the possibility to develop different services with different non-interacting teams, are considered the main reasons for migrating monoliths to microservices. The flexibility to write in different languages and to deploy the services on the most suitable hardware is also considered a very important reason for the migration. Reported migrations from monolithic systems tend to be architected with an API-Gateway architecture, probably due to the fact that, since the systems need to be completely re-developed and re-architected, this was done directly with this approach. Migrations from SOA-based systems, on the other hand, tend to have a hybrid pattern, keeping the Enterprise Service Bus as a communication layer between microservices and existing SOA services. Based on this, the Enterprise Service Bus could re-emerge in future evolutions of microservices.

Deployment: Another outcome is that deployment of microservices is still not clear. As reported for some implementations, sometimes microservices are deployed in a private virtual machine, requiring complete startup of the whole machine during the deployment, thus defeating the possibility of quick deployment and decreasing system maintainability due to the need for maintaining a dedicated operating system, service container, and all VM-related tasks.

Table 3. Classification of advantages and disadvantages of the identified patterns [16].

	Pattern	Advantages	Disadvantages
Orchestration & coordination	General	- Increased maintainability - Can use different languages - Flexibility - Reuse - Physical isolation - Self-healing	- Development, Testing, Complexity - Implementation effort - Network-related issue
	API gateway	- Extension easiness - Market-centric architecture - Backward compatibility	- Potential bottleneck - Development complexity - Scalability
	Service registry	- Increased maintainability - Communic., developm., migration - Software understandability - Failure safety	-Interface design must be fixed - Service registry complexity - Reuse - Distributed system complexity
	Hybrid	- Migration easiness - Learning curve	- SOA/ESB integration issues
Deploy	Multiple service per host	- Scalability - Performance	
	Single service per host	- Service isolation	- Scalability - Performance
Data storage	DB per service	- Scalability - Independent development - Security mechanism	- Data needs to be splitted - Data consistency
	DB cluster	- Scalability - Implementation easiness	- Increase complexity - Failure risks
	Shared DB server	- Migration easiness - Data consistency	- Lack of data isolation - Scalability

Table 4. The implementations reported in the selected works [16].

	Research prototype	Validation-specific implementations	Industrial implementations
Websites	- [S11], [S39]	- [S15], [S24], [S26], [S31]	- [S13], [S32]
Services/API	- IOT integration [S33]	- [S9], [S10], [S14], [S16], [S23], [S37], [S36]	- [S21], [S34]
Others	- Enterprise measurement system [S4] - IP multimedia system [S25]	- Benchmark/Test [S35], [S41], [S42] - Business process modelling [S12]	- Mobile dev. platform [S38] - Deployment platform [S30]

4.2   DevOps Link

Taking into account the continuous delivery process, the DevOps pipeline is only partially covered by research work. Considering the idea of continuous architecting, there is a number of implementations that report success stories regarding how to architect, build, and code microservice-based systems, but there are no reports on how to continuously deliver and how to continuously re-architect existing systems. As reported in our classification schema of the research on DevOps techniques (Table 5), the operation side, monitoring, deployment, and testing techniques are the most investigated steps of the DevOps pipeline. However, only few papers propose specific techniques, and apply them to small example projects. Release-specific techniques have not been investigated in our selected works. No empirical validation have been carried out in the selected works. Therefore, we believe this could be an interesting result for practitioners, to understand how existing testing techniques can adopted in industry.

Table 5. DevOps techniques classification schema.

	Proposed technique
Planning	- Semantic models [S16]
Coding	- Agent-oriented programming language [S40]
Testing	- BDD automated acceptance test [S17], [S18]
	- SVM learning-based testing [S20]
	- Validation on developers' machine [S22]
	- Resiliency test of high-level requirements [S42]
Release	
Deployment	- Automated deployment [S31]
Monitoring	- Self-healing to replace faulty MS [S7], [S19]
Operation	- Context-based anomalies detection [S21]

4.3   Research Trends and Gaps

Industry First: Different research trends have emerged in this study. First of all, we can see that microservices come from practitioners and research comes later, so reports on existing practices are only published with delay. From the architectural point of view, the trend is to first analyze the industrial implementations and then compare them with previous solutions (monolithics or SOA).

Style Variants: A new microservice architectural styles variant was proposed by researchers ([S24] and [S26]), applying a database approach for microservice orchestration. However, because they have just been published, no implementations have adopted these practices yet. Also in this case, we believe that an empirical validation and a set of benchmarks comparing this new style with existing one could be highly beneficial for researchers and practitioners.

Despite the increasing popularity of microservices and DevOps in industry, this work shows the lack of empirical studies in an industrial context reporting how practitioners are continuously delivering value in existing large-scale systems. We believe that a set of studies on the operational side of the DevOps pipeline could be highly beneficial for practitioners and could help researchers understand how to improve the continuous delivery of new services.

We can compile the following **research gaps** and **emerging issues**:

- *Position Papers and Introduction to microservices.* An interesting outcome of this work, obtained thru the reading of the whole literature is the tendency of publishing several position papers, highlighting some microservices properties or reporting about potential issues, without any empirical evidence.
- *Comparison of SOA and Microservices.* The differences have not been thoroughly investigated. There is a lack of comparison from different points of view (e.g., performance, development effort, maintenance).
- *Microservices Explosion.* What happens once a growing system has thousands/millions of microservices? Will all aforementioned qualities degrade?
- *DevOps related techniques.* Which chain of tools and techniques is most suitable for different contexts?
- *Negative Results.* In which contexts do microservices turn out to be counterproductive? Are there anti-patterns [6,15,17]?

4.4 Towards an Integrated Microservice Architecture and Deployment Perspective

Further to the discussion of trends and gaps that we have provided in the previous subsection, we focus a short discussion here on an aspect that has emerged from the discussion of DevOps and Microservices in the section before. Automation and tool support are critical concerns for the deployment of microservices for instance in the form of containers, but also the wider implementation of microservice architectures in a DevOps pipeline with tool support for continuous integration and deployment.

In [7], the success of mmicroservices is linked to the evolution of technology platforms.

- Containerization with LXC or Docker has been the first wave, enabling the independent deployment of microservices.
- Container orchestration based on Mesos, Kubernestes or Docker Swarm enables better management of microservices in distributed environments.
- Continuous delivery platform such as Ansible or Spinnaker have also had its impact as our DevOps discussion shows.

Currently, further technologies are finding their way into architecting software:

- Serverless computing fociussing on function-as-a-service solutions that allow more fine-grained service functions without the need to be concerned with infrastructure resources.
- Service meshes address the need fully integrated service-to-service communication monitoring and management.

This indicates that as the technology landscape evolves, we can expect new patterns to emerge. Thus pattern identification will remain a task for the future.

5 Threats to Validity

Different types of threats to validity need to be addressed in this study.

Construct validity reflects what is investigated according to the research questions. The terms microservices, DevOps, and all sub-terms identified in Table I are sufficiently stable to be used as search strings. In order to assure the retrieval of all papers on the selected topic, we searched broadly in general publication databases, which index most well-reputed publications. Moreover, we included gray literature if their citations were higher than the average, in order to consider relevant opinions reported in non-scientific papers. Reliability focuses on whether the data are collected and the analysis is conducted in a way that can be repeated by other researchers with the same results. We defined search terms and applied procedures that can be replicated by others. Since this is a mapping study and not a systematic review, the inclusion/exclusion criteria are only related to whether the topic of microservices is present in a paper [9].

Internal validity is concerned with data analysis. Since our analysis only uses descriptive statistics, the threats are minimal.

External validity is about generalization from this study. Since we do not draw any conclusions about mapping studies in general, external validity threats are not applicable.

6 Conclusion

In this work, we conducted a systematic mapping study on micro-services-based architectural style principles and patterns, also looking at techniques and tools for continuously delivering new services by applying the DevOps approach when implementing micro-services-based systems.

As main outcome we identified several research gaps, such as the lack of comparison between SOA and Microservices, the investigation of consequences of microservices explosion and the high interest in exploring microservices in DevOps settings. Most of the selected works were published at workshops or conferences, which confirms the novelty of this topic and the interest in conducting this mapping study.

We have used architectural patterns to identify common structural properties of microservice architectures. Three orchestration and data-storage patterns emerged that appear to be widely applied for microservices-based systems. Although some patterns were clearly used for migrating existing monolithic applications (service registry pattern) and others for migrating existing SOA applications (hybrid pattern), adopting the API-Gateway pattern in the orchestration layer in order to benefit from microservice architectures without refactoring a second time emerges as a key recommendation. Overall, a 3-layered catalog of patterns comes out with patterns for orchestration/coordination and storage as structural patterns and for deployment alternatives.

Independent deployability, being based on strong isolation, and easing the deployment and self-management activities such as scaling and self-healing, and also maintainability and reuse as classical architecture concerns are the most widely agreed beneficial principles.

DevOps in the contest of microservices is an hot topic being frequently discussed online among practitioners, despite small number of works, probably because of its novelty. Work in this topic is mainly covering testing and monitoring techniques, while there are not yet papers on release techniques. Nonetheless, the independent deployability property often cited requires microservices to be mapped to a continuous architecting pipeline. Therefore, we believe DevOps would need more empirical validation in the context of microservices.

A further analysis regards the notion of a architecture style itself in case of continuous architecting. The latter becomes an integral element of software architecture these days. Correspondingly, an architectural style requires to cover continuous architecting activities as well in addition to purely development stage regards such as system design usually focused on in architectural styles.

A   The Selected Studies

[S1] Lewis, J. and Fowler, M. 2014. Microservices.
      http://martinfowler.com/articles/microservices.html.
[S2] Richardson, C. 2014. Microservice Architecture http://microservices.io.
[S3] Namiot, D. and Sneps-Sneppe, M. 2014. On micro-services architecture. International Journal of Open Information Technologies V.2(9).
[S4] Vianden, M., Lichter, H. and Steffens, A. 2014. Experience on a Microservice-Based Reference Architecture for Measurement Systems. Asia-Pacific Software Engineering Conference.
[S5] Anwar, A., Sailer, A., Kochut, A., Butt, A. 2015. Anatomy of Cloud Monitoring and Metering: A Case Study and Open Problems. Asia-Pacific Workshop on Systems.
[S6] Patanjali, S., Truninger, B., Harsh, P. and Bohnert, T. M. 2015. CYCLOPS: A micro service based approach for dynamic rating, charging & billing for cloud. Conference on Telecommunications.
[S7] Toffetti, G., Brunner, S., Blöchlinger, M., Dudouet, F. and Edmonds. A. 2015. Architecture for Self-managing Microservices. Int. Workshop on Automated Incident Mgmt in Cloud.
[S8] Chen, H.M., Kazman, R., Haziyev, S.,Kropov, V. and Chtchourov, D. 2015. Architectural Support for DevOps in a Neo-Metropolis BDaaS Platform. Symp. on Reliable Distr Syst Workshop.
[S9] Stubbs, J., Moreira, W. and Dooley, R. 2015. Distributed Systems of Microservices Using Docker and Serfnode. Int. Workshop on Science Gateways.
[S10] Abdelbaky, M., Diaz-Montes, J., Parashar, M., Unuvar, M. and Steinder, M. 2015. Docker containers across multiple clouds and data center. Utility and Cloud Computing Conference.
[S11] Villamizar, M., Garcas, O., Castro, H. et al. 2015. Evaluating the monolithic and the microservice architecture pattern to deploy web applications in the cloud. Computing Colombian Conference
[S12] Alpers, S., Becker, C., Oberweis, A. and Schuster, T. 2015. Microservice Based Tool Support for Business Process Modelling. Enterprise Distributed Object Computing Workshop.

[S13] Le, V.D., Neff, M.M., Stewart,R.V., Kelley, R., Fritzinger, E., Dascalu, S.M. and Harris, F.C. 2015. Microservice-based architecture for the NRDC. Industrial Informatics Conference.

[S14] Malavalli, D. and Sathappan, S. 2015. Scalable Microservice Based Architecture for Enabling DMTF Profiles. Int. Conf. on Network and Service Management.

[S15] Viennot, N., Mathias, M. Lécuyer, Bell, J., Geambasu, R. and Nieh, J. 2015. Synapse: A Microservices Architecture for Heterogeneous-database Web Applications. European Conf. on Computer Systems.

[S16] Versteden, A., Pauwels, E. and Papantoniou, A. 2015. An ecosystem of user-facing microservices supported by semantic models. International USEWOD Workshop.

[S17] Rahman, M. and Gao, J. 2015. A Reusable Automated Acceptance Testing Architecture for Microservices in Behavior-Driven Development. Service-Oriented System Engineering Symp.

[S18] Rahman, M., Chen, Z. and Gao, J. 2015. A Service Framework for Parallel Test Execution on a Developer's Local Development Workstation. Service-Oriented System Engineering Symp.

[S19] Rajagopalan, S. and Jamjoom, H. 2015. App-Bisect: Autonomous Healing for Microservice-based Apps. USENIX Conference on Hot Topics in Cloud Computing.

[S20] Meink, K. and Nycander, P. 2015. Learning-based testing of distributed microservice architectures: Correctness and fault injection". Software Engineering and Formal Methods workshop.

[S21] Bak, P., Melamed, R., Moshkovich, D., Nardi, Y., Ship, H., Yaeli, A. 2015. Location and Context-Based Microservices for Mobile and Internet of Things Workloads. Conference Mobile Services.

[S22] Savchenko, D. and Rodchenko, G. 2015. Microservices validation: Methodology and implementation. Ural Workshop on Parallel, Distributed, and Cloud Computing for Young Scientists.

[S23] Gadea, C., Trifan, M., Ionescu, D., Ionescu, B. 2016. A Reference Architecture for Real-time Microservice API Consumption. Workshop on CrossCloud Infrastructures & Platforms.

[S24] Messina, A., Rizzo, R., Storniolo, P., Urso, A. 2016. A Simplified Database Pattern for the Microservice Architecture. Adv. in Databases, Knowledge, and Data Applications.

[S25] Potvin, P., Nabaee, M., Labeau, F., Nguyen, K. and Cheriet, M. 2016. Micro service cloud computing pattern for next generation networks. EAI International Summit.

[S26] Messina, A., Rizzo, R., Storniolo, P., Tripiciano, M. and Urso, A. 2016. The database-is-the-service pattern for microservice architectures. Information Technologies in Bio-and Medical Informatics conference.

[S27] Leymann, F., Fehling, C., Wagner, S., Wettinger, J. 2016. Native cloud applications why virtual machines, images and containers miss the point. Cloud Comp and Service Science conference.

[S28] Killalea, T. 2016. The Hidden Dividends of Microservices. Communications of the ACM. V.59(8), pp. 42-45.

[S29] M. Gysel, L. Kölbener, W. Giersche, O. Zimmermann. "Service cutter: A systematic approach to service decomposition". European Confeence on Service-Oriented and Cloud Computing.

[S30] Guo, D., Wang, W., Zeng,G. and Wei, Z. 2016. Microservices architecture based cloudware deployment platform for service computing. Symposyum on Service-Oriented System Engineering. 2016.

[S31] Gabbrielli, M., Giallorenzo, S., Guidi, C., Mauro, J. and Montesi, F. 2016. Self-Reconfiguring Microservices". Theory and Practice of Formal Methods.

[S32] Gadea, M., Trifan, D. Ionescu, et al. 2016. A microservices architecture for collaborative document editing enhanced with face recognition. SAC.

[S33] Vresk, T. and Cavrak, I. 2016. Architecture of an interoperable IoT platform based on microservices. Information and Communication Technology, Electronics and Microelectronics Conference.

[S34] Scarborough, W., Arnold, C. and Dahan, M. 2016. Case Study: Microservice Evolution and Software Lifecycle of the XSEDE User Portal API. Conference on Diversity, Big Data & Science at Scale.

[S35] Kewley, R., Keste, N. and McDonnell, J. 2016. DEVS Distributed Modeling Framework: A Parallel DEVS Implementation via Microservices. Symposium on Theory of Modeling & Simulation.

[S36] O'Connor, R., Elger, P., Clarke, P., Paul, M. 2016. Exploring the impact of situational context - A case study of a software development process for a microservices architecture. International Conference on Software and System Processes.

[S37] Jaramillo, D., Nguyen, D. V. and Smart, R. 2016. Leveraging microservices architecture by using Docker technology SoutheastCon.

[S38] Balalaie, A., Heydarnoori, A. and Jamshidi, P. 2015. Migrating to Cloud-Native architectures using microservices: An experience report. European Conference on Service-Oriented and Cloud Computing.

[S39] Lin, J. Lin, L.C. and Huang, S. 2016. Migrating web applications to clouds with microservice architectures. Conference on Applied System Innovation.

[S40] Xu,C., Zhu, H., Bayley, I., Lightfoot, D., Green, M. and Marshall P. 2016. CAOPLE: A programming language for microservices SaaS. Symp. on Service-Oriented System Engineering.

[S41] Amaral, M., Polo, J., Carrera, D., et al. 2015. Performance evaluation of microservices architectures using containers. Int. Symp. on Network Computing and Applications.

[S42] Heorhiadi, V., Rajagopalan, S., Jamjoom, H., Reiter, M.K., and Sekar, V. 2016. Gremlin: Systematic Resilience Testing of Microservices. International Conference on Distributed Computing Systems.

References

1. Apache ZooKeeper: https://zookeeper.apache.org/

2. Balalaie, A., Heydarnoori, A., Jamshidi, P.: Microservices architecture enables DevOps: migration to a cloud-native architecture. IEEE Softw. **33**(3), 42–52 (2016)

3. Bass, L., Weber, I., Zhu, L.: DevOps: A Software Architects Perspective, 1st edn. Addison-Wesley Professional, Boston (2015)

4. Di Cosmo, R., Eiche, A., Mauro, J., Zacchiroli, S., Zavattaro, G., Zwolakowski, J.: Automatic deployment of services in the cloud with aeolus blender. In: Barros, A., Grigori, D., Narendra, N.C., Dam, H.K. (eds.) ICSOC 2015. LNCS, vol. 9435, pp. 397–411. Springer, Heidelberg (2015). https://doi.org/10.1007/978-3-662-48616-0_28

5. ISO/IEC/IEEE   29119   Software   Testing   (2014).   http://www.softwaretestingstandard.org/

6. Jamshidi, P., Pahl, C., Mendonca, N.C.: Pattern-based multi-cloud architecture migration. Softw. Pract. Exp. **47**(9), 1159–1184 (2017)
7. Jamshidi, P., Pahl, C., Mendonca, N.C., Lewis, J., Tilkov, S.: Microservices: the journey so far and challenges ahead. IEEE Softw. **35**(3), 24–35 (2018)
8. Kitchenham, B., Charters, S.: Guidelines for Performing Systematic Literature Reviews in Software Engineering (2007)
9. Kitchenham, B., Brereton, P.: A systematic review of systematic review process research in software engineering. Inf. Softw. Technol. **55**(12), 2049–2075 (2013)
10. Lewis, J., Fowler, M.: MicroServices (2014). www.martinfowler.com/articles/microservices.html
11. Pahl, C., Jamshidi, P.: Microservices: a systematic mapping study. In: International Conference on Cloud Computing and Services Science (2016)
12. Pahl, C., Jamshidi, P., Zimmermann, O.: Architectural principles for cloud software. ACM Trans. Internet Technol. **18**(2), 17 (2018)
13. Petersen, K., Feldt, R., Mujtaba, S., Mattsson, M.: Systematic mapping studies in software engineering. In: EASE (2008)
14. Richardson, C.: Decomposing Applications for Deployability and Scalability, Microservices (2014). https://www.infoq.com/articles/microservices-intro
15. Taibi, D., Lenarduzzi, V., Pahl, C.: Processes, motivations, and issues for migrating to microservices architectures: an empirical investigation. IEEE Cloud Comput. **4**(5), 22–32 (2017)
16. Taibi, D., Lenarduzzi, V., Pahl, C.: Architectural patterns for microservices: a systematic mapping study. In: International Conference on Cloud Computing and Services Science, pp. 221–232 (2018)
17. Taibi, D., Lenarduzzi, V.: On the definition of microservices bad architectural smells. IEEE Softw. **35**(3), 56–62 (2018)
18. Taibi, D., Systä, K.: From monolithic systems to microservices: a decomposition framework based on process mining. In: 8th International Conference on Cloud Computing and Services Science, CLOSER (2019)
19. Wohlin, C.: Guidelines for snowballing in systematic literature studies and a replication in software engineering. In: EASE 2014 (2014)

Towards Pricing-Aware Consolidation Methods for Cloud Datacenters

Gabor Kecskemeti[1] , Andras Markus[2], and Attila Kertesz[2(✉)]

[1] Department of Computer Science, Liverpool John Moores University,
Liverpool, UK
g.kecskemeti@ljmu.ac.uk
[2] Software Engineering Department, University of Szeged,
Dugonics ter 13, Szeged 6720, Hungary
Markus.Andras@stud.u-szeged.hu, keratt@inf.u-szeged.hu

Abstract. Cloud Computing has become the major candidate for commercial and academic compute infrastructures. Its virtualized solutions enable efficient, high-rate exploitation of computational and storage resources due to recent advances in data centre consolidation. Resources leased from these providers are offered under many pricing schemes which are often times influenced by the utilised consolidation techniques. In this paper, we provide a foundation to understand the inter-relationship of pricing and consolidation. This has a potential to reach additional gains for the providers from a new angle. To this end we discuss the introduction of a pricing oriented extension of the DISSECT-CF cloud simulator, and introduce a simple consolidation framework that allows easy experimentation with combined pricing and consolidation approaches. Using our generic extensions, we show several simple but easy to combine pricing strategies. Finally, we analyse the impact of consolidators on the profitability of providers applying our simple schemes with the help of real world workload traces.

Keywords: Cloud computing · Provider pricing ·
Datacentre consolidation · Simulation

1 Introduction

In the last decade Cloud Computing has become mature enough to attract a vast number of infrastructure providers, both in the commercial and academic area. Its virtualized data centre management techniques enable the sharing and on-demand access of software and hardware. In the last five years multi-objective optimization techniques have been developed for data centre consolidation [11] to

The research leading to these results was supported by the Hungarian Government and the European Regional Development Fund under the grant number GINOP-2.3.2-15-2016-00037 ("Internet of Living Things"). This paper is a revised and extended version of the conference paper presented in [14].

V. M. Muñoz et al. (Eds.): CLOSER 2018, CCIS 1073, pp. 152–167, 2019.
https://doi.org/10.1007/978-3-030-29193-8_8

exploit most of the available cloud resources, but the complexity and uncertainty of cloud application workloads represent a burden for further improvements.

The commercial utilization of cloud data centres has also evolved in the past decade, and as a result various provider pricing schemes have appeared that tinges the similarities and differences of cloud providers on the market. In a former work we already developed a model for cloud service pricing based on schemes of the major cloud infrastructure providers [17], and made it available for experimentation with IoT Cloud applications in the extended version of the DISSECT-CF simulator [13]. In this work we further extend the capabilities of this simulation environment by generalising the pricing schemes allowing their easy extensibility and combination. Furthermore, we discuss a framework for introducing advanced consolidation techniques into the simulations enabling experimentation about the influences of consolidators on provider pricing. Our goal is to enable research on novel, pricing-aware data-centre management approaches.

The main contributions of this paper are (i) the generic architecture for pricing as well as for consolidator algorithms, and (ii) their evaluation with 7 different pricing strategies in combination with a simple consolidator technique using real world workload traces. Our proposal is made available through the revised and extended version of the open-source DISSECT-CF simulator.

The remainder of the paper is as follows: in Sect. 2, we introduce related approaches by discussing surveys addressing data centre consolidation. In Sect. 3 we summarize the pricing models made available in the DISSECT-CF simulator, and in Sect. 4 we show how to apply them in consolidator algorithms. Section 5 presents the performed measurements highlighting the trade-offs of profit gains and load balancing. Finally we conclude our paper in Sect. 6.

2   Related Work

Efficient data centre management is crucial for beneficial cloud computing solutions. Such consolidation techniques are highly studied, even comparative surveys are available in this research field, such as the ones authored by Ahmad et al. [10] and Filho et al. [11]. Ahmad et al. summarized that migration and dynamic voltage frequency scaling approaches are the most common solutions for server consolidation. They compared 10 consolidation frameworks that can be used to improve the power management and load balance of data centres that can have an effect on application performance. They also argue that specific solutions exist for bandwidth and storage optimization. The conclusions of their investigations are that application profiling may help in workload prediction, which is crucial for more efficient migration solutions, but it is still not possible to accurately predict application demands, which calls for more lightweight migration techniques. Related to application profiling, we also proposed a solution for workload prediction based on trace file information in a previous work [12].

Filho et al. [11] also presented a survey, in which they summarize virtual machine placement and migration techniques and concerns based on 10 related

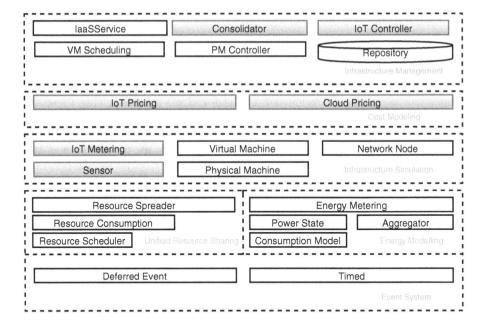

Fig. 1. The architecture of the DISSECT-CF simulator based on [14].

surveys in the field published between 2013 and 2017. They further reviewed 50 works to perform a more detailed analysis than presented in the earlier surveys. They argued that multi-objective optimizations are needed to achieve more accurate results, but they increase the problem complexity at the same time. This survey also highlighted the need for business-aware solutions. To reduce the costs of customers and to achieve higher revenue of providers, cost-aware and profit-aware VM placement strategies may be used. Following this recommendation, in this work we investigate different pricing schemes of cloud providers, and combine them with server consolidation techniques to gain higher profits.

Datacenter consolidation techniques are generally analyzed by means of simulations. Abdullah et al. [9] proposed a heuristic approach for the dynamic server consolidation evaluated using the CloudSim toolkit, and Kertesz et al. also used this framework in [15] to validate an energy efficient virtual machine placement solution. Though similar approaches manage to improve certain properties of cloud data centres, they do not consider provider pricing schemes for consolidation.

3   Our Proposed Cost Model for Cloud Datacentre Management

DISSECT-CF is a compact open source [2] simulator focusing on the internals of IaaS systems. Figure 1 presents its architecture including our latest extensions (denoted with grey colour). There are six subsystems (encircled with dashed lines) implemented, each responsible for a particular functionality: (i) event system – the primary time reference; (ii) unified resource sharing – models low-level resource bottlenecks; (iii) energy modelling – for the analysis of energy-usage patterns of resources (e.g., NICs, CPUs) or their aggregations; (iv) infrastructure simulation – for physical/virtual machines, sensors and networking; (v) cost modelling – for managing IoT and cloud provider pricing schemes, and (vi) infrastructure management – provides a cloud like API, cloud level scheduling and consolidation, and IoT system monitoring and management.

In a recent work [17], we introduced the following new components to model IoT Cloud systems: Sensor, IoT Metering and IoT Controller. Sensors are essential parts of IoT systems, and usually they are passive entities (actuators could change their surrounding environment though). Their performance is limited by their network gateway's (i.e., the device which polls for the measurements and sends them away) connectivity and maximum update frequency. Our network gateway model builds on DISSECT-CF's already existing Network Node model, which allows changes in connection quality as well. In our model, the Sensor component is used to define the sensor type, properties and connections to a cloud system. IoT Metering is used to define and characterize messages coming from sensors, and the IoT Controller is used for sensor creation and management.

To incorporate cost management, we enabled defining and applying provider pricing schemes both for IoT and cloud part of the simulated environments. These schemes are managed by the IoT and Cloud Pricing components of the Cost modeling subsystem of DISSECT-CF, as shown in Fig. 1.

3.1   Configurable Cost Models Based on Real Provider Schemes

In order to enable realistic datacentre consolidation simulations, we considered four of the most popular, commercial cloud providers, namely: Amazon, MS Azure, IBM Bluemix and Oracle. Most providers have a simple pricing method for VM management (beside thaditional virtual machines, some provide containers, compute services or application instances for similar purposes). The pricing scheme of these providers can be found on their websites. We considered the Azure's application service [5], the Bluemix's runtime pricing sheet under the Runtimes section [4], the Amazon EC2 On-Demand prices [1], and the Oracle's compute service [6] together with the Metered Services pricing calculator [7]. The cloud-related cost is based on either instance prices (Azure and Oracle), hourly prices (Amazon) or the mix of the two (Bluemix) provider uses both type of price calculating. For example, Oracle charges depending on the daily uptime of our application as well as the number of CPU cores used by our VMs.

Figure 2 shows the XML structure and the cost values for the applied categories we designed to be used in the simulator. This configuration file contains some providers (for example the amazon element starting in the second line), and the defined values are based on the gathered information from the providers' public websites discussed before. We specified 3 different sizes for applicable VMs (named small, medium and large).

```
<cloudproviders>
 <amazon>
  <medium>
    <ram>8589934592</ram>
    <cpucores>2</cpucores>
    <instance-price>18.15</instance-price>
    <hour-per-price>0.094</hour-per-price>
  </medium>
 </amazon>
 <oracle>
  <medium>
    <ram>16106127360</ram>
    <cpucores>2</cpucores>
    <instance-price>139</instance-price>
    <hour-per-price>0</hour-per-price>
  </medium>
  <large>
    <ram>16106127360</ram>
    <cpucores>4</cpucores>
    <instance-price>268</instance-price>
    <hour-per-price>0</hour-per-price>
  </large>
 </oracle>
 <bluemix>
  <large>
    <ram>4294967296</ram>
    <cpucores>8</cpucores>
    <instance-price>0</instance-price>
    <hour-per-price>0.296</hour-per-price>
  </large>
 </bluemix>
</cloudproviders>
```

Fig. 2. Cost model of Cloud providers based on [14].

This XML file has to contain at least that size category to be used for the experiments. As we can see from the fourth line to the seventh line, a category defines a virtual machine with the given ram and cpucores attributes, and we state the virtual machine prices with the instance-price and hour-per-price attributes. If we select the amazon provider with small category, then in the scenarios a virtual machine will have 1 CPU core and 2 GB of RAM, and the usage of this virtual machine will cost 0.296 Euro per hour.

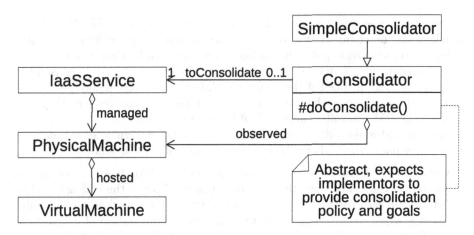

Fig. 3. Consolidation related extension of DISSECT-CF based on [14].

4 Consolidator Algorithms

Data-centre consolidation techniques are heavily used in commercial clouds. Consolidation is built on the migration capabilities of virtual machines, where virtualised workload is moved around in the data-centre according to the cloud operator's goals. In the past years, there were several approaches proposed for consolidating the virtualised workloads of clouds. Most of them were evaluated with simulations. When analysing cost models, the effects of consolidation could not be avoided. Although, the foundations for these consolidator algorithms were laid down in our DISSECT-CF simulator from the beginning [13]. Even with the addition of more precise live-migration modelling [16], the consolidation algorithms were not present in the simulator.

There are two distinct approaches possible to implement a consolidation algorithm in DISSECT-CF: (*i*) create an alternative physical machine (PM) controller which utilizes consolidator related techniques as well or (*ii*) create an independent consolidator which builds on top of the other infrastructure management components of the simulator. While both approaches could apply the same policies and enact the same goals of a cloud provider, they should be implemented differently. In the first case, the PM controller should extend its possible actions from switching on/off PMs to migrating VMs as well. In the second case, the consolidator is dedicated to only decide on migration related actions. This is beneficial as the consolidator algorithm could collaborate with multiple PM controller strategies without the need for a complete rewrite of the consolidation approach. As this second approach is more generic, thus we present it in this paper in more detail. Note, the source of the presented approach is publicly available in the source repository of DISSECT-CF [2].

Figure 3 shows how the extension was implemented. The main addition of the simulator is the `Consolidator` class, which is to be extended by any new consolidation policies in the future. This abstract class handles the basic connection of the future consolidators to the `IaaSService` by monitoring the VM related activities on the cloud. It is also responsible for managing the frequency with which the consolidation policy is run (to be implemented by third parties in the `doConsolidation()` function). In general, it ensures that the custom consolidator policy is only invoked if there are any VMs in the cloud at any particular time. To do so, the consolidator monitors the PMs and observes how they are managed by PM controllers and utilised by the VM schedulers.

The simulator also offers a consolidation policy called `SimpleConsolidator`. This policy packs the VMs to the smallest amount of PMs as follows.

1. Creates an ordered list ($P := \{p_1, p_2, ...p_n\}$) of the PMs (e.g., p_1) currently running in the IaaS (where the number of running PMs in the IaaS is n). This list has the least used PMs in the front and the heaviest used ones at the tail: $u(p_1) \leq u(p_2) \leq ... \leq u(p_n)$. Where we denote the utilisation of a PM with the function : $u : P \rightarrow \mathbb{R}$. Note: the utilisation is determined solely on the resource allocations for the VMs hosted on each PM and it is not dependent on the instantaneous resource usage of any of the VMs in the cloud.
2. Picks the least used not yet evaluated PM (p_i). If there are no more PMs to evaluate, we terminate the algorithm.
3. Picks a VM (v_x) hosted by p_i. Where $v_x \in h(p_i)$ and the function $h : P \rightarrow 2^V$ defines the set of VMs which are hosted by a particular PM. This set is a subset of all VMs (V) in the IaaS service.
4. Picks the heaviest used (but not completely utilised) and not yet tested PM (p_k). Where we have the following limits for k: $i + 1 \leq k \leq n$.
5. Checks if the new PM has enough free resources to host the VM: $r_f(p_k, t) \geq r(v_x, t)$, where $r_f : P \times \mathbb{R} \rightarrow \mathbb{R}^3$ and $r : V \times \mathbb{R} \rightarrow \mathbb{R}^3$. The r_f function tells the amount of free resources available at the specified host at the specified time instance t. Also, the r function tells the amount of resources needed by the virtual machine at the specified time instance. The resource set is modelled by a triplet of real numbers: (i) number of CPU cores, (ii) per core processing power and finally (iii) memory.
   - If the check was successful, then the VM is requested to be migrated from the host p_i to p_k. Then continue on with a new VM pick.
   - If the check fails, we repeat with all untested PMs. If no more PMs are around to test, we pick another VM from the list of $h(p_i)$. If there are no more VMs to pick, we return to step 2.

Thus we can summarize the algorithm as packing the VMs to the heaviest loaded PMs with a first fit approach. This approach is efficient with the PM controller called `SchedulingDependentMachines` which switches off all unused machines once they become freed up (in this case once all their VMs migrate away).

5   Evaluation

During our implementation and evaluation, where applicable, we used publicly available information to populate our experiments. In the next subsection we introduce the applied workloads, then discuss the proposed algorithms and scenarios, and the achieved results.

5.1 Workloads

Though virtual machine management log-based traces would be the best candidates for analysing cloud characteristics, traces collected from other large-scale infrastructures like grids could also be appropriate. Generally two main sources are used for this purpose: the Grid Workloads Archive (GWA [3]) and the Parallel Workloads Archive [8]. For this study we used traces downloadable from GWA (namely: AuverGrid, DAS2, Grid5000, LCG, NorduGrid and SharcNet).

We used the JobDispatchingDemo from the DISSECT-CF examples project[1], to transform the jobs listed in the trace to VM requests and VM activities. This dispatcher asks the simulator to fire an event every time when the loaded trace prescribes. Also, the dispatcher maintains a list of VMs available to serve job related activities (e.g., input & output data transfers, cpu and memory resource use). Initially the VM list is empty. Thus the job arrival event is handled with two approaches: (i) if there is no unused VM in the VM list that has sufficient resources for the prescribed job, then the dispatcher creates a VM according to the resource requirements of the job; alternatively, (ii) if there is an unused VM with sufficient resources for the job, then the job is just assigned to the VM. In the first approach, the job's execution is delayed until its corresponding VM is spawned. In both cases, when the job finishes, it marks the VM as unused. This step allows other jobs to reuse VMs pooled in the VM list. Finally, the VMs are not kept for indefinite periods of time, instead they are kept in accordance with the billing period applied by the cloud provider. This ensures, that the VMs are held for as long as we paid for them but not any longer. So if there is no suitable job coming for a VM within its billing period, then the VM is terminated and it is also removed from the VM list.

5.2 Scenarios

In the following we list the pricing strategies available at the moment. They are applicable alone or in combination as required.

S1 - Fixed Pricing. It uses a constant price for every VM request. This pricing strategy does not consider any factors in its price:

$$M_{fix} = m_c, \tag{1}$$

where M_{fix} is the price (i.e money) returned, and m_c is the constant base price which is configurable for every simulation.

S2 - Resource Constraints Aware Pricing. It implements a linear relationship between the price of a VM and the amount of resources the VM needs. The higher the resource needs are, the more the user should pay.

$$M_{rcaw}(r_{cores}, r_{mem}, r_{proc}) = m_c \frac{r_{cpu} * r_{proc} * r_{mem}}{r_{cpu}^{MAX} * r_{proc}^{MAX} * r_{mem}^{MAX}}, \tag{2}$$

---

[1] https://github.com/kecskemeti/dissect-cf-examples.

where the triple $< r_{cores}, r_{mem}, r_{proc} >$ represents the resources requested by the customer for its VM. The triple $< r_{cpu}^{MAX} * r_{proc}^{MAX} * r_{mem}^{MAX} >$ represents the properties of the largest resource amount any PM has in the cloud provider. Note that all the resource values are represented as the provider sees them fit, for the purpose of the paper we assumed they are all positive real numbers (e.g., $r_{cores} \in \mathbb{R}^+$). Thus, this pricing model, charges m_c if the user requests the largest still serviceable resource set.

S3 - Quantized Pricing. It applies a pricing strategy similar to M_{rcaw}. But instead of scaling the price by a continuous function, we apply a transformation which transforms $(\mathfrak{T} : \mathbb{R}^3 \rightarrow \mathbb{R}^3)$ the original request from the user to some preset values. When defining a quantized pricing, one must define this transformation only, then we can apply the M_{rcaw} model to find out the actual price.

$$M_{quant}(r_{cores}, r_{mem}, r_{proc}) = \\ M_{rcaw}(\mathfrak{T}(r_{cores}, r_{mem}, r_{proc})) \tag{3}$$

This is the technique that is used by most of cloud providers nowadays. In those cases, the providers are often restricting the amount of resources one can request as well. An example transformation function could be:

$$\mathfrak{T}_{ex} = \begin{cases} \text{if } r_{mem} <= 2 \wedge r_{cores} <= 1 \\ r'_{mem} = 2, r'_{cores} = 1, r_{proc} = 1 \\ \text{if } 2 < r_{mem} <= 8 \wedge 1 < r_{cores} <= 2 \\ r'_{mem} = 8, r'_{cores} = 2, r_{proc} = 1 \\ \text{otherwise} \\ r'_{mem} = 32, r'_{cores} = 8, r_{proc} = 1 \end{cases} \tag{4}$$

The simulator implements a pricing model which can be configured to load a particular transformation function for a particular cloud provider. The limits for the transformation functions are stored in an XML file representing certain commercial provider cost models. Later in the measurements we apply the cost model presented in Sect. 3.

S4 - PM Utilization Aware Pricing. This strategy also offers a linear pricing approach. In contrast to the resource constraints aware pricing model, this time, we adjust the price based on the number of PMs in use at cloud provider:

$$M_{utaw} = m_c \frac{|P_U|}{|P|}, \tag{5}$$

where the P_U is the set of PMs that host any VMs: $P_U = \{\forall p_x \in P : u(p_x) \neq 0\}$. Thus the more exploited the cloud provider is, the more the user should pay.

S5 - Load Dependent Pricing. This works similarly to the PM utilization aware pricing. At the cost of additional monitoring requirements, it implements the same policy with a more fine grained utilization calculation:

$$M_{ld} = m_c \frac{\sum_{\forall p \in P} R(p)}{\sum_{\forall p \in P} R^{MAX}(p)}, \tag{6}$$

where $R(p)$ represents the average amount of resources utilised in the last hour from particular physical machine, while $R^{MAX}(p)$ defines the total amount of resources the PM could offer in the same hour. Thus, this pricing model considers how well the VMs actually use the resources and if the VMs are not highly used (even though they are hosted at the cloud at the moment), then the prices will be lowered (this will attract further users and enable the provider to use under provisioning for those VMs that are just paid for but not used at the moment).

S6 - Reliability Aware Pricing. It alters the price based on the ratio of successfully and unsuccessfully hosted VMs at the cloud. A VM is classified unsuccessfully hosted if it is terminated because of a physical machine failure, and not because of a user's request.

$$M_{rel} = m_c \frac{|V_f|}{|V|}, \tag{7}$$

where V_f is the set of VMs which failed due to a hardware issue at the provider side.

S7 - Profit Margin Focused Pricing. It tries to price resources so the profit margin index (i) of the cloud provider stays in a predefined range (i.e. $I_{min} < i < I_{max}$).

$$M_{margin}(t_0) = m_c \tag{8}$$

$$M_{margin}(t_x) =$$
$$M_{margin}(t_{x-1}) \cdot \begin{cases} 0.9, & \text{if } i(t_x) < I_{min} \\ 1.1, & \text{if } i(t_x) > I_{max} , \\ 1, & \text{otherwise} \end{cases} \tag{9}$$

where the function $i(t)$ determines the current (or at a given time, represented by t) profit margin index of a provider. This technique tries to adopt the prices to make sure the provider is profitable even in competitive environments.

5.3   Results

As mentioned before, we investigated how policies considering pricing information can affect consolidation processes. We used 6 different trace files from real world distributed systems to simulate load on the cloud datacentres we aim to consolidate. We also designed 7 different strategies to perform cost-aware consolidation. We have performed numerous experiments by executing the above listed strategies for all previously mentioned trace files. Tables 1 and 2 depict detailed measurement results fro energy consumption for the different workloads represented by different trace files. As we can see from the results, the consolidation algorithms succeeded to balance the load over the system, and in most cases energy and money can be saved by applying them. In the following we highlight the most interesting results.

Concerning experiments run on the *Grid5000* load, Figs. 4 and 5 depict the tradeoff of energy gains and runtime expansions for the given strategies

Table 1. Energy consumption results (kWh) for different trace files I.

	Nordugrid		Grid5000		LCG	
Strategy	Con.	Non-Con.	Con.	Non-Con.	Con.	Non-Con.
S1	453020	527342	295080	303445	7629	9431
S3	453020	527342	295080	303445	7629	9431
S5	453376	527901	295621	303037	7632	9401
S2 + S6	453020	527342	295080	303445	7629	9431
S3 + S4 + S7	453020	527342	295080	303445	7629	9431
S5 + selling	444932	520222	288947	296573	7524	9296

Table 2. Energy consumption results (kWh) for different trace files II.

	Sarchnet		DAS2		Auver	
Strategy	Con.	Non-Con.	Con.	Non-Con.	Con.	Non-Con.
S1	443357	490289	167445	169614	107801	113066
S3	443357	490289	167445	169614	107801	113066
S5	443887	487880	167482	169616	107803	113066
S2 + S6	443357	490289	167445	169614	107801	113066
S3 + S4 + S7	443357	490289	167445	169614	107801	113066
S5 + selling	440110	486964	162884	165033	105174	110438

("S2 + S6" means we applied both strategies, "S5 + selling" means we applied the S5 strategy and sold the shut down PMs to gain money). By migrating certain VMs to other physical machines to balance the load, we managed to reduce the power consumption, however the migration processes took some time which appears in the overall runtime. From the results we can see that the S6 strategy is the most efficient for reducing power consumption, and still it is the fastest solution.

Concerning experiments run on the *NorduGrid* load, Figs. 6 and 7 depict the tradeoff of energy gains and runtime expansions for the same strategies. From these results we can see that we managed to save more energy with all strategies compared to the previous Grid5000 cases.

Figures 8 and 9 depicts the results of our S3 strategy that enables to load and apply different provider pricing schemes. From these results we can see that the highest energy gains could be achieved with the Amazon pricing scheme for this load condition, while the worst result came from applying the Oracle pricing.

We also experienced that the load types represented by the traces highly affect the results. Figure 10 presents measurements performed under different load conditions with the combined S2 + S6 strategy. The depicted balance represents the possible gains of using consolidation in terms of cost (i.e. money) and energy.

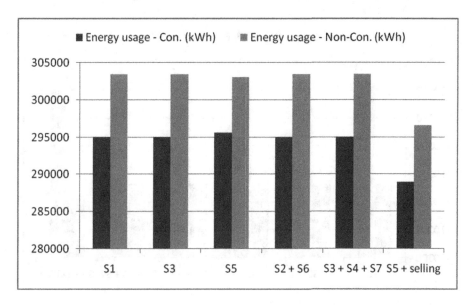

Fig. 4. Energy consumption of experiments with the Grid5000 trace based on [14].

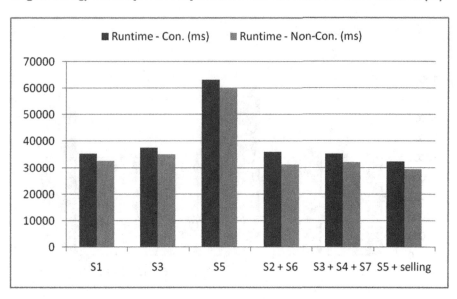

Fig. 5. Runtime of experiments with the Grid5000 trace based on [14].

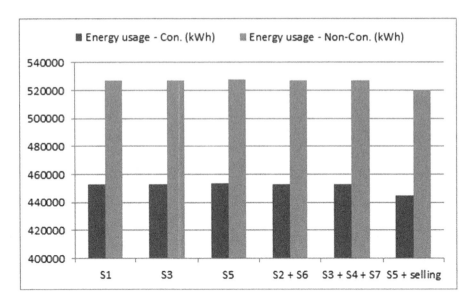

Fig. 6. Energy consumption of experiments with the NorduGrid trace.

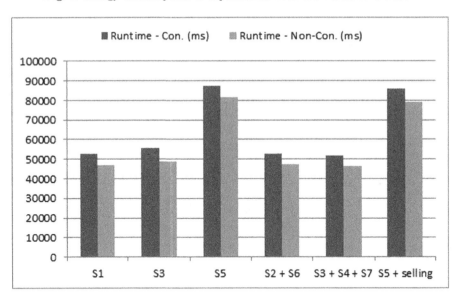

Fig. 7. Runtime of experiments with the NorduGrid trace.

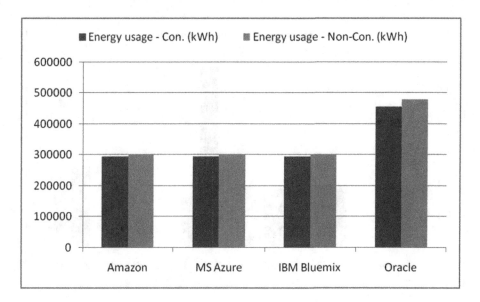

Fig. 8. Energy consumption of experiments with Grid5000 for different cloud provider pricing with the S3 strategy based on [14].

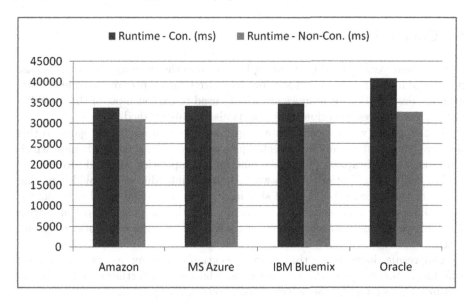

Fig. 9. Runtime of experiments with Grid5000 for different cloud provider pricing with the S3 strategy based on [14].

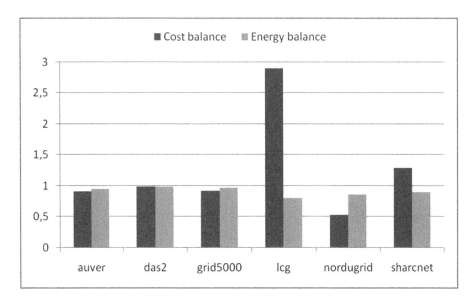

Fig. 10. Load and energy balance for different load conditions with the S2 + S6 strategy based on [14].

6   Conclusions

In the recent years Cloud Computing has become the primary choice for a vast number of infrastructure providers for virtualized data centre management. Datacenter consolidation techniques are widely used to exploit most of the available hardware resources, therefore this field is also highly studied.

In this paper we proposed a novel approach to earn additional gains in this field: we combined consolidation techniques with provider pricing schemes, which have also evolved rapidly due to the emerging competition of cloud providers.

For main contribution of this work, first we introduced a provider pricing model to the DISSECT-CF cloud simulator, then developed novel consolidator algorithms using this model. We also evaluated the proposed algorithms with 7 strategies for cost-aware data centre consolidation using real world workload traces.

Our results have shown that proper selection of the applied pricing method can affect the quality of data centre consolidation, and further cost and power consumption saving can be achieved using our new approach.

Software Availability

This paper described the behaviour and features of DISSECT-CF version 0.9.8. Its source code is open and available (under the licensing terms of the GNU LGPL 3) at the following website:

https://github.com/kecskemeti/dissect-cf

References

1. Amazon pricing. https://aws.amazon.com/ec2/pricing/on-demand/
2. DISSECT-CF. https://github.com/kecskemeti/dissect-cf. Accessed Jan 2018
3. Grid Workloads Archive. http://gwa.ewi.tudelft.nl/. Accessed Sept 2018
4. IBM Bluemix pricing sheet. https://www.ibm.com/cloud-computing/bluemix. Accessed Jan 2018
5. MS Azure price calculator. https://azure.microsoft.com/en-gb/pricing/calculator/. Accessed Jan 2018
6. Oracle pricing. https://cloud.oracle.com/en_US/opc/compute/compute/pricing. Accessed Jan 2018
7. Orcale Metered Services pricing calculator. https://shop.oracle.com/cloudstore/index.html?product=compute. Accessed Jan 2018
8. Parallel Workloads Archive. http://www.cs.huji.ac.il/labs/parallel/workload/. Accessed Sept 2018
9. Abdullah, M., Lu, K., Wieder, P., Yahyapour, R.: A heuristic-based approach for dynamic VMS consolidation in cloud data centers. Arab. J. Sci. Eng. **42**(8), 3535–3549 (2017). https://doi.org/10.1007/s13369-017-2580-5
10. Ahmad, R.W., Gani, A., Hamid, S.H.A., Shiraz, M., Yousafzai, A., Xia, F.: A survey on virtual machine migration and server consolidation frameworks for cloud data centers. J. Netw. Comput. Appl. **52**(Suppl. C), 11–25 (2015). https://doi.org/10.1016/j.jnca.2015.02.002. http://www.sciencedirect.com/science/article/pii/S1084804515000284
11. Filho, M.C.S., Monteiro, C.C., Inacio, P.R., Freire, M.M.: Approaches for optimizing virtual machine placement and migration in cloud environments: a survey. J. Parallel Distrib. Comput. **111**(Suppl. C), 222–250 (2018). https://doi.org/10.1016/j.jpdc.2017.08.010. http://www.sciencedirect.com/science/article/pii/S074373151730240X
12. Kecskemeti, G., Kertesz, A., Nemeth, Z.: Cloud workload prediction by means of simulations. In: ACM International Conference on Computing Frontiers 2017, CF 2017, pp. 279–282 (2017). https://doi.org/10.1145/3075564.3075589
13. Kecskemeti, G.: DISSECT-CF: a simulator to foster energy-aware scheduling in infrastructure clouds. Simul. Model. Pract. Theory **58P2**, 188–218 (2015). https://doi.org/10.1016/j.simpat.2015.05.009
14. Kecskemeti, G., Markus, A., Kertesz, A.: Cost-efficient datacentre consolidation for cloud federations. In: Proceedings of the 8th International Conference on Cloud Computing and Services Science, CLOSER 2018, Funchal, Madeira, Portugal, 19–21 March 2018, pp. 213–220 (2018). https://doi.org/10.5220/0006775302130220
15. Kertesz, A., Dombi, J.D., Benyi, A.: A pliant-based virtual machine scheduling solution to improve the energy efficiency of IaaS clouds. J. Grid Comput. **14**(1), 41–53 (2016). https://doi.org/10.1007/s10723-015-9336-9
16. Maio, V.D., Kecskemeti, G., Prodan, R.: An improved model for live migration in data centre simulators. In: 2016 IEEE/ACM 9th International Conference on Utility and Cloud Computing (UCC), pp. 108–117, December 2016
17. Markus, A., Kertesz, A., Kecskemeti, G.: Cost-aware IoT extension of DISSECT-CF. Future Internet **9**(3) (2017). https://doi.org/10.3390/fi9030047. http://www.mdpi.com/1999-5903/9/3/47

Optimising QoS-Assurance, Resource Usage and Cost of Fog Application Deployments

Antonio Brogi[1], Stefano Forti[1(✉)], and Ahmad Ibrahim[2]

[1] Department of Computer Science, University of Pisa, Pisa, Italy
{brogi,stefano.forti}@di.unipi.it
[2] School of Computer Science, University of Birmingham, Birmingham, UK
a.ibrahim@bham.ac.uk

Abstract. Identifying the best application deployment to distribute application components in Fog infrastructures – spanning the IoT-to-Cloud continuum – is a challenging task for application deployers. Indeed, it requires fulfilling all application requirements, whilst determining a trade-off among different objectives (i.e., QoS assurance, Fog resource consumption and cost), resulting in a complex and time-consuming decision-making process to be tuned manually. In this paper, we present a simple multi-objective optimisation scheme that permits selecting the best placement of application components, balancing the trade-off among QoS-assurance, Fog resource consumption and monthly deployment costs. We exploit our prototype, extended with parallel Monte Carlo simulations, and a motivating example to show how IT experts can benefit from our approach.

Keywords: Fog computing · Application deployment ·
Multi-objective optimisation · Cost models · Monte Carlo method

1 Introduction

Fog computing [5] aims at moving computation closer to the source of IoT data by relying on a multitude of heterogeneous devices (e.g., personal devices, gateways, micro-data centres, embedded servers) spanning the continuum from the Cloud to the IoT[1]. Meanwhile, modern applications are made from a set of independently deployable components (or services, or micro-services) that interact together and must meet some requirements. The interactions (component-component or component-Things) may have firm Quality of Service (QoS) requirements – latency, bandwidth – to be fulfilled for the application to work as expected [16].

---

[1] Hereinafter, the word *Things* is used to refer to IoT devices, both sensors and actuators.

© Springer Nature Switzerland AG 2019
V. M. Muñoz et al. (Eds.): CLOSER 2018, CCIS 1073, pp. 168–189, 2019.
https://doi.org/10.1007/978-3-030-29193-8_9

Deployment of Fog applications requires placing their components (e.g., control loops, operational support, business intelligence) over the available infrastructure that consists of Cloud, Fog and IoT devices (spread over a possibly large geographical area, and inter-connected via heterogeneous communication technologies), based upon specific application and user requirements. Determining eligible deployments of multi-component applications to given Fog infrastructure is proved to be NP-hard [7].

Naturally, financial considerations play a role too in deployment selection as industry and businesses usually aim at maximising their revenues, whilst minimising deployment operational costs [39]. If Cloud offerings are limited to a few large providers, Fog computing envisions many other small and medium players (e.g., single Fog node or Things owners) that will offer virtual instances or IoT capabilities at different pricing schemes, making it more challenging to identify cost-effective deployments among the possible ones.

Overall, there is a need for tools that can actually support application deployment to the Fog and that should feature *(i) QoS-awareness* to achieve latency reduction, bandwidth savings and to enforce business policies, *(ii) context-awareness* to suitably exploit local and remote resources, *(iii) cost-awareness* to enact cost-effective deployments.

To support all these objectives, we developed a prototype (FogTorchΠ) [7–9] that given a Fog infrastructure (1) determines application deployments that meet all (hardware, software IoT and QoS) requirements, (2) estimates their *QoS-assurance* and *Fog resource consumption* by simulating latency and bandwidth variations of communication links as per given probability distributions, and (3) estimates the monthly cost of application deployments over the input infrastructure. It is worth noting that, even after a set of eligible deployments has been identified, the application deployers still have to identify a best candidate deployment. Trading-off among different metrics like QoS assurance, Fog resource consumption and cost can make this complex decision making process time-consuming and difficult to be tuned manually (since some constraints are orthogonal to each other). Indeed, suppose application deployers aim at minimising deployment cost and Fog resource consumption for a given application deployment. Such preferences may lead their choice to a candidate deployment that minimises the two considered metrics, missing to actually guarantee a good level of compliance to QoS-requirements (i.e., QoS-assurance). With the support of trade-off analysis tools, application deployers might discover some other eligible deployments that can provide a more balanced compromise between all considered metrics.

In this paper, we extend the work of [9] – in which we introduced a cost model to estimate monthly deployment cost of Fog applications – so to include a simple multi-objective optimisation scheme that permits selecting the best placement of application components, balancing the trade-off among QoS-assurance, Fog resource consumption and monthly costs. With respect to [9] we also extended FogTorchΠ to perform parallel Monte Carlo simulations when estimating deployment QoS-assurance, thus taming the complexity of the described algorithms.

We show, over a motivating example, how these extensions of our methodology, particularly the multi-objective optimisation, can further help IT experts (or new businesses coming onto the Fog market) in deciding how to distribute application components to Fog infrastructures in a QoS-, context- and cost-aware manner.

The rest of this paper is organised as follows. After introducing a motivating example of a smart building application (Sect. 2), we briefly describe FogTorchΠ (Sect. 3) and present the cost model extension (Sect. 4). Then, we discuss multi-objective optimisation (Sect. 5), present the results obtained by applying the extended version of FogTorchΠ methodology to the motivating example (Sect. 6), and discuss some related work (Sect. 7). Finally, we draw some concluding remarks (Sect. 8).

2   Motivating Example

A simple Fog application (Fig. 1) manages fire alarm, heating and A/C systems, interior lighting, and security cameras of a smart building and is made from three microservices:

- IoTController, directly controlling the connected cyber-physical systems,
- DataStorage, storing all sensed data for future use and employing machine learning techniques to update sense-act rules at the IoTController so to optimise heating and lighting management based on previous experience and/or on people behaviour, and
- Dashboard, aggregating and visualising collected sensor data and videos, as well as providing an interface to users interacting with the application.

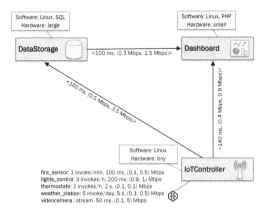

Fig. 1. Fog application of the motivating example as in [9].

Each microservice is an independently deployable component of the application [37] and has some hardware and software requirements to be fulfilled in order to function properly (the grey box associated with each component). Hardware requirements are expressed in terms of the virtual machine (VM) types[2] that will host the component once deployed. Table 1 lists all VM types used in this example and the corresponding hardware specification.

Table 1. Hardware specification for different VM types [9].

VM type	vCPUSs	RAM (GB)	HDD (GB)
Tiny	1	1	10
Small	1	2	20
Medium	2	4	40
Large	4	8	80
Xlarge	8	16	160

Furthermore, end-to-end communication links supporting component-component interactions need to feature suitable latency and bandwidth (e.g., the latency between IoTController and DataStorage should be less than 160 ms and the free bandwidth should be at least 0.5 Mbps download and 3.5 Mbps upload[3]). Finally, interactions between the IoTController and Things are subject to similar constraints, and also specify the expected sampling rate for the component to query Things at runtime.

System integrators in charge of deploying the smart building application for one of their customers have two Cloud data centres, three Fog nodes and nine Things (Fig. 2) available in the target infrastructure. The deployed application will have to utilise the Things connected to Fog 1 and the weather_station_3 at Fog 3. For the system integrators, deploying components to Fog 2 involves no additional cost since their customers own that node, and can use it free of charge.

All Fog and Cloud nodes are associated with their pricing schemes. Those scheme consider the possibility of either buying a ready-made instance of a certain VM type (e.g., a *small* instance at Cloud 2 costs €25 per month) as well as the possibility of assembling on-demand instances (by selecting the required number of cores and the needed amount of memory and storage to support a given component).

Fog nodes offer software capabilities with limited hardware resources (i.e., RAM, HDD, CPUs), as indicated in Fig. 2. Cloud nodes also offer software capabilities and we assume that they offer potentially unbounded hardware resources (under the assumption that one can always purchase extra or larger instances on-demand).

QoS profiles of the available communication links[4] are listed in Table 2. They are based on real data[5] and represented as probability distributions to account

---

[2] Adapted from OpenStack Mitaka flavours: https://docs.openstack.org/.

[3] Arrows on the links in Fig. 1 indicate the upload direction.

[4] Arrows on the links in Fig. 2 indicate the upload direction.

[5] Satellite: https://www.eolo.it/, 3G/4G: https://www.agcom.it, VDSL: http://www.vodafone.it.

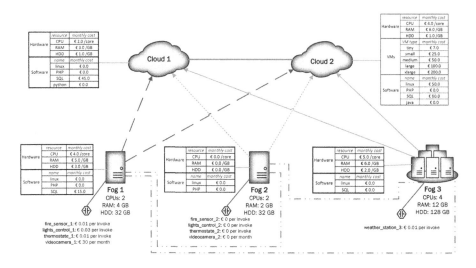

Fig. 2. Fog infrastructure of the motivating example as in [9]. (Color figure online)

for QoS variations. Green color links at Fog 2 initially feature a 3G Internet access. We assume Fog and Cloud nodes are able to access directly connected Things as well as Things (or the data they produce) at neighbouring nodes via a specific middleware layer (through the associated communication links) which is in accordance with the current technical proposals (e.g., [5] and [40]).

Table 2. QoS profiles of communication links as in [9].

Dash Type	Profile	Latency	Download	Upload
· — —	Satellite 14M	40 ms	98%: 10.5 Mbps 2%: 0 Mbps	98%: 4.5 Mbps 2%: 0 Mbps
··············	3G	54 ms	99.6%: 9.61 Mbps 0.4%: 0 Mbps	99.6%: 2.89 Mbps 0.4%: 0 Mbps
	4G	53 ms	99.3%: 22.67 Mbps 0.7%: 0 Mbps	99.4%: 16.97 Mbps 0.6%: 0 Mbps
——	VDSL	60 ms	60 Mbps	6 Mbps
▬▬▬	Fibre	5 ms	1000 Mbps	1000 Mbps
— · · —	WLAN	15 ms	90%: 32 Mbps 10%: 16 Mbps	90%: 32 Mbps 10%: 16 Mbps

The system integrators, planning to sell the deployed solution for €1,500 a month, set the limit of the monthly deployment cost at €850. On the other hand, the customer is willing to pay them only if the application can comply to the specified QoS requirements at least 98% of the time. Then, interesting questions for the system integrators before the first deployment of the application are, for instance:

Q1(a) — *Is there any eligible deployment of the application reaching the needed Things at Fog 1 and Fog 3, and meeting the financial (at most €850 per month) and QoS-assurance (at least 98% of the time) constraints mentioned above?*

Q1(b) — *Which eligible deployment represent the most balanced trade-off optimising QoS-assurance, Fog resource consumption and monthly deployment cost of the smart building application?*

Suppose that with an extra monthly investment of €20, system integrators can exploit a 4G connection at Fog 2. Then:

Q2 — *Does the upgrade from 3G to 4G at Fog 2 make it possible to determine a deployment with better trade-off on QoS-assurance, Fog resource consumption and monthly deployment cost?*

In Sect. 6, we will show how the FogTorchΠ – suitably extended with the cost model described in Sect. 4 – can be exploited, along with multi-objective optimisation techniques, to obtain answers to all the above questions.

3   Overview of **FogTorchΠ**

FogTorchΠ [8] is an open-source Java prototype[6] that permits describing Fog infrastructures and applications so to determine QoS-, context-, and cost-aware application deployments. Before detailing the cost-aware extension to FogTorchΠ, we summarise the overall functioning of our prototype. FogTorchΠ takes as input:

1. a *Fog infrastructure I*, with the specification of the Fog and Cloud nodes available for deployment (each with its hardware, software and IoT capabilities), the probability distributions of the network QoS (viz., latency, bandwidth) featured by end-to-end communication links interconnecting such nodes[7], and the cost for purchasing sensed data and Cloud/Fog virtual instances,
2. a *multi-component application A*, specifying all hardware (i.e., CPU, RAM, storage), software (i.e., OS, libraries, frameworks) and IoT requirements (i.e., which type of Things to exploit) of each component, and the minimum QoS (i.e., latency and bandwidth) needed to suitably support component-component and component-Thing interactions at runtime,
3. a *Things binding* ϑ, mapping each IoT requirement of an application component to an actual Thing in *I*, and
4. a *deployment policy* $\delta(\gamma)$, white-listing the nodes where component γ of *A* can be deployed[8] in accordance to security or business-related considerations.

---

[6] Available at https://github.com/di-unipi-socc/FogTorchPI/tree/multithreaded/.

[7] Actual implementations in Fog landscapes can rely on monitoring tools (e.g., [6], [22]) to update the information available on *I*.

[8] When δ is not specified for a component γ of *A*, γ can be deployed to any compatible node in *I*.

```
 1: procedure MONTECARLO(A, I, ϑ, δ, n)
 2:     D ← ∅                                          ▷ dictionary of ⟨Δ, counter⟩
 3:     parallel for n times do
 4:         I_s ← SAMPLELINKSQOS(I)
 5:         E ← FINDDEPLOYMENTS(A, I_s, ϑ, δ)
 6:         D ← UNIONUPDATE(D, E)
 7:     end parallel for
 8:     for Δ ∈ keys(D) do
 9:         D[Δ] ← D[Δ]/n
10:     end for
11:     return D
12: end procedure
```

Fig. 3. Pseudocode of the parallel version of the Monte Carlo simulation in FogTorchΠ [9].

Based on such input, FogTorchΠ determines all eligible deployments of the components of A to Cloud or Fog nodes in I. An *eligible deployment* Δ maps each component γ of A to a Cloud or Fog node n of I so that (1) $n \in \delta(\gamma)$ and it meets the hardware and software requirements of γ, (2) hardware resources are enough to deploy *all* components of A simultaneously mapped to n, (3) Things exploited by γ (and specified in ϑ) are reachable from n, and (4) component-component and component-Thing interactions mapped to the same end-to-end communication link do not exceed the available bandwidth and meet their latency requirements.

FogTorchΠ relies on the Monte Carlo method [21] to estimate the *QoS-assurance* of output deployments, by aggregating the eligible deployments obtained when varying the QoS of communication links according to the associated probability distributions for latency and bandwidth. Figure 3 lists the pseudocode of FogTorchΠ functioning. First, an empty dictionary D is created (line 2) to contain key-value pairs $\langle \Delta, \texttt{counter} \rangle$, where the key ($\Delta$) represents an eligible deployment and the value (`counter`) keeps track of how many times Δ will be generated during the Monte Carlo simulation. Then, at the beginning of each run of the simulation, a new state I_s of the infrastructure is sampled based on the probability distributions of the QoS of the communication links in I (line 4).

The function FINDDEPLOYMENTS(A, I_s, ϑ, δ) (line 5) employs an exhaustive (backtracking) search [7] to determine the set E of eligible deployments Δ of A to I_s, i.e. deployments of A that meet all hardware, software, IoT, and QoS requirements in that particular state of the infrastructure. In order to tame the worst-case exponential complexity of such search step, the current version of FogTorchΠ features a multi-thread implementation of the *for* loop of lines 3–7, which assigns n/w runs to each of the w threads available on the system and executes them in parallel afterwards [10].

The objective of the Monte Carlo step is to look for eligible deployments in different underlying network conditions. At the end of each run, the set E of eligible deployments of A to I_s is used to update D. The function UNIONUPDATE(D,

E) (line 6) updates D by adding deployments $\langle \Delta, 1 \rangle$ discovered during the last run ($\Delta \in E \setminus keys(D)$) and by incrementing the **counter** of those deployments that had already been found in a previous run ($\Delta \in E \cap keys(D)$).

After the simulation has run for a significantly large number of times ($n \geq 100,000$), the QoS-assurance of each deployment $\Delta \in keys(D)$ is obtained by dividing the **counter** associated to Δ by n (lines 8–10). Thus, the QoS-assurance is the percentage of runs a certain deployment Δ was output by FIND-DEPLOYMENTS($A, I_s, \vartheta, \delta$). Such percentage offers an estimate on how likely Δ is to satisfy all QoS constraints of A, against variations in the communication links as per their historical behaviour. Finally, dictionary D is output (line 11).

Each output deployment Δ also contains information about its Fog resource consumption, which is computed during the search as the aggregate percentage averaging RAM and HDD consumed over the set F of all Fog nodes[9]:

$$\frac{1}{2}\left(\frac{\sum_{\gamma \in A} RAM(\gamma)}{\sum_{f \in F} RAM(f)} + \frac{\sum_{\gamma \in A} HDD(\gamma)}{\sum_{f \in F} HDD(f)}\right)$$

The next section details the cost model exploited by FogTorchII, which permits predicting the monthly deployment cost of output deployments. As for the resource consumption, FINDDEPLOYMENTS($A, I_s, \vartheta, \delta$) computes and associates each eligible deployment Δ with an estimate of its monthly cost[10], which we detail in the next section.

4   Cost Model

Our cost model [9] extends to Fog computing previous efforts in Cloud VM cost modelling [20], and includes software costs, and costs typical of the IoT [39]. With respect to related work, which – to the best of our knowledge – only exploited linear cost models based on unit cost for different types of hardware resource, we also consider the possibility of purchasing bundle offers at the IoT, the Cloud and the Fog layer (i.e., for data, hardware and software).

A hardware offering H, available at any Cloud or Fog node n, can be either a *default VM* (Table 1) featuring a fixed monthly price or an *on-demand VM*, assembled by selecting any amount of processors (CPU), memory (RAM) and storage (HDD). By assuming that $R = \{CPU, RAM, HDD\}$ is the set of resources considered when assembling on-demand instances, our cost model estimates the monthly cost for a hardware offering H at node n as

$$p(H, n) = \begin{cases} c(H, n) & \text{if } H \text{ is a default VM} \\ \sum_{\rho \in R} [H.\rho \times c(\rho, n)] & \text{if } H \text{ is an on-demand VM} \end{cases}$$

---

[9] FogTorchII permits to compute Fog resource consumption also on a specified subset of Fog nodes $\overline{F} \subset F$.

[10] Cost computation is performed *on-the-fly*. This is done during the search step, considering the possibility to rely on the cost prediction as a heuristic to lead backtracking towards best candidate deployments.

where $c(H, n)$ is the monthly cost of a default VM H at Fog or Cloud node n, whilst $H.\rho$ indicates the amount of resource $\rho \in R$ used by[11] the on-demand VM represented by H, and $c(\rho, n)$ is the unit monthly cost at n for resource ρ.

Analogously, a software offering S at any Cloud or Fog node n can be either a ready-made *bundle* or an *on-demand* subset of the software capabilities offered by n (each purchasable as a separate item). The monthly cost for S at node n is estimated as

$$p(S, n) = \begin{cases} c(S, n) & \text{if } S \text{ is a bundle} \\ \sum_{s \in S} c(s, n) & \text{if } S \text{ is on-demand} \end{cases}$$

where $c(S, n)$ is the price for the software bundle S at node n, and $c(s, n)$ is the monthly cost of a single software s at n.

Finally, in Sensing-as-a-Service [41] scenarios, a Thing offering T exploiting an actual Thing t can be made available at a monthly *subscription* fee (i.e., covering a certain amount of data exchanges) or through a *pay-per-invocation* mechanism (i.e., per exchanged message) [34]. Hence, the cost for offering T at Thing t can be estimated as

$$p(\text{T}, t) = \begin{cases} c(\text{T}, t) & \text{if T is subscription based} \\ \text{T}.k \times c(t) & \text{if T is pay-per-invocation} \end{cases}$$

where $c(\text{T}, t)$ is the monthly subscription fee for T at t, while $\text{T}.k$ is the number of monthly invocations expected over t and $c(t)$ is the cost per invocation at t (including Thing exploitation and/or data transfer costs).

In what follows, we assume that Δ is an eligible deployment for an application A to an infrastructure I, as defined in Sect. 3. In addition, let $\gamma \in A$ be a component of the considered application A, and let $\gamma.\overline{\mathcal{H}}$, $\gamma.\overline{\Sigma}$ and $\gamma.\overline{\Theta}$ be its hardware, software and Things requirements, respectively. By summing up all the presented pricing schemes, the monthly cost for a given deployment Δ can be first approximated as:

$$cost(\Delta, \vartheta, A) = \sum_{\gamma \in A} \left[p(\gamma.\overline{\mathcal{H}}, \Delta(\gamma)) + p(\gamma.\overline{\Sigma}, \Delta(\gamma)) + \sum_{r \in \gamma.\overline{\Theta}} p(r, \vartheta(r)) \right]$$

This first estimate of the monthly deployment cost, however, does not feature a way to match application (hardware, software and IoT) requirements to "best" (Cloud, Fog and IoT) offerings at chosen nodes or Things. Particularly, it may lead the choice always to on-demand and pay-per-invocation offerings when the application requirements do not match exactly default or ready-made offerings, or when a Cloud provider does not offer a particular VM type (e.g., starting its offerings from *medium*). This may incur in overestimating monthly deployment costs.

---

[11] Bounded by the maximum amount purchasable from any chosen Cloud or Fog provider.

As an example, consider the infrastructure of Fig. 2 and this hardware requirements $r = \{\texttt{CPU} : 1, \texttt{RAM} : \texttt{1GB}, \texttt{HDD} : \texttt{20GB}\}$ of a component to be deployed to Cloud 2. Since no exact matching between the requirement and an offering at Cloud 2 exists, this first version the current cost model selects an on-demand instance, and estimates a cost of €30[12]. However, Cloud 2 also provides a *small* instance that can accommodate the component requirements at a (lower) cost of €25.

Indeed, larger VM types always satisfy smaller hardware requirements, bundled software offerings may satisfy multiple software requirements at a lower price, and subscription-based Thing offerings can be more or less convenient depending on the number of invocations on a given Thing. Therefore, some mechanism must be adopted to choose the "best" offering that can fulfil all software, hardware and Thing requirements of an application component. In what follows, we propose a small refinement to our cost model, necessary to capture this important aspect.

A *requirement-to-offering matching policy* $p_m(r, n)$ matches hardware or software requirements r of a component ($r \in \{\gamma.\overline{\mathcal{H}}, \gamma.\overline{\Sigma}\}$) to the estimated monthly cost of the offering that will support them at Cloud or Fog node n, and a Thing requirement $r \in \gamma.\overline{\Theta}$ to the estimated monthly cost of the offering that will support r at Thing t.

Overall, this refinement to our cost model permits estimating the monthly cost of Δ including a cost-aware matching between application requirements and infrastructure offerings (for hardware, software and IoT), that are chosen as per p_m. Hence, we get:

$$cost(\Delta, \vartheta, A) = \sum_{\gamma \in A} \left[p_m(\gamma.\overline{\mathcal{H}}, \Delta(\gamma)) + p_m(\gamma.\overline{\Sigma}, \Delta(\gamma)) + \sum_{r \in \gamma.\overline{\Theta}} p_m(r, \vartheta(r)) \right]$$

The cost-aware version of FogTorchΠ, including the described cost model, exploits a *best-fit lowest-cost* policy for choosing hardware, software and Thing offerings. Indeed, it selects the cheapest between the first default VM (from *tiny* to *xlarge*) that can support $\gamma.\overline{\mathcal{H}}$ at node n and the on-demand offering built as per $\gamma.\overline{\mathcal{H}}$. Similarly, software requirements in $\gamma.\overline{\Sigma}$ are matched with the cheapest compatible version available at n, and Thing per invocation offer is compared to monthly subscription so to select the cheapest[13] offering possible. The requirement-to-offering matching policy used in FogTorchΠ can be defined formally as:

$$p_m(\overline{\mathcal{H}}, n) = \min\{p(H, n) \mid H \in \{\text{default VMs, on-demand VM}\} \wedge H \models \overline{\mathcal{H}}\}$$

$$p_m(\overline{\Sigma}, n) = \min\{p(S, n) \mid S \in \{\text{on-demand, bundle}\} \wedge S \models \overline{\Sigma}\}$$

---

[12] €30 = 1 CPU × €4/core + 1 GB RAM × €6/GB + 20 GB HDD × €1/GB.

[13] Other policies are also possible such as, for instance, selecting the largest offering that can accommodate a component, or always increasing the component's requirements by some percentage (e.g., 10%) before selecting the matching.

$$p_m(r,t) = \min\{p(T,t) \mid T \in \{\text{subscription, pay-per-invocation}\} \wedge T \models r\}$$

where $O \models R$ reads as offering O *satisfies requirements R*.

It is worth noting that the proposed cost model is general enough to include both IaaS and PaaS Cloud offerings since it separates the cost of purchasing virtual instances from the cost of purchasing software. Furthermore, even if we referred to VMs as the only deployment unit for application components, a straightforward extension to the model can account for other types of virtual instances (e.g., containers).

5   Multi-objective Optimisation

Exploiting the cost model of Sect. 4, it is naturally possible to minimise the obtained estimate for the monthly deployment cost and choose a candidate application deployment accordingly. However, decision makers in Fog application deployment processes (like the system integrators in Sect. 2), have often to determine a best placement of application components as a trade-off among various – sometimes orthogonal – requirements and metrics.

As described in Sects. 3 and 4, FogTorchΠ methodology enables to predict QoS-assurance, Fog resource consumption and monthly cost of eligible application deployments, i.e. those meeting application hardware, software and QoS constraints. Each of the mentioned metrics represents an objective that application deployers aim at optimising along with the others. Indeed, we are facing a multi-objective optimisation (MOO) problem [18].

MOOs are generally defined as

$$\min_\Delta F(\Delta) = [f_1(\Delta), f_2(\Delta), \cdots, f_m(\Delta)]$$

subject to : $\Delta \in \overline{D}$

where $f_i(\cdot)$ denote a set objective functions and $\overline{D}$ denote a feasible design space in which $F(\cdot)$ should be optimised. Usually, as it can be in our Fog application deployment scenarios, no solution Δ exists that minimises all set objectives at the same time. In this situations, Pareto optimal solutions are looked for. A solution is Pareto optimal when it is not possible to improve (at least) one objective function without making another worst. The set of all Pareto optimal solutions forms a so-called Pareto frontier.

A common aggregation technique to solve MOOs and to determine the best trade-off among all set objectives is the *linear weighted sum* method [35]. Such strategy allows to convert MOOs into single objective problems by linearly combining their (normalised) objective functions. As we will show over our motivating example in the next section, this permits to determine a best solution deployment, also accounting for the user preferences specified for some of the objectives (e.g., the minimum QoS-assurance of 98% and the maximum monthly cost of €850 required by system administrators) which specify the feasible design space $\overline{D}$. Last but not least, under the assumptions that functions weights are positive, the found solution is Pareto optimal.

Therefore, in this work, similarly to [26], given a deployment Δ, we will try to optimise the objective function

$$r(\Delta) = \sum_{f_i \in F} \omega_i \cdot \widehat{f_i(\Delta)}$$

where F is the set of m metrics to be optimised, ω_i is the weight[14] assigned to each metrics (so that $\sum_{i=1}^{m} \omega_i = 1$) and $\widehat{f_i(\Delta)}$ is the normalised value of the objective function $f_i(\cdot)$ for deployment Δ, which – given the set D of candidate deployments – is computed as:

- $\widehat{f_i(\Delta)} = \frac{f_i(\Delta) - \min_{d \in D}\{f_i(d)\}}{\max_{d \in \overline{D}}\{f_i(d)\} - \min_{d \in D}\{f_i(d)\}}$ when the $f_i(\Delta)$ is to be maximised, and
skip
- $\widehat{f_i(\Delta)} = \frac{\max_{d \in D}\{f_i(d)\} - f_i(\Delta)}{\max_{d \in D}\{f_i(d)\} - \min_{d \in D}\{f_i(d)\}}$ when $f_i(\Delta)$ is to be minimised.

Since, in this case, we assumed that the higher the value of $r(\Delta)$ the better is deployment Δ, we will choose $\overline{\Delta}$ such that $r(\overline{\Delta}) = \max_{\Delta \in D}\{r(\Delta)\}$.

Considering our problem, deployers will most probably aim at maximising QoS-assurance, whilst minimising monthly deployment costs (in which we include the cost for the 4G connection at Fog 2 when needed). However, different system integrators may want to either maximise or minimise the Fog resource consumption of their deployment, i.e. they may look for *Fog-ward* or for *Cloud-ward* deployments. Hence, in the next section, we will consider both situations and compare the results obtained when trying to maximise Fog resource usage (i.e., Fog-ward deployments) to those obtained when trying to minimise it (i.e., Cloud-ward deployments).

6   Motivating Example (Continued)

In this section, we discuss the results of running the cost-aware version of FogTorchΠ over the smart building example of Sect. 2. We rely on the linear weighted sum method presented in Sect. 5 to answer all questions coming from the system integrators.

FogTorchΠ outputs the eligible deployments (as per Sect. 3) along with their predicted QoS-assurance, Fog resource consumption and monthly deployment cost (as per Sect. 4). Table 3 lists all eligible deployments output[15] by FogTorchΠ, entries indicated with a * are only output when 4G is available at Fog 2.

Figure 4 shows a 3D-plot of the same output deployments along the predicted metrics (i.e., the objective functions) that FogTorchΠ can estimate for them.

---

[14] For the sake of simplicity, we assume here $\omega_i = \frac{1}{|F|} = \frac{1}{m}$, which can be tuned differently depending on the needs of the application operator.

[15] Results and Python code to generate 3D plots as in Figs. 4, 5 and 6 are available at: https://github.com/di-unipi-socc/FogTorchPI/tree/costmodel/results/SMARTBUILDING18/.

Table 3. Eligible deployments generated by FogTorchΠ for **Q1** and **Q2** as in [9].

Dep. ID	IoTController	DataStorage	Dashboard
Δ1	Fog 2	Fog 3	Cloud 2
Δ2	Fog 2	Fog 3	Cloud 1
Δ3	Fog 3	Fog 3	Cloud 1
Δ4	Fog 2	Fog 3	Fog 1
Δ5	Fog 1	Fog 3	Cloud 1
Δ6	Fog 3	Fog 3	Cloud 2
Δ7	Fog 3	Fog 3	Fog 2
Δ8	Fog 3	Fog 3	Fog 1
Δ9	Fog 1	Fog 3	Cloud 2
Δ10	Fog 1	Fog 3	Fog 2
Δ11	Fog 1	Fog 3	Fog 1
Δ12*	Fog 2	Cloud 2	Fog 1
Δ13*	Fog 2	Cloud 2	Cloud 1
Δ14*	Fog 2	Cloud 2	Cloud 2
Δ15*	Fog 2	Cloud 1	Cloud 2
Δ16*	Fog 2	Cloud 1	Cloud 1
Δ17*	Fog 2	Cloud 1	Fog 1

Before continuing, we recall the questions posed by the system integrators in Sect. 2:

Q1(a) — *Is there any eligible deployment of the application reaching the needed Things at **Fog 1** and **Fog 3**, and meeting the financial (at most €850 per month) and QoS-assurance (at least 98% of the time) constraints mentioned above?*
Q1(b) — *Which eligible deployment represent the most balanced trade-off optimising QoS-assurance, Fog resource consumption and monthly deployment cost of the smart building application?*
Q2 — *Does the upgrade from 3G to 4G at **Fog 2** make it possible to determine a deployment with better trade-off on QoS-assurance, Fog resource consumption and monthly deployment cost?*

Figure 5 shows the feasible space for questions **Q1(a)** and **Q1(b)**, as defined by the QoS-assurance and budget constraints declared by the system integrators. Only Δ2, Δ3, Δ4, Δ7 and Δ10 meet those constraints. Analogously, Fig. 6 shows the feasible space for **Q2**, obtained when upgrading **Fog 2** to 4G, and also includes Δ16 as feasible.

The answer to question **Q1(a)** is positive. Indeed, FogTorchΠ outputs eleven deployments (Δ1 — Δ11 in Table 3) which are in the feasible solution space, determined as per the algorithms of Sect. 3.

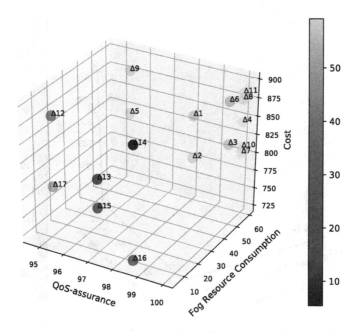

Fig. 4. FogTorchΠ output deployments and predicted metrics.

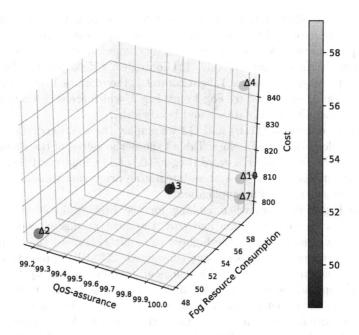

Fig. 5. Feasible space for **Q1(a)–(b)** as in [9]. Colormap refers to Fog resource consumption.

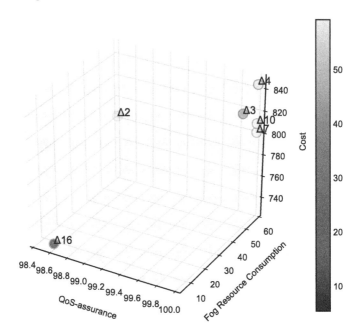

Fig. 6. Feasible space for **Q2** as in [9]. Colormap refers to Fog resource consumption.

It is worth recalling that we consider remote access to IoT devices connected to Fog nodes from other Cloud and Fog nodes. Indeed, some output deployments map components to nodes that do not directly connect to all the bound Things. As an example, in the case of $\Delta 1$, IoTController is deployed to Fog 2 but the required Things (fire_sensor_1, light_control_1, thermostate_1, video_camera_1, weather_station_3) connected to Fog 1 and Fog 3, which are still reachable with suitable network QoS (viz., latency and bandwidth).

To answer questions **Q1(b)** and **Q2** we employ the multi-criteria optimisation methodology described before. Table 4 shows the values of the single objectives, and of the aggregate Fog-ward (i.e., $r_F(\Delta)$) and Cloud-ward (i.e., $r_C(\Delta)$) objective functions, which the system integrators are trying to optimise, when deploying the smart building application.

In the Fog-ward case, when looking for the best trade-off among QoS-assurance, resource consumption and cost, the most promising deployment is always $\Delta 7$, i.e., the one with the highest value for $r_F(\Delta)$. In the Cloud-ward case, when the upgrade to 4G is not considered, $\Delta 7$ still represents the best candidate deployment. These considerations all together answer **Q1(b)**.

The 4G upgrade at Fog 2, which makes it possible to enact also $\Delta 16$, is not worth the investment when looking for Fog-ward deployments due to the much lower score achieved in the ranking with respect to $\Delta 7$. Conversely, when upgrading to 4G in the Cloud-ward case, despite investing €20 more every month, $\Delta 16$ is the best option (actually leading to €50 of monthly savings with respect to $\Delta 7$). These considerations all together answer **Q2**.

Table 4. Ranking of eligible deployments.

Dep. ID	IoTController	DataStorage	Dashboard	QoS	Cost	Resources	$r_F(\Delta)$	$r_C(\Delta)$
$\Delta2$	Fog 2	Fog 3	Cloud 1	98.6%	€798.7	48.4%	0.42	0.22
$\Delta3$	Fog 3	Fog 3	Cloud 1	100%	€829.7	48.4%	0.65	0.45
$\Delta4$	Fog 2	Fog 3	Fog 1	100%	€844.7	59.2%	0.67	0.33
$\Delta7$	Fog 3	Fog 3	Fog 2	100%	€801.7	59.2%	0.81	0.48
$\Delta10$	Fog 1	Fog 3	Fog 2	100%	€809.7	59.2%	0.79	0.45
$\Delta16^*$	Fog 2	Cloud 1	Cloud 1	98.6%	€727.7 (+20)	5.4%	0.33	0.67

In [9], $\Delta2$ and $\Delta16$ were chosen by the system integrators, in the 3G and 4G scenario respectively. However, their goal in [9] was to minimise deployment costs and Fog resource consumption (going Cloud-ward), only guaranteeing QoS-assurance above 98% (without trying to maximise it). Here, we are instead looking for the most balanced trade-off among the predicted metrics (which are all weighted equally[16]) and $\Delta7$ clearly constitutes a better compromise towards this end, guaranteeing 100% QoS-assurance and costing only a few euro more than $\Delta2$, despite using 10% more Fog resources.

7   Related Work

Few approaches have been proposed so far to specifically model Fog infrastructures and applications, as well as to determine and compare eligible deployments for an application to a Fog infrastructure under different metrics. On the other hand, the problem of deciding how to deploy multi-component applications has been extensively studied in Cloud scenarios. Projects like SeaClouds [12], Aeolus [19] or Cloud-4SOA [14], for instance, proposed model-driven optimised planning solutions to deploy software applications across different (IaaS or PaaS) Clouds. [32] proposed to use OASIS TOSCA [13] to model IoT applications in Cloud+IoT scenarios. Also, solutions to automatically provision and configure software components in Cloud (or multi-Cloud) scenarios are currently used by the DevOps community to automate application deployment or to lead deployment design choices (e.g., Puppet [2] and Chef [1]). However, only few efforts in Cloud computing considered non-functional requirements *by-design* [15,36] or uncertainty of execution (as in Fog nodes) and security risks among interactive and interdependent components [28,48].

Fog introduces new problems with respect to the Cloud paradigm, mainly due to its pervasive geo-distribution and heterogeneity, need for QoS-awareness, dynamicity and support to interactions with the IoT, that were not taken into account by previous works (as reported in [3,44,47]).

---

[16] By tuning ω_i differently and by considering the Cloud-ward case, we can obtain the same results of [9], e.g. assigning weight 0.50 to both resource consumption and cost, and 0.0 to QoS-assurance $\Delta2$ is ranked 0.34 whilst $\Delta7$ scores 0.22.

[42] was among the first attempts to evaluate service latency and energy consumption of the new Fog paradigm applied to the IoT, as compared to traditional Cloud scenarios. The model of [42], however, deals only with the behaviour of software already deployed over Fog infrastructures and simulates it mathematically.

Also investigating this new lines, [27] proposed a Fog-to-Cloud search algorithm as a first way to determine an eligible deployment of (multi-component) DAG applications to tree-like Fog infrastructures. Their placement algorithm proceeds Edge-ward, i.e. it attempts the placement of components *Fog-to-Cloud* by considering hardware capacity only. An open-source simulator – iFogSim – has been released to test the proposed policy against Cloud-only deployments. Building on top of iFogSim, [33] refines the Edge-ward algorithm to guarantee the application service delivery deadlines and to optimize Fog resource exploitation. Limiting their work to linear application graphs and tree-like infrastructure topologies, [46] used iFogSim to implement an algorithm for optimal online placement of application components, with respect to load balancing. An approximate extension handling tree-like application was also proposed. Recently, exploiting iFogSim, [25] proposed a distributed search strategy to find the best service placement in the Fog, which minimises the distance between the clients and the most requested services, based on request rates and available free resources. Their results showed a substantial improvement on network usage and service latency for the most frequently called services. [29] proposed a (linearithmic) heuristic algorithm that attempts deployments prioritising placement of smaller applications to devices with less free resources. Along the same line, [43] proposed an Edge-ward linearithmic algorithm that assigns application components to the node with the lowest capacity that can satisfy all application requirements.

Cost is an important parameter in choosing an eligible deployment, yet pricing models for the Fog are still to be developed. In the case of Cloud scenarios, pricing models are well established (e.g., [20,39] and references therein) yet they do not consider costs generated by the usage of IoT devices. Cloud pricing models are generally divided into two types, pay per use scheme and subscription-based. For both types, the total cost of deployment is calculated based on user requirements (e.g., the number of CPU cores, VM types, time duration, type of instance (reserved or pre-emptible). Since multiple offers among cloud providers can satisfy user needs, a cloud broker can be needed to choose a best VM instance(s) based upon the pricing model [20]. In the case of IoT, the providers normally process data coming from the IoT devices and sell the processed information as value added service to the users. IoT providers can sometime federate their services and create new offers for the end-users [39]. Depending upon data demand end-users can estimate the total cost of using IoT services by comparing pay-per-use and subscription-based offers. A cost model that considers various parameters (e.g., the type and number of sensors, number of data request and uptime of VM) to estimate the cost of running an application for IoT+Cloud scenario over a certain period of time was proposed in [34]. In Fog scenario, however, there is a need to compute IoT costs at a finer level, also accounting for data-transfer costs (i.e., event-based).

Trade-off analysis is needed to allow application deployers to identify the best candidate deployment and prioritise some metrics over the rest. The principles of Pareto optimality are widely used in this regard [18]. Such optimization has been applied in the cloud to optimize resource utilization and Virtual machine placement [24,50]. It is also employed in Fog scenario to address other challenges [4,30,38]. For instance, [30] used multi-objective optimization to extend iFogSim [27] to support the automated gateways selection and fog devices clustering. [4,38] applied the optimization principle for virtual machine (VM) placement and resource utilization on fog nodes to satisfy the application requirement. To summarise, most of the surveyed approaches focussed on one among Cloud, Fog or IoT, mainly considered linear cost models based on unit cost for different types of hardware resource. Our attempt is, to the best of our knowledge, the first to model costs in the Fog scenario that extends Cloud pricing schemes to the Fog layer, integrates them with costs of IoT deployments and at the same time enable the trade-off analysis between different metrics.

Inspired by our work on FogTorchΠ methodologies [7,8,10], Xia et al. [49] proposed a backtracking solution to minimise the average response time of deployed IoT applications. Two new heuristics were devised. The first one sorts the nodes considered for deploying each component in ascending order with respect to the (average) latency between each node and the IoT devices required by the component. The second one considers a component that caused backtracking as the first one to be mapped in the next search step. Despite discussing improved results on latency with respect to exhaustive backtracking and first-fit strategies, no prototype implementations were released. Finally, FogTorchΠ was also modularly extended by De Maio et al. to simulate mobile task offloading in Edge computing scenarios [17].

8   Concluding Remarks

In this paper, we extended the work presented in [9] by illustrating how the proposed cost model for Fog application deployments can be used in a multi-objective optimisation framework to determine deployments that achieve a *best* trade-off among predicted QoS-assurance, Fog resource consumption and monthly deployment cost.

Indeed, finding a good compromise among those (often orthogonal) objectives is not a trivial task to be accomplished without actual support or, worst, by trial-and-error. By means of a lifelike motivating example, we have shown how our prototype, FogTorchΠ, can help (multi-component) application deployers to determine such optimal trade-off according to their preferences. The deployment resulting from the multi-objective optimisation are clearly QoS- (i.e., accounting for variations in the QoS of communication links), context- (i.e., exploiting the contextually available resources), and cost-aware (i.e., considering Cloud, Fog and IoT related costs).

We envision the possibility of exploiting such optimisation methodology to evaluate, at design time, the feasibility of different application deployments, whilst taming the complexity, scale and intrinsic heterogeneity of Fog infrastructures. Furthemore, new businesses coming to market can use tools like FogTorchΠ not only to decide on where to deploy their application components but also to design their SLAs and billing schemes for the services they will offer.

We see three main directions for future work:

- since security represents a concern that should be addressed *by-design* at all architectural levels of Fog computing [40], we aim at devising a novel methodology to perform quantitative assessments of the security level of Fog application deployments and to show how it can synergically work with FogTorchΠ,
- by approximating the estimate of the proposed objectives (in particular of the QoS-assurance) and by envisioning the possibility for application components to be deployed in different flavours (like in *Osmotic Computing*[45]), we aim at exploiting other optimisation frameworks such as bio-inspired or swarm intelligence techniques, and
- finally, to assess our predictive analyses in support of Fog application deployment we aim at using them in available simulation environments for the management of Fog applications (e.g., [23,27,31] and, if possible, in experimental testbed settings (e.g., using as a starting point the Fog application of [11]).

References

1. Opscode. Chef. http://www.opscode.com/chef/
2. Puppetlabs. Puppet. http://puppetlabs.com
3. Arcangeli, J.P., Boujbel, R., Leriche, S.: Automatic deployment of distributed software systems: definitions and state of the art. J. Syst. Softw. **103**, 198–218 (2015)
4. Aryal, R.G., Altmann, J.: Dynamic application deployment in federations of clouds and edge resources using a multiobjective optimization AI algorithm. In: Third International Conference on Fog and Mobile Edge Computing, FMEC 2018, Barcelona, Spain, 23–26 April 2018, pp. 147–154 (2018). https://doi.org/10.1109/FMEC.2018.8364057
5. Bonomi, F., Milito, R., Natarajan, P., Zhu, J.: Fog computing: a platform for internet of things and analytics. In: Bessis, N., Dobre, C. (eds.) Big Data and Internet of Things: A Roadmap for Smart Environments. SCI, vol. 546, pp. 169–186. Springer, Cham (2014). https://doi.org/10.1007/978-3-319-05029-4_7
6. Breitbart, Y., Chan, C.Y., Garofalakis, M., Rastogi, R., Silberschatz, A.: Efficiently monitoring bandwidth and latency in IP networks. In: Proceedings IEEE INFOCOM 2001. Twentieth Annual Joint Conference of the IEEE Computer and Communications Societies, vol. 2, pp. 933–942. IEEE (2001)
7. Brogi, A., Forti, S.: QoS-aware deployment of IoT applications through the fog. IEEE Internet Things J. **4**(5), 1185–1192 (2017). https://doi.org/10.1109/JIOT.2017.2701408
8. Brogi, A., Forti, S., Ibrahim, A.: How to best deploy your fog applications, probably. In: Rana, O., Buyya, R., Anjum, A. (eds.) Proceedings of 1st IEEE International Conference on Fog and Edge Computing (ICFEC), Madrid, pp. 105–114, May 2017. https://doi.org/10.1109/ICFEC.2017.8

9. Brogi, A., Forti, S., Ibrahim, A.: Deploying Fog applications: how much does it cost, by the way? In: Proceedings of the 8th International Conference on Cloud Computing and Services Science - vol. 1: CLOSER, pp. 68–77. INSTICC, SciTePress (2018). https://doi.org/10.5220/0006676100680077

10. Brogi, A., Forti, S., Ibrahim, A.: Predictive analysis to support fog application deployment. In: Buyya, R., Srirama, S.N. (eds.) Fog and Edge Computing: Principles and Paradigms. Wiley, Hoboken (2018)

11. Brogi, A., Forti, S., Ibrahim, A., Rinaldi, L.: Bonsai in the fog: an active learning lab with fog computing. In: 2018 Third International Conference on Fog and Mobile Edge Computing (FMEC), pp. 79–86. IEEE (2018)

12. Brogi, A., et al.: SeaClouds: a European project on seamless management of multi-cloud applications. ACM SIGSOFT SEN **39**(1), 1–4 (2014)

13. Brogi, A., Soldani, J., Wang, P.W.: TOSCA in a nutshell: promises and perspectives. In: Villari, M., Zimmermann, W., Lau, K.-K. (eds.) ESOCC 2014. LNCS, vol. 8745, pp. 171–186. Springer, Heidelberg (2014). https://doi.org/10.1007/978-3-662-44879-3_13

14. Corradi, A., Foschini, L., Pernafini, A., Bosi, F., Laudizio, V., Seralessandri, M.: Cloud PaaS brokering in action: the Cloud4SOA management infrastructure. In: VTC 2015, pp. 1–7 (2015)

15. Cucinotta, T., Anastasi, G.F.: A heuristic for optimum allocation of real-time service workflows. In: 2011 IEEE International Conference on Service-Oriented Computing and Applications (SOCA), pp. 1–4. IEEE (2011)

16. Dastjerdi, A.V., Buyya, R.: Fog computing: helping the internet of things realize its potential. Computer **49**(8), 112–116 (2016)

17. De Maio, V., Brandic, I.: First Hop Mobile Offloading of DAG Computations (2018, in press)

18. Deb, K.: Multi-objective optimization. In: Burke, E., Kendall, G. (eds.) Search Methodologies. Springer, Boston, MA (2014). https://doi.org/10.1007/978-1-4614-6940-7_15

19. Di Cosmo, R., Eiche, A., Mauro, J., Zacchiroli, S., Zavattaro, G., Zwolakowski, J.: Automatic deployment of services in the cloud with aeolus blender. In: Barros, A., Grigori, D., Narendra, N.C., Dam, H.K. (eds.) ICSOC 2015. LNCS, vol. 9435, pp. 397–411. Springer, Heidelberg (2015). https://doi.org/10.1007/978-3-662-48616-0_28

20. Díaz, J.L., Entrialgo, J., García, M., García, J., García, D.F.: Optimal allocation of virtual machines in multi-cloud environments with reserved and on-demand pricing. Future Gener. Comput. Syst. **71**, 129–144 (2017)

21. Dunn, W.L., Shultis, J.K.: Exploring Monte Carlo Methods. Elsevier, Amsterdam (2011)

22. Fatema, K., Emeakaroha, V.C., Healy, P.D., Morrison, J.P., Lynn, T.: A survey of cloud monitoring tools: taxonomy, capabilities and objectives. J. Parallel Distrib. Comput. **74**(10), 2918–2933 (2014)

23. Forti, S., Ibrahim, A., Brogi, A.: Mimicking FogDirector application management. Comput. Sci. Res. Dev. **34**(2–3), 151–161 (2018)

24. Gao, Y., Guan, H., Qi, Z., Hou, Y., Liu, L.: A multi-objective ant colony system algorithm for virtual machine placement in cloud computing. J. Comput. Syst. Sci. **79**(8), 1230–1242 (2013)

25. Guerrero, C., Lera, I., Juiz, C.: A lightweight decentralized service placement policy for performance optimization in fog computing. J. Ambient Intell. Humanized Comput. **10**(6), 2435–2452 (2019). https://doi.org/10.1007/s12652-018-0914-0

26. Guerrero, C., Lera, I., Juiz, C.: Resource optimization of container orchestration: a case study in multi-cloud microservices-based applications. J. Supercomput. **74**(7), 2956–2983 (2018)
27. Gupta, H., Dastjerdi, A.V., Ghosh, S.K., Buyya, R.: iFogSim: a toolkit for modeling and simulation of resource management techniques in internet of things, edge and fog computing environments. Softw. Pract. Exp. **47**(9), 1275–1296 (2017). https://doi.org/10.1002/spe.2509
28. Haithem, M., Mokhtar, S., Jaber, K.: Security-aware SaaS placement using swarm intelligence. J. Softw. Evol. Process **30**(8), e1932 (2018). https://doi.org/10.1002/smr.1932. https://onlinelibrary.wiley.com/doi/abs/10.1002/smr.1932
29. Hong, H.J., Tsai, P.H., Hsu, C.H.: Dynamic module deployment in a fog computing platform. In: 2016 18th Asia-Pacific Network Operations and Management Symposium (APNOMS), pp. 1–6, October 2016. https://doi.org/10.1109/APNOMS.2016.7737202
30. Kimovski, D., Ijaz, H., Surabh, N., Prodan, R.: An Adaptive Nature-inspired Fog Architecture. CoRR abs/1803.03444 (2018)
31. Lera, I., Guerrero, C.: YAFS - Yet Another Fog Simulator (for python). https://yafs.readthedocs.io/en/latest/
32. Li, F., Vögler, M., Claeßens, M., Dustdar, S.: Towards automated IoT application deployment by a cloud-based approach. In: SOCA 2013, pp. 61–68 (2013)
33. Mahmud, R., Ramamohanarao, K., Buyya, R.: Latency-aware application module management for fog computing environments. ACM Trans. Internet Technol. (TOIT) **19**(1), 9 (2018)
34. Markus, A., Kertesz, A., Kecskemeti, G.: Cost-aware IoT extension of DISSECT-CF. Future Internet **9**(3), 47 (2017). https://doi.org/10.3390/fi9030047. http://www.mdpi.com/1999-5903/9/3/47
35. Marler, R.T., Arora, J.S.: The weighted sum method for multi-objective optimization: new insights. Struct. Multi. Optim. **41**(6), 853–862 (2010)
36. Nathuji, R., Kansal, A., Ghaffarkhah, A.: Q-Clouds: Managing Performance Interference Effects for QoS-Aware Clouds. Association for Computing Machinery, Inc., April 2010
37. Newman, S.: Building Microservices: Designing Fine-Grained Systems. O'Reilly Media, Inc., Sebastopol (2015)
38. Nguyen, D.T., Le, L.B., Bhargava, V.: Price-based resource allocation for edge computing: a market equilibrium approach. CoRR abs/1805.02982 (2018)
39. Niyato, D., Hoang, D.T., Luong, N.C., Wang, P., Kim, D.I., Han, Z.: Smart data pricing models for the internet of things: a bundling strategy approach. IEEE Netw. **30**(2), 18–25 (2016)
40. OpenFog: OpenFog Reference Architecture (2016)
41. Perera, C.: Sensing as a Service for Internet of Things: A Roadmap (2017). Lulu.com
42. Sarkar, S., Misra, S.: Theoretical modelling of fog computing: a green computing paradigm to support IoT applications. IET Netw. **5**(2), 23–29 (2016)
43. Taneja, M., Davy, A.: Resource aware placement of IoT application modules in fog-cloud computing paradigm. In: 2017 IFIP/IEEE Symposium on Integrated Network and Service Management (IM), pp. 1222–1228, May 2017. https://doi.org/10.23919/INM.2017.7987464
44. Varshney, P., Simmhan, Y.: Demystifying fog computing: characterizing architectures, applications and abstractions. In: 2017 IEEE 1st International Conference on Fog and Edge Computing (ICFEC), pp. 115–124, May 2017. https://doi.org/10.1109/ICFEC.2017.20

45. Villari, M., Fazio, M., Dustdar, S., Rana, O., Ranjan, R.: Osmotic computing: a new paradigm for edge/cloud integration. IEEE Cloud Comput. **3**(6), 76–83 (2016)
46. Wang, S., Zafer, M., Leung, K.K.: Online placement of multi-component applications in edge computing environments. IEEE Access **5**, 2514–2533 (2017). https://doi.org/10.1109/ACCESS.2017.2665971
47. Wen, Z., Yang, R., Garraghan, P., Lin, T., Xu, J., Rovatsos, M.: Fog orchestration for internet of things services. IEEE Internet Comput. **21**(2), 16–24 (2017). https://doi.org/10.1109/MIC.2017.36
48. Wen, Z., Cała, J., Watson, P., Romanovsky, A.: Cost effective, reliable and secure workflow deployment over federated clouds. IEEE Trans. Serv. Comput. **10**(6), 929–941 (2017)
49. Xia, Y., Etchevers, X., Letondeur, L., Coupaye, T., Desprez, F.: Combining hardware nodes and software components ordering-based heuristics for optimizing the placement of distributed IoT applications in the fog. In: Proceedings of the 33rd Annual ACM Symposium on Applied Computing, pp. 751–760. ACM (2018)
50. Xu, J., Fortes, J.A.: Multi-objective virtual machine placement in virtualized data center environments. In: IEEE/ACM GreenCom and CPSCom, pp. 179–188. IEEE (2010)

Right Scaling for Right Pricing: A Case Study on Total Cost of Ownership Measurement for Cloud Migration

Pierangelo Rosati[1(✉)], Frank Fowley[1], Claus Pahl[2], Davide Taibi[3], and Theo Lynn[1]

[1] Irish Centre for Cloud Computing and Commerce,
Dublin City University, Dublin, Ireland
{pierangelo.rosati,frank.fowley,theo.lynn}@dcu.ie
[2] Faculty of Computer Science, Free University of Bozen-Bolzano,
Bolzano, Italy
claus.pahl@unibz.it
[3] Laboratory of Pervasive Computing, Tampere University of Technology,
Tampere, Finland
davide.taibi@tut.fi

Abstract. Cloud computing promises traditional enterprises and independent software vendors a myriad of advantages over on-premise installations including cost, operational and organizational efficiencies. The decision to migrate software configured for on-premise delivery to the cloud requires careful technical consideration and planning. In this chapter, we discuss the impact of right-scaling on the cost modelling for migration decision making and price setting of software for commercial resale. An integrated process is presented for measuring total cost of ownership, taking in to account IaaS/PaaS resource consumption based on forecast SaaS usage levels. The process is illustrated with a real world case study.

Keywords: Cloud migration · Total cost of ownership · Pricing · Architecture migration · Software producer

1 Introduction

Cloud computing is increasingly the computing paradigm of choice for enterprises worldwide. Cloud computing is particularly attractive from a business perspective since it requires lower upfront capital expenditure, and improves operational and organizational efficiencies and agility [4, 9, 39, 45]. Similarly, from a technical perspective, the benefits of the cloud are well documented including on-demand and self-service capabilities, resource pooling and rapid elasticity [4]. However, the success of cloud computing investments highly depends on accurate and efficient decision making; the implications of investment decisions need to be quantifiable to allow a comparison of alternatives, both from the consumer's and from the vendor's perspective [27].

Cloud computing adoption may generate significant challenges particularly for software producers (SPs) offering a Software-as-a-Service (SaaS) model. SPs typically

© Springer Nature Switzerland AG 2019
V. M. Muñoz et al. (Eds.): CLOSER 2018, CCIS 1073, pp. 190–214, 2019.
https://doi.org/10.1007/978-3-030-29193-8_10

migrate their software to a third-party platform (Infrastructure-as-a-Service – IaaS – or Platform-as-a-Service – PaaS) and their customers access it from this new multi-tenant architecture. In a cloud environment both SPs and their customers are typically charged on a pay-per-use or subscription basis. Furthermore, SPs do not have control of customers' service usage; in such a context, it is crucial for SPs to identify the right architectural configuration to meet service level agreement (SLA) obligations at the minimum cost. Being charged on a per-use basis also represents a radical change in the producers' cost and revenue models and introduces additional uncertainty in cash flow forecasting [15]. Furthermore, the actual cost of the migration process might be substantial for SPs and for their legacy customers, while nonexistent for cloud-native SPs. According to the Cloud Native Computing Foundation, modern cloud-native systems have the following properties:

- Container-packaged;
- Dynamically managed by a central orchestrating process;
- Microservice-oriented.

Cloud-native architectures have technical advantages in terms of isolation and reusability, thus reducing cost for maintenance and operations. PaaS clouds with their recent support for containerized micro-service architectures are the ideal environments to create cloud-native systems. While the service and payment/revenue model are the same in both migrated and native scenarios, the total cost of ownership (TCO) is substantially different due to the migration costs. Rationally, SPs should offer their software at a higher price to compensate for their migration costs, however this may not always be competitively feasible or desirable.

While architectural challenges in migration have been addressed [7, 33, 49, 57, 58], research exploring the link between cloud architecture and TCO, and therefore on pricing cloud services from an SP perspective is lacking. The main objective of this chapter is to extend our previous work [53] exploring the impact of two cloud architectural options, IaaS (basic virtualization) and a range of PaaS-related technology options on SPs' operating costs. We present an initial process for architecture-related cost estimation and informing pricing strategy.

This chapter is organized as follows. Section 2 reviews related work and presents the cloud migration context. Section 3 introduces the overall process. Section 4 focuses on the I/PaaS-based architecture cost calculation. In Sect. 5, we validate and illustrate our contribution using a case study. Section 6 presents different pricing structures available for SPs. The chapter concludes with a summary of contributions and suggestions for future research.

2 Architecture Migration Context

2.1 Context and Related Work

Cloud computing has attracted significant attention from the research community. Despite this, most of the research focuses on technical aspects with a limited number of studies examining the business implications of cloud adoption [36, 65]. This is somewhat surprising given the significant changes that cloud computing can generate in organizations' processes and business model, particularly for SPs [16]. Even more surprising is the lack of studies linking the value generated by cloud investments to the technical aspects of the services adopted or provided. This chapter aims to fill this gap by focusing on the impact of architectural decisions on the TCO of cloud services that SPs consume (i.e. I/PaaS) in order to provide SaaS services to their customers.

Traditionally, enterprise software was licensed under a packaged, perpetual or server license, and customers were typically required to purchase technical support and maintenance packages for a predefined period [21]. The cost of software development, production and marketing was offset against the license fees, typically paid upfront by the customer. The introduction of cloud computing accelerated the adoption of two new licensing models: subscription and utility-based licensing. The former involves an enterprise customer purchasing a license for a pre-defined time period whereas the latter involves charging the customer on a pay-per-use basis. Key advantages for the enterprise customer include (i) less upfront expenditure in licensing and (ii) no additional fees for fixes, upgrades or feature enhancements [21]. The shift from a product orientation to a service orientation is a significant disruption for SPs, not only from a strategic perspective but also from a cost- and revenue- recognition perspective, and requires in many instances a significant business model readjustment [14]. For example, cost and revenues are spread over time and producers do not receive additional fees for upgrades. Obviously, the impact of such discontinuities and shifts are not experienced by cloud-native SPs such as start-ups. Indeed, Giardino et al. [23] observe that cloud computing is particularly beneficial for start-up companies since it significantly lowers the initial investment in IT infrastructure.

It is now generally accepted that cloud computing generates a wide range of benefits and estimating the overall value generated by these type of investments is receiving growing attention from both consumers and providers [52]. Academic research has proposed a number of different approaches to estimate the business value of information technology (IT) [52]. The need for robust methodologies to assess the value generated by IT investments is driven by a trend towards value-based management, a managerial approach finalized to maximize shareholder value [5]. Value assessment techniques can be both *ex-ante* and *ex-post* [51], but it is clear that a proper *ex-ante* evaluation can better inform investment decision-making therefore potentially maximizing the return on investment or avoiding losses.

Farbey et al. [20] and Farbey and Finkelstein [19] classify value assessment methodologies in two categories:

- Quantitative/comparative methods: these typically leverage accounting methodologies to translate costs and benefits of IT investments in economic terms therefore allowing comparison between alternative investments. As such, these methods are also referred to as "objective" methods;
- Qualitative/exploratory methods: these mostly focus on the opportunities and threats that an IT investment may bring to some stakeholders. The aim in this case is to obtain an agreement over objectives through a process of exploration. These methods are also referred to as "subjective" methods given the high degree of subjectivity they may include.

Tables 1 and 2 provides a summary of different methodologies for each category as proposed by Farbey et al. [20] and Farbey and Finkelstein [19].

Table 1. Quantitative/Comparative methods (adapted from [51]).

Method	Detail	Process management	Data	Features
Total cost of ownership (TCO)	Very detailed	Accounting and costing staff	Cost accounting and work study method	Focus on cost savings
Return on investment (ROI)	High	Calculation by professionals; cash flows as the aggregation of tangible cost and benefits	Cost accounting; direct and objective costs	Future uncertainty is considered; middle to high cost of implementation
Cost-benefit analysis	High	Carried out by experts; money values for decision makers by incorporating surrogate measures	Cost and benefit elements expressed in monetary value form	Cost-effective solutions; includes "external" and "soft" costs and benefits; numbers more important than process; high implementation cost
Return on management (ROM)	Low	Calculation by professionals; manipulates accounting figures to estimate the value added by management	Accounting totals (e.g. total revenue, total labor cost)	Ex-post only; no cause and effect relations can be postulated; focus on management activities; low implementation cost
Boundary values and spending ratios	Low	Top-down approach; senior stakeholders involved; calculation by professionals	Ratios of aggregated numbers (e.g. IT expense per employee)	Supporting benchmarking analysis; low implementation cost
Information economics (IE)	Very detailed	Many stakeholders involved; detailed analysis required	Ranking and rating of objectives, both tangible and intangible	All options are comprehensively dealt with; complex to implement

For the purpose of this chapter, we focus on quantitative methods since these are the most used in practice. Among them, TCO, CBA and ROI are the most widely adopted while others like ROM, Boundary Values, Spending Ratios and Information Economics are not frequently adopted due to a perceived lower level of analysis [51] or subjectivity [63].

Despite the wide range of benefits that the adoption of cloud computing may generate for organizations, cost savings, rather than strategic return-on-investment, still represents a major factor in cloud adoption [8, 11] and TCO is *de facto* the most adopted costing model in both research and practice [52, 56]. TCO has been defined as

Table 2. Qualitative/Exploratory methods (adapted from [51]).

Method	Detail	Process management	Data	Features
Multi-Objective, Multi-Criteria (MOMC)	Any level	Top-down; consensus seeking; all stakeholders involved; best choice is computed	Priorities are stated by stakeholders; subjective evaluations of intangibles	Ex-ante; good for extracting software requirements; process is more important than numbers; selection of (a) preferred set of design goals, (b) best design alternative; high implementation cost
Value analysis	Any level; usually very detailed	Iterative process; senior to middle management involved; variables identified with Delphi method	Indirect; subjective evaluations of intangibles; utility scores	Ex-ante; iterative and incremental process; focus more on added value than cost saving; process is more important than numbers; high implementation cost
Critical success factors (CSFs)	Short list of factors	Senior management define CSFs	Interview or self-expression; quick process but requires senior management time	Ex-ante; highly selective; high implementation cost
Experimental methods	From detailed to abstract	Management scientists working with stakeholders	Exploratory; uncertainty reduction	Ex-ante

"a procedure that provides the means for determining the total economic value of an investment, including the initial capital expenditures (*CapEx*) and the operational expenditures (*OpEx*)" [22]. The metering nature of cloud computing provides the perfect basis for extremely low-granularity TCO analysis and the opportunity to reimagine how the business value of IT is measured in both research and practice [52]. Despite its apparently simplicity and the availability of different online tools offered by cloud service providers, *ex-ante* TCO estimation is not straightforward due to the presence of long-term and hidden costs of operating in the cloud which tend to be ignored or underestimated [32]. TCO estimation frameworks used for traditional on-premise infrastructure need to be adapted to the cloud world to reflect different cost drivers [46, 62]. Rosati et al. [52] further highlight significant methodological flaws in current TCO estimation frameworks which tend to focus merely on operational cost and usually consider a small number of cost drivers.

From an SP perspective, this represents a major concern. Being both cloud consumers and cloud providers, properly mapping the costs of the cloud represents the basis for adequate and effective pricing strategies. SPs price their SaaS services in many ways [12]. Even though monthly or annual subscription fees is the most common pricing structure, other structures include, for example, transaction based revenue (i.e. customers are charged based on the number of transactions they perform) and premium based revenue (users are charged for premium versions besides the free versions) [13, 16, 48]. Irrespective of the pricing structure an SP adopts, a reliable estimate of the infrastructure costs it has to sustain to provide the service is required in order to ensure the existence of adequate margins [37]. This process has become more and more important for SPs due to increasing competition in the cloud environment, where SPs are sometimes forced to deliver services whose costs exceed revenues [17].

Strebel and Stage [56] applied a TCO-based decision model for business software application deployment while running simulations on hybrid cloud environments. They found that the cost-effectiveness of cloud services, from a user perspective, is positively related to the cloud-readiness of business applications and processes. The decision model they proposed was limited to a comparison of operational IT costs, such as server and storage expenses, and the external provisioning by means of cloud computing services. Li et al. [41] focused on the provider perspective. They formulated a TCO model to calculate set-up and maintenance costs (e.g. costs of hardware, software, power, cooling, staff and real-estate) of a cloud service and identified the factors involved in the utilization cost. This model consists of the total cost of all servers and resources used to provide the service. Cloud implementation and operating costs were divided into eight different categories that mainly represent fixed costs, such as set-up and maintenance costs that providers need to bear during the whole lifecycle. Han [25] presents a cost comparison between virtual managed nodes and local managed servers and storage, but neglects important cost components like licensing, training, and maintenance. Finally, Walterbusch et al. [62] presents a comprehensive TCO model for the three main cloud service models (i.e. IaaS, PaaS and SaaS), and map into their model different cost components across four phases of cloud computing i.e. initiation, evaluation, transition, operation. Costs related to system failure, backsourcing or discarding are listed but not included in the model since they are, by their nature, contingent on situation contexts and therefore difficult to translate in a mathematical formula.

Despite the large number of studies on software architecture-related factors for consideration in migration, and, likewise, the large number of studies related to TCO for cloud computing, there is a lack of papers seeking to estimate the TCO for cloud migration in conjunction with architecture concerns. The extant literature is typically focused on ex-post calculation of costs and profits independently from the wider situational context, and typically considers only cloud operational cost. For example, Andrikopoulos et al. [2] proposes a decision support system which includes a cost calculator based on per-use cost components only. Jinesh [35] presents a TCO estimation of migrating to Amazon Web Services (AWS) that includes per-use charges only. Similarly, Anwar et al. [3] examine cost-aware cloud metering for scalable services.

2.2 Two Migration Business Cases

Cloud computing adoption can dramatically change a company's business model and internal organization, and requires investing a significant amount of resources in the migration process. In such a context, an *ex-ante* evaluation of costs and potential benefits that such an investment may generate is crucial for effective decision-making. In this chapter, we consider two discernible business cases:

- The migration of existing legacy software and associated customers with perpetual licenses;
- Adoption of cloud-native software by new customers with no existing economic relationship with the SP.

In the first case, there is a significant post-migration discontinuity in the vendor-customer relationship and the nature of the billing. From the customer perspective, the business case can be made by comparing the as-is and the to-be solution, however this is anything but a trivial process [32]. There may be time, effort and additional hidden costs related to the migration that needs to be included in the ex-ante evaluation and recovered by both SPs and their customers [32]. In the second case, customers can make their choice on the basis of the perceived value of the service *per se*. In both cases a key consideration for SPs is the amount of cost they can sustain to generate a positive margin on their sale over a defined time period.

TCO is used to estimate the cost of cloud investments from the initial sourcing through to the end of the cloud usage, whether that is the backsourcing of information, or the client switching to other services or providers. While the measured nature of the cloud allows for a detailed *ex-post* cost analysis, *ex-ante* cost estimation can be complicated due to the uncertainty associated with multi-tenancy and resource pooling. Similarly, while there are clear cost savings in cloud computing there are also intangible cost components which are more difficult to estimate [32].

By its very nature, cloud computing enables enterprise customer scale up and down on-demand without the ties associated with a substantial upfront investment. Thus, forecasting the customer lifetime (and associated value) for a cloud customer can be difficult. Suddenly, they can leave or radically modify their usage, since switching costs in the cloud are significantly lower than on-premise. Notwithstanding this, enterprise customers and SPs require a practical approach to measuring cloud TCO.

3 Integrated Migration Framework and Process

Typically, a cloud migration is organized around an architectural transformation of the legacy system, independent of cost and pricing considerations. We propose an integrated process for migration planning and pricing:

Step 1: Analyze and model – Use a set of migration patterns to determine structural cloud architecture aspects;

Step 2: Right-scaling – Conduct a feasibility study to size the predicted workload to a machine (configuration) profile based on analysis of direct operational costs driven by predicted usage and experimental consumption figures;

Step 3: Right-pricing – Determine pricing for the software service based on the TCO calculation generated from the feasibility study.

3.1   Step 1: Analyze and Model

In the analysis and modelling step, we examine both the pre-migration context (including migration concerns) and use a set of migration patterns to determine structural cloud architecture aspects. This phase is not relevant in the context of native cloud software. For each use case, we examine the context as per Pahl et al. [49], namely:

- Setting/Application – description of the sector and classification of the application in question;
- Expectation/Drivers – the drivers and a distinction of migration benefits and expectations that potential users are aware of (their vision);
- Ignorance – factors that have been overlooked;
- Concerns – specific problems/constraints that need to be addressed.

We then conduct a multi-level analysis of requirements e.g. technology review, business analytics, migration and architecture and test and evaluation. Once this preliminary contextual analysis is completed, a set of cloud migration patterns, processes and issues as presented by Jamshidi et al. [34] and Taibi et al. [57] can be used to inform a detailed migration plan.

3.2   Step 2: Right-Scaling of SaaS Software

SPs seeking to migrate to the cloud need to find the right architectural configuration to meet the necessary service level agreement (SLA) obligations at the minimum cost. Therefore, a key question for a decision maker is:

How many components can I host on a fixed cloud compute resource with a pre-defined latency performance target for a forecasted number of users of a particular application with a forecasted mix of application operation usage?

Changes in usage require changes in the number and/or configuration of cloud resources used, which may result in additional costs. Estimation of the expected usage level or patterns is needed to predict when scaling, and related additional costs, may occur.

Furthermore, storage and networking charges are akin to commodities that can be consumed on a per-unit of usage basis. The compute costs are more difficult to predict since they are determined by the users' use of the application. In this chapter, we consider a virtual SLA-backed service that is not entirely fixed in terms of computational and storage resources allocated. Finally, the actual capacity of the offered cloud service may fluctuate over time affecting potential economies of scale and application performance. Only the cloud service provider, and not the SP, can monitor the underlying service availability thus, the first problem is right-scaling i.e., to size a predicted workload to a machine (configuration) profile. This requires usage prediction to configure IaaS or PaaS through an experimental pre-migration feasibility study, and represents the basis for an accurate estimation of operational costs. For SPs, right-scaling reduces overprovisioning and therefore usage cost of their cloud infrastructure.

3.3   Step 3: Right-Pricing of SaaS-Delivered Products

Monetization refers to how organizations capture value i.e. when, what and how value is converted into money [6]. Despite the fact that how SPs price and monetize their cloud offering is beyond the scope of the TCO process adopted in this chapter, it is important to understand as the TCO represents a critical component of SPs' pricing decision. A monetization framework for SPs usually comprise three models, namely:

- Architecture model: the source and target architecture need to be considered together with planned changes in functional or non-functional properties;
- Cost model: the expected direct operational costs need to be estimated including basic infrastructure and platform costs, additional features for external access and networking, internal quality management, and development and testing costs, and mapped into the TCO estimation;
- Revenue model: expected revenues based on a selected pay-per-use or subscription model.

From an SP perspective, the relationship between cloud cost and price (P) can represented as follows:

$$P = TCO \times (1 + \mu) \tag{1}$$

Where μ represents the percentage of profit the producer aims to obtain. Understanding how SaaS usage translates in to IaaS costs is of primary importance for SPs since the SaaS income should cover the corresponding infrastructure costs. The interplay between these three models ultimately determines the attractiveness of the cloud offering of an SP in the marketplace. In this context, relevant questions to consider are:

- Which factors are static and might be considered as a baseline for the cost calculation?
- What are the additional costs for scaling up beyond the baseline?
- What is the best combination of cost and revenue model that maximize profit in the short- and long-term?

3.4   Total Cost of Ownership and Cost Factors

TCO, in a strict sense, is the sum of the initial investment required to purchase an asset (*CapEx*) plus the operating costs that the cloud generates (*OpEx*). When choosing among alternatives, SPs should look at both components of TCO to evaluate the investment properly. Migration costs tend to be omitted in cloud TCO estimations even though they can be substantial and change the overall return on investment. TCO calculation can be formalized as follows:

$$TCO = CapEx + OpEx \qquad (2)$$

In the context of our study, *OpEx* includes fixed (e.g. location and size) and variable (i.e. usage) IaaS cost components while *CapEx* includes migration and implementation costs (e.g. development and testing, project management etc.). Walterbusch et al. [62] provide a comprehensive list of cost components that may be considered for estimating TCO of SP cloud migration.

In order to estimate the cost associated with the expected SaaS usage, we consider costs at the SP level. In terms of IaaS operational costs for an SP we focus on compute, storage and network resources since they usually represent the most significant cost components. IaaS costs can be categorized as either (i) fixed (size of the reserved/allocated resources, availability, location, and other supplemental and/or premium services) or (ii) variable (i.e., usage of all respective IaaS resources). Like other fixed cost factors, reconfiguration is possible, but not considered in this chapter. Availability is considered as a contractually guaranteed property and it is also assumed to be fixed.

4 I/PaaS Cost Calculation Process

The nature of the cloud makes it difficult to determine the input variables of the TCO model, but, as we will see, architecture quality concerns such as performance and availability can drive this process. Cloud architecture qualities, and corresponding costs, can be influenced by compute, storage and network resources. Therefore, a reliable TCO estimation requires at least two mappings from SaaS (service provided) to I/PaaS (service consumed): (i) map SaaS to I/PaaS metrics in order to link expected (SLA) and actual level of quality; and (ii) map SaaS to I/PaaS usage patterns in order to link SaaS usage variation to the required level of I/PaaS resources. Figure 1 summarizes the cost estimation process that we will now apply.

Fig. 1. Costing SaaS usage - estimation process [53].

4.1 Cost Estimation Process

In a cloud migration scenario, an SP needs to migrate the system architecture of the target on-premise software product and change the corresponding cost and revenue models at the same time. As highlighted before, the new models heavily depend on expected or predicted usage, both of which are difficult to estimate. In fact, any estimation of SaaS usage volumes will determine IaaS usage requirements but customers' usage can be subject to temporary peaks that might generate spikes in costs due to ineffective IaaS usage.

Estimation complexity varies between the two business cases identified earlier, i.e. migrated or cloud-native application. Usage patterns of the existing customer base can be determined with reasonably high accuracy, as opposed to the future behavior of an unknown customer cohort in the cloud-native scenario. The initial two phases relate to usage estimation at both the SaaS and IaaS level. SaaS usage can be mapped onto IaaS by experimental means using feasibility studies or other mechanisms. A third phase is concerned with IaaS cost estimation, which is driven by the usage estimation and SLA obligations. IaaS configuration heuristics can be used to identify the most efficient infrastructure configuration. The fourth and final phase is related to pricing the SaaS service based on the outcome of the previous stages.

4.2 Architecture Selection and Cost/Revenue Prediction

From an SP perspective, the list of selection criteria of a cloud provider includes both fees and the associated billing model. Many IaaS providers offer monthly basic subscription fees with additional fees for premium services such as scalability, access monitoring (e.g., IP endpoint, network bandwidth), and advanced self-management. An SP requires a clear comparison of costs and revenues resulting from the cloud adoption. This has to be an "apples to apples" comparison [32]. Even though we primarily discuss IaaS, similar assumptions can be made for PaaS services. PaaS-level costs need to address both development and deployment and need to be aligned with SaaS-level income. In order to determine a profitable and sustainable pricing model, the following steps need to be taken:

- Estimation of the TCO of consumed cloud services on the basis of the expected usage of the provided SaaS service;
- Estimation of the expected level of revenues on the basis of expected usage of suitable fees level;
- A sensitivity analysis of I/PaaS costs to potential changes in SaaS usage;
- Assessment of the alignment of the selected pricing model with the market strategy of the SP;
- Assessment of the sustainability of the selected pricing model both in the short- and long-term.

4.3 Assumptions – Resource Cost Modeling and Right-Scaling

In order to make this more practically relevant, we can look at the different resource types and compare them in terms of utilization and cost fluctuations in common deployments (and resulting impact on cost estimation). Cost modeling for compute versus storage services are fundamentally different. Storage usage is more predictable and current cloud service pricing models support a commodity-style costing. Compute usage and related cost is more complicated to predict since it can fluctuate significantly over time and contributes disproportionately to the achievement of economies of scale.

SPs need to make configuration assumptions which may or may not prove to be accurate. Scenario analysis may help to achieve better estimation.

For illustration purposes, a simple initial configuration of IaaS resources could be based on 80% reserved and 20% on-demand instances. This combines reliable core provisioning without overprovisioning for extra demand (in which case on-demand instances are acquired). The benefits of this strategy are:

- 60–80% utilization of used instances is achievable if the reserved instances deal with peak demand;
- Up to 50% cost reduction compared to on-demand instances only.

Another factor impacting resource requirement is the nature of the architecture. Stateless, loosely-coupled architectures help accommodate extra demand and enable scalability by just using additional resources on-demand without much start-up costs (transfer of state to other resources).

4.4   An Exemplar Costing Model

In order to understand pricing models of IaaS and PaaS providers, we report exemplar categories and common pricing models (Table 3). This is largely built on Microsoft Azure pricing information, but is typical of other providers. Relevant costing models focus primarily on storage in GB and transactions (read/write). A proper estimation of IaaS costs associated with a SaaS application provisioning is needed in order to (i) select the technically best option, and (ii) estimate the costs for hosting the SaaS application, for example, in a PaaS cloud. Quality concerns other than the expected workload (e.g. availability expectations, failover strategy etc.) have to be considered in the process as well. Effectively, the estimation process needs to include the number of storage units and total size as an input, and the costs, estimated over a defined period, with predicted growth, and for different replication options as an output.

A further complication is that pricing models between platform providers are difficult to compare due to different definitions of price components. Consequently, a formal and clear estimation framework for an economic evaluation of different solutions to deliver a SaaS service is needed.

5   Illustration and Validation – Case Study

We now illustrate the estimation process presented in Sect. 4 using a case study. The estimation process was applied to an SP migrating a legacy client-server on-premise single-tenant enterprise application to the cloud by re-designing, re-engineering and recoding the system as a cloud application. The SP is a small-medium enterprise which provides a document management application. Its application has over 1,000 existing client installs and in this case study, we present the TCO estimation of migrating 240 of these to the new cloud platform over a 3-year period. The main business requirements for the SP to adopt the cloud were (i) to pursue flexibility across different devices and situational contexts, and (ii) to increase the customer base through efficient entry in to new geographical markets. The solution requires meeting high-volume data storage and processing needs.

Table 3. Storage cost component (adapted from [53]).

Component	Description
Region	A region is a set of datacenters deployed within a latency-defined perimeter and connected through a dedicated regional low-latency network
Replication	Cloud providers usually create multiple copies of each database in order to ensure durability and high availability. Cloud users can choose the replication option that best fits its needs but each option come with different a different price. Sample configurations include: • Local Redundant – a number of copies are stored in the same data-center and region of the storage account, but across different fault or upgrade domains • Zone Redundant – a number of copies are stored in different data-centers, which have slightly less throughput than Local redundancy • Geo Redundant – a number of copies are stored in different data-centers, with a back-up, separate multiple saves in a specific secondary region to allow to recover from potential region failure • Read-Only Geo Redundant – Similar to geo redundancy with read access to secondary data All replication operations are done asynchronously
Size	Storage cost is positively related with the volume of data stored in a database
Transactions	Storage cost depends on the number of transactions - i.e. read/write blob operations – performed in each database. The higher the number of transactions, the higher the cost
Data transfer	Storage cost is positively related with volume of data being transferred from/to the database. However, the cost of data transfer is usually charged only when data is moved out from the geographical region where it was stored. In-region transfers are usually free

5.1   Application Overview

The case site is a small-to-medium sized SP that overs document management services to the logistics sector. The application is a Document Management System (DMS), which enables a user to scan paper documents from enterprise-grade scanners and save them on a cloud store as electronic images. Documents are classified under custom types, such as invoice or delivery docket, and specific metadata templates are used to store search-able tagged data against the documents for future retrieval and reporting. The SP wishes to deploy the software in the cloud and due to the commercially sensitive nature of the documents being scanned, data location is major concern. The SP does not have enough information on the cost of migration and cloud deployment specifically to inform a migration decision and/or pricing strategy. Specifically:

• Technology review - the SP has network concerns regarding the upload and download data transfer speeds and services for in-cloud document processing.

- Business analysis – the SP has concerns about security and data privacy regulations e.g. GDPR.
- Migration and architecture – the preferred solution is a two-stage incremental migration plan (IaaS and PaaS) to migrate document scanning, storage and processing to a scalable cloud architecture.
- Test and evaluation – scalability, performance, integration and security must meet agreed criteria.

A summary migration plan with stepwise migration from on-premise via IaaS into a PaaS cloud could be implemented as follows:

1. IaaS Compute Architecture: The application can be packaged in-to VMs. License fees for components of the application are incurred as usual. The business problem is scaling out; adding more VMs means adding more license fees for every replicated component. From a technical point of view, multiple copies of data storage that are not in sync might cause integrity problems.
2. DaaS Storage: Refactor and extract storage i.e. use a virtual data-as-a-service (DaaS) solution for storage needs. This alleviates the technical integrity problem cited above.
3. PaaS Cloud Data Storage: Package the whole DBMS into a single virtual machine. This alleviates the business license fee problem for the DBMS and simplifies data management, but other license fees may still occur.
4. Full Application Migration: Migrate to a PaaS service. Apart from solving technical problems, this significantly mitigates the licensing fees issue.

Ultimately and for the purposes of this case, the application has been redesigned and coded specifically to run as a cloud application on the Microsoft Azure public cloud platform.

5.2   TCO Calculation

The TCO is made up of the implementation costs of the new cloud application and the cloud charges incurred in running the new system on Microsoft Azure. Estimated implementation costs (*CapEx*) were classified into seven implementation phases: Business Analysis, Cloud Architecture Design, Data Design, Security Framework Design, Development and Test (see Table 10), Performance and Costs Analysis (see Tables 11, 12 and 13). It should be noted that the calculations do not include the operational costs of migrating the customers to the new cloud web application.

The application is a multi-process system since it comprises a web server compute resource and a separate image processing compute resource. However, the functional dependency between these do not need to be considered in the TCO analysis since the image processing worker VM acts completely asynchronously to the web server role web requests which continue regardless of the state of the image processor. Therefore, we have calculated the multi-tenant VM requirements based on a simple linear multiplication of the CPU load per tenant.

IaaS usage charges (*OpEx*) are estimated considering the two most relevant cost components:

- A cloud data store – made up of a NoSQL Table structure (using the Microsoft Azure Table service) and an object store (using the Microsoft Azure Blob Storage service). Table and blob storage are platform services that allow a more fine-grained costing. As such, these need to be considered on an individual service base.
- A cloud compute architecture – made up of a separate compute resource for the web server of the web application (Web Role Virtual Machine), and a separate compute component for carrying out the image processing functions, such as barcode reading (Worker Role Virtual Machine).

Our calculation is based on the Microsoft Azure services pricing reported in Tables 4, 5, and 6. In order to forecast the usage of cloud storage resources, we used actual historical data over an eleven-month period from an existing average-sized tenant with a typical application usage pattern. To estimate the computing resources required, we monitored the usage and performance statistics during a snapshot of the operational use of the application by the same typical user. Tables 7, 8, and 9 summarize the usage profile adopted in the calculation.

Table 4. Blob storage prices (adapted from [53]).

Service	Redundancy	Cool tier price	General purpose price
Price per GB/Month space	Local	€ 0.013	€ 0.020
	Geo	€ 0.025	€ 0.041
Price per 10,000 transactions	Local	€ 0.084	€ 0.003
	Geo	€ 0.169	€ 0.003
Price per GB data access write	Local	€ 0.002	-
	Geo	€ 0.004	-

Table 5. Table storage prices (adapted from [53]).

	Redundancy	Price
Price per Entity/GB/Month	Local redundant	€ 0.059
	Geo redundant	€ 0.085
Price per 10,000 transactions (PUT)	Local redundant	€ 0.003
	Geo redundant	€ 0.003

Table 6. Compute prices (adapted from [53]).

VM type	No. of CPU cores	Annual cost Azure VM (€)	VM type	No. of CPU cores	Annual cost Azure VM (€)
a1	1	598.18	d4	8	8,936.93
a2	2	1,205.28	d1 v2	1	1,107.07
a3	4	2,401.63	d2 v2	2	2,232.00
a4	8	4,812.19	d3 v2	4	4,464.00
d1	1	1,107.07	d4 v2	8	8,936.93
d2	2	2,232.00	d5 v2	16	17,873.86
d3	4	4,464.00	d2 v3	2	1,589.18

Table 7. Usage profile of a typical tenant (adapted from [53]).

Items	Size
Total number of scanned documents per annum	145,853
Average number of document table entities per month	14,675
Number of peak entities per day	3,551
Number of peak entities per hour	1,137
Average table entity size (in bytes)	2,160
Average scanned image file size (in Kilobytes)	666
Average template file size (in bytes)	2,200

Table 8. Forecasted input parameters (adapted from [53]).

Per tenant	End of year		
	1	2	3
Number of documents	176,105	352,210	528,314
Document table size (in Gigabytes)	0.380	0.761	1.141
Number of image blobs	176,105	352,210	528,314
Image blobs size (in Gigabytes)	117	235	352
Document template file blobs	2	3	6
Total template blob storage (in bytes)	4,400	8,800	13,200

Table 9. Summary parameter values (adapted from [53]).

Workload	%
Web role peak CPU load	67.1%
Web role average CPU load	31.5%
Worker role peak CPU load	24.3%
Worker role average CPU load	10.4%

Table 10. Migration and implementation costs (adapted from [53]).

Implementation phase	Cost (€)
Implementation consultancy costs – business analysis (Contract hours)	16,078
Implementation consultancy costs – security design (Contract hours)	27,237
Implementation consultancy costs – design and development (Contract hours)	80,662
Project management and implementation design (Staff Salaries)	16,265
Development and Testing (Staff Salaries)	17,465
Non-staff or non-contractor costs (Cloud Testbed subscription, test equipment, travel)	10,940
Total	168,647

5.3   Experimentation – Usage and Cost

Table 10 summarizes the estimated implementation and migration costs for the SP (€168,647). The most significant cost component, which represents 47.83% of the overall migration costs, is by far consultancy costs for design and development, followed by security design (16.15%). Such a significant amount of upfront migration costs further highlights the need to include such costs into TCO estimation to inform both adoption and pricing decisions.

Tables 11, 12, and 13 summarize IaaS usage costs estimated as a linear combination of usage parameters and price of each service. Note that these pragmatic/empirical observations stem from experiments in a live feasibility study and have been implemented on the basis of the following assumptions:

Table 11. Blob storage costs (adapted from [53]).

Costs per tenant	Space cost (€)		Transactions cost (€)	
Redundancy	Local	Geo	Local	Geo
End year 1	8.87	17.80	1.48	2.97
End year 2	26.60	53.41	1.48	2.97
End year 3	44.33	89.02	1.48	2.97
	Data access write cost (€)		Total cost (€)	
Redundancy	Local	Geo	Local	Geo
End year 1	1.48	2.96	11.83	23.73
End year 2	4.43	8.87	32.52	65.25
End year 3	7.39	14.78	53.21	106.77

Note: Blob storage costs for template files were ignored due to their negligible amount.

Table 12. Table storage costs (adapted from [53]).

Costs per tenant	Space Cost (€)		Transactions Cost (€)		Total Cost (€)	
Redund.	LR	GR	LR	GR	LR	GR
End year 1	0.13	0.19	0.05	0.05	0.19	0.25
End year 2	0.40	0.58	0.05	0.05	0.46	0.63
End year 3	0.67	0.97	0.05	0.05	0.73	1.02

Note: LR (Local Redundant); GR (Geo Redundant); Redund. (Redundancy)

Table 13. Compute costs (adapted from [53]).

End year	Clients migrated	Number of VMs (WeR)	Number of VMs (WoR)	Storage costs (LR) (€)
1	80	6	2	946
2	80	18	4	3,548
3	80	30	6	7,805
		Storage costs (GR) (€)	Compute costs (WS) (€)	Compute costs (IP) (€)
1	80	1,898	9,536	3,179
2	80	7,118	28,606	6,357
3	80	15,660	47,676	9,536

Note: WeR (Web Role); WoR (Worker Role); LR (Local Redundant); GR (Geo Redundant); WS (Web Server VMs); IP (Image Processing VMs).

- The existing deployment does not include any data caching which would obviously reduce the CPU overhead and data storage access costs.
- There is no optimization of the queries to the table service to optimize CPU load over the TCO estimation period.
- There is no performance tuning on the application and/or on the platform during the TCO estimation period.
- There is no smoothing effect of multiple tenants sharing the same application compute resources.

The use case we present in this chapter involves a significant image-processing component resulting in high upload- and download- volumes and the in-cloud processing of images. The most critical challenge at the architectural level was to select the optimal Virtual Machine type from the available types on the Microsoft Azure platform; we carried out a benchmark study of the performance of the different "flavors" of the role VMs when running the data layer functions of the new application. The costs presented in Tables 11, 12, and 13 are based on the D2-V3 VM type which represented

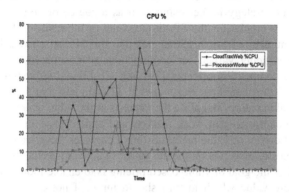

Fig. 2. Compute usage over a twenty-minute monitoring period [53].

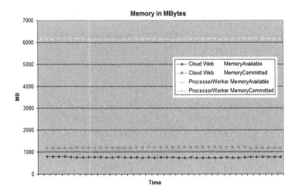

Fig. 3. Storage usage over a twenty-minute monitoring period [53].

the best trade-off between TCO and SLA requirements on the basis of the average tenant usage.

Among different TCO components, compute is by far the most significant (€129,701), and also the most fluctuating resource (see Fig. 2). As such, its efficient and effective usage should be the main concern of the SP. Storage, as predicted, is relatively stable and predictable with essentially fixed costs (see Fig. 3), and accounts for a very tiny portion of the TCO (€293.31 – 0.001%). The heavy image processing results in higher-than-normal network bandwidth and storage requirements. As a consequence, the observations should also hold for applications with less data volume and would thus cover the majority of typical transactional business applications.

6   Right-Pricing of SaaS Service

Once a SP has established the costs of cloud delivery including compute, storage, and migration, if appropriate, the price can be determined using Eq. 1 as outlined in Sect. 3.3.

At this point in time, the SP typically must decide on their pricing strategy driven by their overall strategic objectives i.e. determine the value for μ. The selection of an appropriate pricing strategy is increasing seen as a source of competitive advantage thus right-pricing is crucial for the SP, in the cloud or otherwise [30].

There are a number of pricing strategies that the SP can choose from, the most common strategies being variants or combinations of cost-based, demand-driven or value-based, and competition-oriented [29, 38]. Cost-based strategies determine the price level using cost accounting. Harmon et al. [26] suggest that these approaches are short-term, tactical in nature, and place the interests of the seller over the interests of the buyer leading to overpricing in weak markets and underpricing in strong markets. In contrast, demand-driven or value-based costing recognizes the price that a customer is willing to pay, mostly, depends on the customer's value requirements, not the SP. For Harmon et al. [26], the goal of value-based pricing is to enable more profitable pricing by capturing more value which in turn should input, if not determine, the level of product (development) costs that the company is willing to incur or not. While commentators suggest that this is the best overall approach to take [29, 31], it is not without drawbacks. Hinterhuber [29] notes the difficulty in obtaining and interpreting the necessary data to measure customer value and that in some cases, value-based pricing can lead to relatively high prices. Competition-oriented pricing is based on anticipated or observed price levels of competitors for determining price points [29]. The weakness in competition-based pricing is that again customer willingness to pay or costs are not necessarily taken in to account [29]. Each of these pricing strategies are prevalent in cloud computing [1]. It should be noted that profitability may or not be a goal in initial pricing strategies. SPs may offer unprofitable software services (including zero pricing) for a variety of reasons in order to drive market expansion or maintain customer satisfaction levels [30, 59]. As such, μ may be negative. For each pricing strategy outlined, TCO remains a useful calculation and indeed can help address the drawbacks in each strategy.

For our purposes, right pricing is combinatorial approach taking in to account the costs of cloud deployment but also scalability. Scalability, in this context, represents future customer demand. μ therefore becomes a variable that can be used to support the testing all pricing strategies at different levels through scenario analysis or even lean startup methodologies. Additionally, once a pricing strategy has been decided, a specific pricing structure must be agreed e.g. pay-per-use, annual or monthly subscription per user etc.

7 Conclusions and Future Developments

Our literature review highlighted a clear lack of processes integrating software architecture and costing within a cloud migration scenario. This chapter aims to fill such a gap by investigating the link between architectural decisions and the impact on costing in cloud migration and therefore making an initial contribution in this context [42]. Specifically, we have identified the major determinants of SaaS usage costs and integrated them into one single process to estimate the corresponding I/PaaS costs. This would represent the basis for defining the pricing a SaaS licensing model, and ultimately impact the profit margins of an SP. Due to the differences in factors and account types between the IaaS/PaaS providers, a generic, formalized model cannot exist. Thus, our aim was to identify the factors influencing this calculation and to illustrate this through a real-life case study.

As no single formula to easily determine right-scaling and right-pricing was identified in our literature review, in this chapter we propose an initial process for estimating operating costs and dependencies, and architecture-related costs.

Cloud adoption, like all technology investments, results in direct tangible costs such as cloud resources but also in intangible costs, e.g., change management, vendor management, risk mitigation etc. [47]. In our case study, we have moved beyond merely operating costs by including some of these indirect cost components. However, our example does not aim to provide a comprehensive list of such costs. Furthermore, the research presented in this chapter is subject to a series of limitations which curtail its generalizability, but it also presents avenues for future research. First, we have focused on a business-to-business SP targeting small and medium enterprises, and to a single cloud service provider. As such, our conclusion is not directly generalizable to business-to-consumer SPs. Further studies may account for more complex models suitable for larger and more mature organizations or may seek to compare functionality, quality and costs across multiple providers [24].

Second, we did not consider recent developments in cloud architectures like container technology and microservices architectures, which are an increasing feature in the enterprise cloud and enabling new provisioning and payment models, new services like serverless computing (also referred to as 'function-as-a-service'), which will radically change how SPs conceptualize costs and pricing. The adoption of serverless computing, for example, is growing significantly in order to increase efficiencies and provisioning speeds. This relatively new paradigm of cloud computing envisages a model of computing where effectively all resources are pooled including hardware, operating systems and runtime environments [28]. As a result, an SP only concerns themselves with relatively lightweight, single purpose stateless functions that can be executed on demand without consuming any resources until the point of execution. The serverless paradigm introduces greater separation of concerns between cloud service providers and SPs to the extent that much more responsibility is transferred to the cloud service provider. In addition, the SP benefits from much less complexity but also benefits from a lower cost of deployment related to the lightweight nature of functions and by cloud service pricing driven at the level of execution runtime for computer code rather than how long an instance is running [18]. The market for serverless computing is expected to grow to US$7.72 billion by 2021 [44]; as such, it is not surprising that many of the major cloud service providers have entered the market including AWS (Lambda), Microsoft (Azure Function), Google (Cloud Function), and IBM (Bluemix OpenWhisk). Research on serverless computing is at a very early stage of development and is primarily based on AWS Lambda [43]. While most of the research is focused on use cases, Lynn et al. [43] report a small number of studies that report cost efficiencies resulting from serverless implementations [40, 60, 61]. Given the novelty of serverless computing, the novelty of serverless pricing models, emerging use cases, and the dearth of research on business value and serverless migration, this area would seem to be a fruitful area for research moving forward. As other novel cloud services emerge, there will be a need for business value research, and TCO research specifically, not least fog computing [10], edge computing [54], cloud service brokerage and enterprise app marketplaces [50], quantum computing as a service [55], and self-organizing self-managing heterogeneous clouds [64].

Our work shows that there is a need for an integrated perspective accommodating architecture and cost in order to provide a clear basis for service pricing and revenue, and that the traditional TCO approaches cannot be applied without adaptation. Even though this chapter focuses on TCO, the same need for adaptation applies to other value assessment methodologies. As such, they present additional avenues for future research. Our chapter also highlights the need for collaboration between business, accounting and computer science researchers. As businesses become more and more reliant on cloud computing, such a collaboration is essential for providing a comprehensive understanding of the financial implications of adopting specific software architectures in the cloud computing context. This likely requires not only adaptation in common activity-based and resource-based costing methodologies but also in software and systems design.

Acknowledgements. The research work described in this chapter was supported by the Irish Centre for Cloud Computing and Commerce, an Irish National Technology Centre funded by Enterprise Ireland and the Irish Industrial Development Authority.

References

1. Al-Roomi, M., Al-Ebrahim, S., Buqrais, S., Ahmad, I.: Cloud computing pricing models: a survey. Int. J. Grid Distrib. Comput. **6**(5), 93–106 (2013)
2. Andrikopoulos, V., Song, Z., Leymann, F.: Supporting the migration of applications to the cloud through a decision support system. In: IEEE Sixth International Conference on Cloud Computing (2013)
3. Anwar, A., Sailer, A., Kochut, A., Schulz, C.O., Segal, A., Butt, A.R.: Cost-aware cloud metering with scalable service management infrastructure. In: IEEE 8th International Conference on Cloud Computing, pp. 285–292 (2015)
4. Armbrust, M., et al.: A view of cloud computing. Commun. ACM **53**(4), 50–58 (2010)
5. Arnold, G., Davies, M.: Value-Based Management: Context and Application. Wiley, New York (2000)
6. Baden-Fuller, C., Haefliger, S.: Business models and techno-logical innovation. Long Range Plan. **46**(6), 419–426 (2013)
7. Balalaie, A., Heydarnoori, A., Jamshidi, P., Tamburri, D.A., Lynn, T.: Microservices migration patterns. Softw. Pract. Exp. **48**, 1–24 (2018)
8. Bain and Company: The Changing Faces of the Cloud (2017). http://www.bain.com/publications/articles/the-changing-faces-of-the-cloud.aspx. Accessed 28 Jan 2018
9. Berman, S.J., Kesterson-Townes, L., Marshall, A., Srivathsa, R.: How cloud computing enables process and business model innovation. Strategy Leadersh. **40**(4), 27–35 (2012)
10. Bonomi, F., Milito, R., Zhu, J., Addepalli, S.: Fog computing and its role in the internet of things. In: Proceedings of the First Edition of the MCC Workshop on Mobile Cloud Computing, pp. 13–16 (2012)
11. CFO Research: The Business Value of Cloud Computing: A Survey of Senior Finance Executives. CFO Publishing (2012). http://lp.google-mkto.com/rs/google/images/CFO%2520Research-Google_research%2520report_061512.pdf. Accessed 20 Jan 2018
12. Cusumano, M.A.: The changing labyrinth of software pricing. Commun. ACM **50**(7), 19–22 (2007)
13. Cusumano, M.A.: The changing software business: moving from products to services. Computer **41**(1), 20–27 (2008)
14. DaSilva, C.M., Trkman, P., Desouza, K., Lindic, J.: Disruptive technologies: a business model perspective on cloud computing. Technol. Anal. Strateg. Manag. **25**(10), 1161–1173 (2013)
15. Dillon, T., Wu, C., Chang, E.: Cloud computing: issues and challenges. In: IEEE International Conference on Advanced Information Networking and Applications, pp. 27–33 (2010)
16. D'souza A., Kabbedijk, J., Seo, D., Jansen, S., Brinkkemper, S.: Software-as-a-service: implications for business and technology in product software companies. In: Pacific Asia Conference on Information Systems (2012)
17. Durkee, D.: Why cloud computing will never be free. Commun. ACM **53**(5), 62–69 (2010)

18. Eivy, A.: Be wary of the economics of "serverless" cloud computing. IEEE Cloud Comput. **4**(2), 6–12 (2017)
19. Farbey, B., Finkelstein, A.: Evaluation in software engineering: ROI, but more than ROI. Working Paper Series - Department of Computer Science University College London – LSE, (2000). http://is.lse.ac.uk/all_wp.htmS
20. Farbey, B., Land, F., Targett, D.: How to Assess Your IT Investment: A study of Methods and Practice. Butterworth-Heinemann, Oxford (1993)
21. Ferrante, D.: Software licensing models: what's out there? IT Prof. **8**(6), 24–29 (2006)
22. Filiopoulou, E., Mitropoulo, P., Tsadimas, A.: Integrating cost analysis in the cloud: a SoS approach. In: 11th International Conference on Innovations in Information Technology (IIT) (2015)
23. Giardino, C., Bajwa, S.S., Wang, X., Abrahamsson, P.: Key challenges in early-stage software startups. In: Lassenius, C., Dingsøyr, T., Paasivaara, M. (eds.) XP 2015. LNBIP, vol. 212, pp. 52–63. Springer, Cham (2015). https://doi.org/10.1007/978-3-319-18612-2_5
24. Gilia, P., Sood, S.: Automatic selection and ranking of cloud providers using service level agreements. Int. J. Comput. Appl. **72**(11), 45–52 (2013)
25. Han, Y.: Cloud computing: case studies and total costs of ownership. Inf. Technol. Libr. **30**(4), 198–206 (2011)
26. Harmon, R., Demirkan, H., Hefley, B., Auseklis, N.: Pricing strategies for information technology services: a value-based approach. In: Hawaii International Conference on System Sciences (HICSS), pp. 1–10 (2009)
27. Heilig, L., Voß, S.: Decision analytics for cloud computing: a classification and literature review. In: Bridging Data and Decisions, pp. 1–26 (2014)
28. Hendrickson, S., Sturdevant, S., Harter, T., Venkataramani, V., Arpaci-Dusseau, A.C., Arpaci-Dusseau, R.H.: Serverless computation with openlambda. Elastic **60**, 1–7 (2016)
29. Hinterhuber, A.: Customer value-based pricing strategies: why companies resist. J. Bus. Strategy **29**(4), 41–50 (2008)
30. Hinterhuber, A., Liozu, S.M.: Is innovation in pricing your next source of competitive advantage? Bus. Horiz. **57**, 413–423 (2014)
31. Ingenbleek, P., Debruyne, M., Frambach, R.T., Verhallen, T.M.: Successful new product pricing practices: a contingency approach. Mark. Lett. **14**(4), 289–305 (2003)
32. ISACA: Calculating Cloud ROI: From the Customer Perspective (2012). https://www.isaca.org/knowledge-center/research/researchdeliverables/pages/calculating-cloud-roi-from-the-customer-perspective.aspx. Accessed 20 Jan 2018
33. Jamshidi, P., Ahmad, A., Pahl, C.: Cloud migration research: a systematic review. IEEE Trans. Cloud Comput. **1**(2), 142–157 (2013)
34. Jamshidi, P., Pahl, C., Chinenyeze, S., Liu, X.: Cloud migration patterns: a multi-cloud service architecture perspective. In: International Workshop on Engineering Service Oriented Applications – WESOA 2014 (2014)
35. Jinesh, V.: Migrating your existing applications to the AWS cloud. A Phase-driven Approach to Cloud Migration (2010). http://docs.huihoo.com/amazon/aws/whitepapers/Migrating-your-Existing-Applications-to-the-AWS-Cloud-October-2010.pdf. Accessed 21 Jan 2018
36. Karunakaran, S., Krishnaswamy, V., Rangaraja, P.S.: Business view of cloud: decisions, models and opportunities–a classification and review of research. Manag. Res. Rev. **38**(6), 582–604 (2015)
37. Laatikainen, G., Ojala, A.: SaaS architecture and pricing models. In: IEEE International Conference on Services Computing (SCC), pp. 597–604 (2014)
38. Lehmann, S., Buxmann, P.: Pricing strategies of software vendors. Bus. Inf. Syst. Eng. **1**(6), 452–462 (2009)

39. Leimbach, T., et al.: Potential and Impacts of Cloud Computing Services and Social Network Websites. Science and Technology Options Assessment (STOA) (2016). http://www.europarl.europa.eu/RegData/etudes/etudes/join/2014/513546/IPOL-JOIN_ET(2014) 513546_EN.pdf. Accessed 15 Aug 2016

40. Leitner, P., Cito, J., Stöckli, E.: Modelling and managing deployment costs of microservice-based cloud applications. In: Proceedings of the 9th International Conference on Utility and Cloud Computing, pp. 165–174 (2016)

41. Li, X., Li, Y., Liu, T., Qiu, J., Wang, F.: The method and tool of cost analysis for cloud computing. In: IEEE International Conference on Cloud Computing, pp. 93–100 (2009)

42. Li, H., Zhong, L., Liu, J., Li, B., Xu, K.: Cost-effective partial migration of VoD services to content clouds. In: IEEE International Conference on Cloud Computing, pp. 203–210 (2011)

43. Lynn, T., Rosati, P., Lejeune, A., Emeakaroha, V.: A preliminary review of enterprise serverless cloud computing (function-as-a-service) platforms. In: IEEE International Conference on Cloud Computing Technology and Science (CloudCom), pp. 162–169 (2017)

44. Market and Markets: Function-as-a-Service Market by User Type (Developer-Centric and Operator-Centric), Application (Web & Mobile Based, Research & Academic), Service Type, Deployment Model, Organization Size, Industry Vertical, and Region - Global Forecast to 2021 (2017). https://www.marketsandmarkets.com/Market-Reports/function-as-a-service-market-127202409.html. Accessed 2 Aug 2018

45. Marston, S., Li, Z., Bandyopadhyay, S., Zhang, J., Ghalsasi, A.: Cloud computing - the business perspective. Decis. Support Syst. **51**(1), 176–189 (1999)

46. Martens, B., Walterbusch, M., Teuteberg, F.: Costing of cloud computing services: a total cost of ownership approach. In: 45th Hawaii International Conference on System Science (HICSS), pp. 1563–1572 (2012)

47. Misra, S.C., Mondal, A.: Identification of a company's suitability for the adoption of cloud computing and modelling its corresponding return on investment. Math. Comput. Model. **53** (3), 504–521 (2011)

48. Ojala, A.: Software renting in the era of cloud computing. In: IEEE 5th International Conference on Cloud Computing (CLOUD), pp. 662–669 (2012)

49. Pahl, C., Xiong, H., Walshe, R.: A comparison of on-premise to cloud migration approaches. In: Lau, K.-K., Lamersdorf, W., Pimentel, E. (eds.) ESOCC 2013. LNCS, vol. 8135, pp. 212–226. Springer, Heidelberg (2013). https://doi.org/10.1007/978-3-642-40651-5_18

50. Paulsson, V., Morrison, J., Emeakaroha, V., Lynn, T.: Cloud service brokerage: a systematic literature review using a software development lifecycle. In: 22nd Americas Conference on Information Systems (AMCIS) (2016)

51. Ronchi, S., Brun, A., Golini, R., Fan, X.: What is the value of an IT e-procurement system? J. Purchasing Supply Manag. **16**(2), 131–140 (2010)

52. Rosati, P., Fox, G., Kenny, D., Lynn, T.: Quantifying the financial value of cloud investments: a systematic literature review. In: IEEE International Conference on Cloud Computing Technology and Science (CloudCom), pp. 194–201 (2017)

53. Rosati, P., Fowley, F., Pahl, C., Taibi, D., Lynn, T.: Making the cloud work for software producers: linking architecture, operating cost and revenue. In: 8th International Conference on Cloud Computing and Services Science (CLOSER) (2018)

54. Shi, W., Cao, J., Zhang, Q., Li, Y., Xu, L.: Edge computing: vision and challenges. IEEE Internet Things J. **3**(5), 637–646 (2016)

55. Singh, H., Sachdev, A.: The quantum way of cloud computing. In: International Conference on Optimization, Reliability, and Information Technology (ICROIT), pp. 397–400 (2014)

56. Strebel, J., Stage, A.: An economic decision model for business software application deployment on hybrid cloud environments. Multikonferenz Wirtschaftsinformatik, MKWI (2010)

57. Taibi, D., Lenarduzzi, V., Pahl, C.: Processes, motivations and issues for migrating to microservices architectures: an empirical investigation. IEEE Cloud IEEE Cloud Comput. J. **4**(5), 22–32 (2017)
58. Taibi, D., Lenarduzzi, V., Pahl, C.: Architectural patterns for microservices: a systematic mapping study. In: 8th International Conference on Cloud Computing and Services Science (CLOSER) (2018)
59. Terho, H., Suonsyrjä, S., Karisalo, A., Mikkonen, T.: Ways to cross the rubicon: pivoting in software startups. In: Abrahamsson, P., Corral, L., Oivo, M., Russo, B. (eds.) PROFES 2015. LNCS, vol. 9459, pp. 555–568. Springer, Cham (2015). https://doi.org/10.1007/978-3-319-26844-6_41
60. Villamizar, M., et al.: Cost comparison of running web applications in the cloud using monolithic, microservice, and AWS lambda architectures. SOCA **11**(2), 233–247 (2017)
61. Wagner, B., Sood, A.: Economics of resilient cloud services. In: IEEE International Conference on Software Quality, Reliability and Security Companion (QRS-C), pp. 368–374 (2016)
62. Walterbusch, M., Martens, B., Teuteberg, F.: Evaluating cloud computing services from a total cost of ownership perspective. Manag. Res. Rev. **36**(6), 613–638 (2013)
63. Willcocks, L.P.: Evaluating the outcomes of information systems plans managing information technology evaluation—techniques and processes. In: Strategic Information Management: Challenges and Strategies in Managing Information Systems, pp. 271–294 (2001)
64. Xiong, H., et al.: CloudLightning: a self-organized self-managed heterogeneous cloud. In: Federated Conference on Computer Science and Information Systems (FedCSIS), pp. 749–758 (2017)
65. Yang, H., Tate, M.: A descriptive literature review and classification of cloud computing research. Commun. Assoc. Inf. Syst. **31**(1), 35–60 (2012)

Malicious Behavior Classification in PaaS

Cemile Diler Özdemir$^{(\boxtimes)}$, Mehmet Tahir Sandıkkaya, and Yusuf Yaslan

Computer Engineering Department, Istanbul Technical University,
Sarıyer, 34469 Istanbul, Turkey
{ozdemirc,sandikkaya,yyaslan}@itu.edu.tr

Abstract. PaaS delivery model let cloud customers share cloud provider resources through their cloud applications. This structure requires a strong security mechanism that isolates customer applications to prevent interference. For concurrent configurations of common providers, cloud applications are mostly deployed as server side web applications that share a common thread pool. In this paper, a malicious thread behavior detection framework that utilizes machine learning algorithms is proposed to classify whether the cloud platform executes a malicious flow in the currently active thread. The framework uses CPU metrics of worker threads and N-Gram frequencies of basic, privacy-friendly user operations as its features during machine learning phase. The proof of concept results are evaluated on a real-life cloud application scenario using Random Forest, Adaboost and Bagging ensemble learning algorithms. The scenario results indicate that the malicious request detection accuracy of the proposed framework is up to 87.6%. It is foreseen that better feature selection and targeted classifiers may end up with better ratios.

Keywords: Cloud security · PaaS · Malicious behavior ·
Machine learning

1 Introduction

The popular cloud computing concept permits cloud customers, which are mostly small to medium enterprises, rapidly enable an Internet-based service for their users on the resources of the cloud provider. This minimum-effort on-demand approach is highly adopted for the past ten years; therefore a Cisco report indicates that cloud data center workloads will be tripled from 2015 to 2020 [13]. On the other hand, there are still some prospective customers who have security concerns. Also, cloud providers are always in a quest for better security mechanisms to protect their valuable resources [2].

Most of the common PaaS providers offer web application platforms to their customers. The reason for that is twofold: First, many customers require web-oriented services to provide to their users. Second, there exists a well-known technology for this; therefore, adoption is considerably easy. As a result, this strategy is beneficial both for the PaaS providers and the PaaS customers. Since popular scripting languages (such as Ruby and Python) as well as virtualized

V. M. Muñoz et al. (Eds.): CLOSER 2018, CCIS 1073, pp. 215–232, 2019.
https://doi.org/10.1007/978-3-030-29193-8_11

platforms (such as Java and .NET) are commonly used in web development in recent years, providers build their servers on these popular technologies. Cloud customers can quickly customize their existing web applications, then deliver them to the providers to be served in the cloud. Thus, deploying many cloud applications is straight-forward when PaaS is built on top of web application servers.

The common benefit of rapid adoption to the cloud comes with a major flaw. Different cloud customers share PaaS platform resources (the most important resource is probably being the memory space from security perspective) and it requires isolation between customer applications to prevent interference between different applications. This interference can occur unconsciously or maliciously. For instance, a faulty application can consume most of the memory or CPU on the provided platform for many customers. Therefore, other customers are influenced; even there is no conscious attack to the PaaS platform. In addition, it is possible that maliciously acting customers can execute code to attack other customers or to the platform. Availability, confidentiality and integrity of PaaS are threaten for these reasons [12]. PaaS providers need a strong security mechanism to protect and isolate their customer applications and the platform itself.

Theoretically, a cloud application provision platform could be designed with different approaches. For instance, each cloud application may be a separate operating system process or each cloud application may reside in its own operating system for better isolation. On the other side of the spectrum, a cloud application may be organized as a single uninterrupted thread —as in cooperative fibers instead of preemptive threads. Both ends of the spectrum are acceptable when the crucial point is satisfied; the flow of execution must be as defined as the cloud customer programmed. The sole difference is, placing each cloud application in a separate operating system is extremely expensive in one hand and leaving the control of whole execution to cloud customer is too risky for the cloud provider on the other hand. The cloud providers are trying to balance the ease of adoption and lesser security risk for their resources when they choose their designs.

Currently, PaaS customers are limited to web applications due to leading PaaS providers Google[1], Heroku[2] and Amazon[3]. This approach has the advantage of rapid adoption as discussed before. Moreover, the providers may limit customer applications' access to trivial resources such as files or sockets via carefully set up permissions. However, memory and CPU are shared among multiple threads in web applications as well as per-request user behavior cannot be traced [17]. This vulnerability is left behind as a trade-off for ease of adoption instead of isolating memory and CPU via process containers [16].

The aim of this paper is to propose a security mechanism that can classify malicious flow of execution independent of the underlying approach; being a thread, a process or a separate operating system by observing simple, basic privacy-friendly access sequences of a task and the respective CPU metrics. This

---

[1] https://cloud.google.com/appengine/.

[2] https://www.heroku.com/.

[3] https://aws.amazon.com/elasticbeanstalk/.

is done by carefully setting entry and exit points for critical provider resources and observing them. In case of anomalies, these entry or exit points could also be used to terminate the execution of the malicious thread. Entry or exit points are not chosen to be resource specific, but rather operation specific. As a result, the detection mechanism cannot collect private data of the cloud customers; but only a statistical view of sequential resource access operations. This statistical view is enriched using machine learning techniques, then classified to detect malicious or benign behaviors.

1.1 Comparison with Other Security Mechanisms

Many intrusion detection mechanisms have been proposed for the security of PaaS clouds; including host based intrusion detection systems [1], network based intrusion detection systems [8], distributed intrusion detection systems [18] and hypervisor based intrusion detection systems [7]. One may note, aforementioned security mechanisms are not designed to isolate threads running on the same web application server. Intrusion detection systems are designed to detect intrusions from outside of a pre-defined secure perimeter, which does not exist in the cloud deployments. Further, the mentioned systems focus on network perimeter, operating system or virtualized set of operating systems rather than monitoring thread behavior. Therefore, they cannot consider isolation of customer applications hosted in the same process virtual machine.

Besides, it should be noted that an intrusion detection system could be beneficial in a PaaS deployment. Figure 1 presents PaaS service model in a layered approach. It can be observed that the customer has the responsibility only for the application and data layers. The bottom layers are managed by the cloud provider. Recalling where intrusion detection systems are affective, it is obvious that the cloud provider can effectively deploy an intrusion detection system to protect all resources from third parties. However, it will hardly help to protect the cloud applications or the underlying platform from another cloud application.

Apart from intrusion detection systems, there are other widely used security mechanisms in PaaS. These are either hardware or software based isolation mechanisms. Software mechanisms may isolate threads, processes or virtual machines of different users [3]. For instance, Heroku uses container-based isolation which groups operating system processes by kernel namespaces and resource allocations to isolate from other groups. Docker[4] is one of the most popular open-source container platform providers, which has been adopted by many PaaS providers. In addition, Cloud Foundry[5] also isolates its tenants using user-based isolation mechanisms. It is a traditional and widely used technique that each application runs as a different user within the operating system. However, sharing the same process virtual machine environment by multiple users requires runtime isolation mechanisms [23].

---

[4] https://www.docker.com/.
[5] https://www.cloudfoundry.org/.

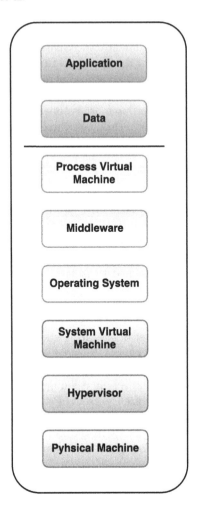

Fig. 1. The PaaS deployment model: The physical computer resides a hypervisor to monitor the operating systems through system virtual machines. This level of abstraction is mostly known as IaaS. On top of operating systems, many process virtual machine instances could be run. Each of these process virtual machines (E.g. JVM) may isolate an application, but not the threads within the same application. This level of abstraction is mostly known as PaaS. The process virtual machine may be configured as a web application server and the threads may belong to different cloud applications of different cloud customers [14].

Another widely used security mechanism that could be relevant might be virus or malware scanners. As malware scanners also seek for malicious behavior of executable files, historically they do this search mostly offline, simply via pattern matching. For sure, malwares evolved in time and their current codebase are so complex to be matched by patterns. Modern malware scanners search for malicious behavior by emulating malware behavior in a sandbox —still offline, before actually executing the file. This is conceptually different than cloud applications executed on a PaaS deployment. The application is paid to run as a web application within the same process scope with others. Moreover, cloud users may misbehave or feed malicious input that cannot be detected by offline checks. Therefore, the detection must be at runtime on the cloud.

1.2 Contributions

Note that, this paper is an extended version of authors' previously published work [14].

This paper presents a runtime-based security framework for multitenant PaaS providers to detect malicious behaviors using machine learning. The main contributions of this paper are summarized as follows:

- *Thread behavior detection framework*: A thread behavior detection framework is proposed. The functionality of this framework could be easily integrated into cloud applications through the provided PaaS platform. The framework is designed for PaaS providers which have many customer web applications in the same application server. In this deployment scenario, customers' web applications reside on the same process virtual machine, which is a single process from the operating system's perspective. The proposed framework is effective within this process virtual machine. It measures worker threads' CPU usage metrics and resource access sequence during a task to reason about an anomaly.
- *Well-selected privacy-friendly metrics*: The selected metrics that are required to classify the malicious execution are observable in the runtime. The collected features are independent from underlying mechanisms, yet dependent on the flow of the execution to complete a task. Being independent from threads, operating systems, programming languages or cloud infrastructures has two advantages. First, this approach does not leak any personally identifiable information. Second, it is adaptable to almost any architecture. Therefore, the features that are collected without any dependency are used to classify malicious or benign behaviors in a PaaS cloud.

Based on our contributions, things that makes the proposed security mechanism unique and novel are: First, the proposed mechanism does not assume there exists a secure perimeter as in intrusion detection systems. Therefore, it does not monitor network activity or collect any feature from network interfaces. The main focus is the current running thread. Second, the proposed mechanism does not make the assumption that every execution of an application are identical. Each execution of a cloud application may be radically different than others and only one of them may cause trouble in runtime. Regular malware scanners are far from detecting such cases even though they inspect customer code line by line.

The rest of this paper is organized as follows: Sect. 2 spots some light to the historical and recent studies on the topic. The proposed security mechanism is presented in the following Sect. 3. The experimental setup of the study is detailed in Sect. 4. Section 5 describes the selected feature set and classification algorithms applied to the extracted data. The results of the experiments are presented in Sect. 6. Finally, Sect. 7 concludes the paper and presents a discussion on the results.

2   Related Work

Many malicious behavior detection systems exist in the literature that utilizes machine learning algorithms [6,12]. Most of these are focused on intrusion detection systems to protect a perimetrized computer network infrastructure. Therefore, they mostly rely on categorizing transported packets by identifying their headers or part of their contents. These models generally extract the feature vector from data, packets, user input command sequences, log files, low-level system information and CPU/memory usage [22]. As a result, they might have a huge feature set that may probably cause privacy issues when used all together. Besides, as mentioned before, these intrusion detection systems differ from the proposed mechanism as they always assume a trusted perimeter to be protected. They hardly detect malicious activity that originates from the insiders. Note that, in PaaS deployments, the providers are willingly to accept the customers as tenants, thus insiders. Then, malicious activities may originate from these tenants or tenants' users. Therefore, an intrusion detection system cannot detect malicious user behavior after the request is once accepted to access internal resources. In practice, an intrusion detection system may exist independent of the proposed mechanism and controlled by the PaaS provider to protect the whole PaaS deployment against third party attackers; e.g. denial-of-service attackers.

Another protection mechanism that is worthy of mentioning for operating systems is malware scanners. These approach is beneficial when the user of a program is known beforehand. In that case, the program execution could be emulated offline, right before the program actually executes. Then, application's execution is permitted if the emulation does not match any known malicious pattern. During intelligent malware scanning, application programming interface (API) calls and machine instructions are widely used features [4]. Pirscoveanu et al. [15] used sequence, frequency and count of the windows platform system calls as main features to classify with Random Forest algorithm. This study can classify several malwares simultaneously with this approach. Fan et al. [6] also used API calls as features of their Malicious Sequential Pattern Malware Detection (MSPMD) framework. They applied modified Generalized Sequential Pattern algorithm for sequence mining with All-Nearest-Neighbor classifier to Windows Portable Executable (PE) samples. Uppal et al. [21] applied N-Gram algorithm to extract features from API sequences. Shabtai et al. [19] move to a lower level and utilized machine instruction data to extract features with N-Gram pattern from opcodes. Then, several classification algorithms are applied to extracted feature vector to detect unknown malicious applications. The given list of malware detection studies are close to the proposed approach as they monitor user behavior from their resource access then classify them. Still, they should go through the all code sequence to extract information about examined application. On the other hand, the proposed application collects information in runtime when resource access happens.

The main feature enrichment algorithm used in this study is N-gram. N-Gram algorithm has a history in prediction models as it is suitable for sequential data. Su et al. [20] utilized N-Gram model to predict future requests of users. This probabilistic prediction model aims to make best estimate for the users' next actions based on previous actions. Su et al.'s study does neither have a security focus nor they try to estimate malicious requests. Still, it is foreseen that N-Gram prediction model is adaptable to predict malicious behavior of users. Supporting that, N-Gram is applied to API calls and machine instructions data in the security domain [19,21]. These studies can provide only system level detection and prevention in the cloud deployments.

Malicious thread execution detection in PaaS clouds is a necessity even though the mentioned malware detection techniques' results are favorable. This necessity is a result that the proposed system covers an unexplored area for cloud computing security and may lead to cost benefits for cloud providers. The framework runs in the PaaS provider side, together with PaaS customers' cloud applications. This framework monitors thread behavior and collected information is analyzed offline to train a classifier that is used for runtime decision making afterwards.

3   Proposed Mechanism

The proposed mechanism is designed to cover the widest possible range of scenarios offered in the current PaaS ecosystem. Current PaaS providers offer their computational resources to their customers through threads as they offer web application provisions. The customers sometimes reside in the same process virtual machine. In that case, there is a risk of interference as they share the same process scope. Either the customers' cloud applications may interfere or the cloud applications may access provider's resources without permission. In such an adversarial model, the aim of the proposed method is not completely isolate cloud customers' access to the platform resources. The aim of the proposed model is to determine if the cloud customer is acting maliciously. This malicious act can occur consciously or unconsciously. An unconscious malicious act may occur as a result of an error or even if the customer application is programmed correctly, customer's user may misbehave. The aim is to detect the anomalous flow of execution independent from how the unwanted flow occurs. The maliciously acting threads can be stopped or at least kept away from accessing more resources right after they are classified as malicious by the proposed security framework.

Checkpoints are used to enable control over threads. As stopping threads prematurely could cause security problems on its own, the framework waits for the thread stop itself for a while after marking it as malicious. If the thread does not stop in the given interval, framework waits for the thread to be trapped in one of the checkpoints, then the execution is interrupted. Checkpoints are the methods where the application accesses any provider resources. Access to each PaaS resource is wrapped in a separate method. This could be easily managed through aspects [10]. Checkpoints are defined in enter and exit of resource consuming system methods and are identified using aspects because of its numerous advantages. First, time consumption of each resource access can be collected per-request without affecting privacy of the customers. The only leaked data is the sequence of the resource access and the time consumption in each resource. Second, the checkpoints are programmed to disrupt the execution of a thread if its behavior after it is classified as malicious by the framework. This is beneficial because the threads cannot request any more resources if they are classified as malicious.

The anatomy of a web application server must be noted to better describe the proposed mechanism. A web application server is not different from a regular web server when compared by its input and output. The difference lies how it responds to requests internally. For each request it receives, instead of a static file to respond back, it executes an application and responds the output of that application. Simply, a web application server stitches the input and output streams of applications to web requests and responses. The web application might be designed dynamic and behave dynamically with respect to user input carried on user requests. Then, a web application might produce several dynamic responses. From the operating system perspective, a web application server is a single process. It holds a pool of threads. When it receives a request, it chooses a random thread from the pool, dispatches relevant user and execution flow to thread and waits for the execution to conclude. Then, the thread is sent back to the pool to serve another user for another execution.

The framework focuses on web application users' request based analysis as the main execution cycle takes place on a request-oriented execution. Fundamentally, the mechanism distinctively analyses each worker thread per request of each user, so even capable of classify one-time unconscious malicious activity of a trustworthy user. This feature of the proposed mechanism is especially useful in the scenario of adversaries capture someone's credentials then logged into an application to cause harm.

Proposed mechanism detects maliciously acting threads on the cloud platform using machine learning techniques. First, classification features are selected to be measured by proposed framework. Instant CPU usage and cumulative CPU usage per request are two attributes of the feature vector. Moreover, feature vector contains three more attributes per request. These attributes are resource access duration, resource access type and resource access sequence. Access type feature is mapped to CRUD (create, read, update, delete) functions and contains information about requested function. Sequence feature holds order of requested functions. It is so informative to have sequence of these operations to obtain frequency of the operation and transaction between each operation.

Note that, collection of the mentioned data is a time and resource consuming process. The framework performs some optimizations to enhance data collection, such as using running averages instead of storing each value separately or setting up epochs for cumulative metrics. Otherwise, data collection itself turn out to be the main consumption of resources. Moreover, privacy of the cloud customer or user is considered during data collection. Proposed mechanism observes only thread behavior and collects processor usage and requested operation sequences on runtime. Finally framework classifies malicious behavior of the cloud customer or user using collected feature vector. It is considered that, for the cloud customer, this feature set is far less invasive than a malware analysis tool that inspects each line of code or an intrusion detection system that inspects each packet separately. The cloud user's privacy concerns mostly rely on their relationship with the cloud customer. Still, it could be considered that a cloud user who is willing to use cloud customer's application in the cloud is probably signed a service level agreement to support this privacy decision.

Proposed mechanism processes the collected data using N-Gram algorithm to enrich the feature set. N-Gram represents a contiguous sequence of N items from a given list of items and predicts the next item. In natural language processing these items can be letters or words, in speech recognition items can be phonemes and in malware analysis they can be system calls or machine instruction sequence. In the proposed mechanism, operation sequence is one the features that is beneficial to be enriched and the set of operations is represented as $O = \{Create, Read, Update, Delete\}$. Table 1 represents sample tokenized operation sequences data and their types to visualize structure of the train data. This sequence data is represented as string and these tokens are converted into a set of new attributes using Weka NGramTokenizer API with the values $N_{min} = 1$ and $N_{max} = 5$. After this filtering process, new feature vector has 132 new attributes according to occurrence frequency of the transactions between each operation from the sequence text data. Operation transactions are visualized in Fig. 3.

Many classification algorithms are utilized with the enriched feature set where some of them stand out. The classifiers performed better with the training data after feature vector measured and tokenized with the N-Gram. In order to detect malicious thread, different classification algorithms have been evaluated. After the comparison of test results, Random Forest classifier is integrated into proposed framework as the most accurate classifier.

Classification is made in the proposed framework based on the aforementioned trained classifiers. Proposed framework uses runtime observation to classify a request. Figure 2 shows classification process of runtime observations. Proposed framework is integrated into an experimental cloud web application that is explained in detail in Sect. 4. Note that, the proposed behavior based system does not require a heavy signature database. The framework could be integrated into a PaaS deployment easily with previously known good parameters, then updated accordingly.

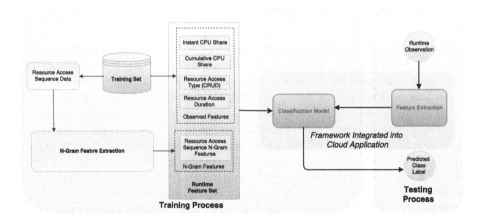

Fig. 2. The overall architecture of the proposed framework for malicious thread behavior detection. The framework extracts four features from any PaaS web application server deployment in a cost-effective and privacy-friendly way. The collected metrics are: instant CPU share of a thread in the web application server, CPU share of a thread over a period of time, a thread's access type (create, read, update, delete) to critical resources (databases, files, sockets, etc.) and finally the duration of this access. These features are enriched with N-Gram algorithm based on access sequence during training phase. In the test phase, a thread's behavior is classified as benign or malicious based on trained knowledge [14].

4   Experimental Setup

The proposed mechanism is tested on a demo cloud system that contains an event ticketing application connected to a relational database. Conventional paths of usage are recorded and repeated with Apache JMeter to reproduce a set of regular requests. Realistic attack scenarios are considered and also added to the query set of JMeter. Experimental ticketing cloud application is composed of basic user operations that may be mapped to CRUD (create, read, update, delete) operations on a database. These four main operations are: add, delete, read, and update. Depending on the payload of the request an event, a user, a ticket may be added, read, updated or deleted from the cloud application. The application also includes many meta elements such as text, graphics, audio, and video. Training set contains add, delete, read and update functions either as a regular or a malicious operation. Regular requests are defined as common user behavior depending on cloud application's scope and goal. On the other hand, malicious operations are selected from a wide set of possibilities. Among many other possibilities, an unexpected content may be added to the database, whole table may be dropped, a large set of bogus data may be inserted. The attack scenarios are produced by considering cross-site scripting, SQL-injection, database modification and file system access scenarios.

The final set contains ten sets that include nearly 1% malicious requests and the total number of queries is 100 000. Each experiment is conducted with 10 000 requests of which nearly 100 of the requests are malicious. Each experiment is repeated 10 times. In the final set, there are exactly 1000 malicious requests and 99 000 regular requests. The results are presented as the average of 10 independent experiments.

Note that, it is assumed that, a PaaS customer's cloud application reside in a JVM and deployed the proposed framework. This is amongst the most common approaches in the current PaaS deployments. Therefore, utilizing Java in the experiments is realistic even though the proposed mechanism could be adopted to other systems as well. Java Management Extensions (JMX) is utilized to measure processor shares, memory and average time consumption for a user request.

5   Used Feature Set and Classification Algorithms

In this paper, N-Gram feature extraction algorithm is applied to feature set and its brief description is given in Subsect. 5.1. After the feature extraction, ensemble learning algorithms, Random Forest, Bagging and AdaBoost, are run on the data to evaluate their accuracy in proposed framework. These classification algorithms are described respectively in Subsects. 5.2, 5.3 and 5.4.

5.1   N-Gram Features

N-Gram models sequence of n elements, which is usually sequential tokens such as letters, words or phonemes. Though, this paper utilizes N-Gram probabilistic model to predict the type of the next operation X_i based on previous operation sequence $X_{i-(n-1)}, X_{i-(n-2)}, \ldots X_{i-1}$. Likelihood of the next element in the sequence is symbolized as $P(X_i \mid X_{i-(n-1)}, X_{i-(n-2)}, \ldots X_{i-1})$ and it is based on $(n-1)$ order Markov model.

The proposed framework uses Weka API's NGramTokenizer filter to the collected operation sequence data to enrich the sequence information to be used in the classifiers feature sets. NGramTokenizer's output is a new features vector that contains probability of each gram. An example data is shown in Table 1. N-Gram splits the given sequence data with the minimum and maximum grams. The frequencies and transitions of each operation that illustrated in Fig. 3 is calculated. When N-Gram is configured with larger n values, it stores more context with larger sequence information. Storing more context provides better prediction but it requires more memory usage and time consumption. However, prediction gets worse with the small N while memory usage and time consumption decrease. Eventually, N is given with the interval of $[1, 5]$ that provides reasonable efficiency of prediction accuracy, time consumption and memory usage in the proposed framework during training phase.

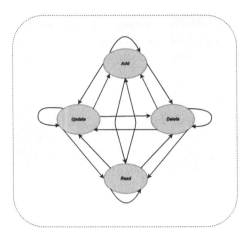

Fig. 3. Transitions, $S_t \rightarrow S_{t+1}$, between states. States represent resource access types and transitions can be evaluated with this state machine [14].

Table 1. Sample data is shown below for N-Gram classification. N-Gram classifies regular or malicious threads only by the sequence of their access types. It does not check which resource threads access or for how long. It also does not check the parameters of the operations. Such information is fed into the classification model by other features.

Operation sequence	Request type
Read → Read	Regular
Read → Read → Add → Update	Regular
Delete → Delete → Delete	Malicious
Update	Regular

5.2 Random Forest Classifier

Random Forest is an ensemble learning method that grows many random classification or regression trees. Trees vote for the most popular class and the result is the combination of these tree predictors. One advantage of Random Forest is it runs efficiently on large datasets. Moreover, Random Forest algorithm has randomness in tree construction which minimizes the correlation. This property is especially useful when dealing with several execution traces in which some of them could be malicious. In addition, Random Forest algorithm does not overfit to data [5]. Rapidly increasing cloud data traffic requires memory and time efficient algorithms to run with big data. These characteristics make random forest algorithm applicable to classify malicious behavior in cloud deployments. The pseudo code of the random forest algorithm is given in Algorithm 1.

Algorithm 1. Random Forest generates ensemble of trees using randomly selected instances and features.

```
 1: procedure RANDOMFOREST
 2:     f ← features
 3:     N ← number of trees
 4:     H ← ∅
 5:     for i = 1 to T do
 6:         n_i ← bootstrap samples from original data
 7:         g_i ← GROWTREE(n_i, f)
 8:         H ← H ∪ g_i
 9: procedure GROWTREE(n,f)
10:     f_i ← subset of f
11:     best split among f_i
12:     return tree
```

5.3 Bagging

Bagging [11], also called Bootstrap Aggregating, is an ensemble technique that uses classifiers trained on instances generated by randomly drawn examples, with replacement. Therefore, each classifier in the ensemble is obtained with a different random sampling of the training dataset. The final decision is given by majority vote over individual classifiers' outputs.

5.4 AdaBoost

$$H(x) = sign\left(\sum_{t=1}^{T} \alpha_t h_t(x)\right) \quad (1)$$

AdaBoost, short for Adaptive Boosting, is a successful boosting algorithm that constructs a strong classifier $H(x)$ as linear combination of weak classifiers $h_t(x)$ shown in Eq. 1. Prediction of the class label $H(x)$ is made by calculating the weighted average of the weak predictions $h_t(x)$. The weight, α_t, is based on the classifier's error rate which infers the number of misclassified instances over the training set divided by the training set size.

Adaboost algorithm is known to be used effectively in intrusion detection systems as it has low computational complexity, high detection rate, and low false-alarm rate [9]. Therefore, it is chosen as one of the candidate classifiers to compare its accuracy in the proposed framework.

6 Experimental Results

Each published result is obtained after ten-fold cross validation for statistical correctness. Experimental results are evaluated based on the percentage of incorrectly classified instances, precision values, recall values and F-measure. These measurements are calculated with respect to the True Positive (TP), False Positive (FP), True Negative (TN) and False Negative (FN) rates as shown on the confusion matrix presented in Table 2.

$$Misclassified = \frac{FP + FN}{FP + TP + FN + TN} \tag{2}$$

$$Precision = \frac{TP}{TP + FP} \tag{3}$$

$$Recall = \frac{TP}{TP + FN} \tag{4}$$

$$F\text{-}Measure = 2 \times \frac{Precision \times Recall}{Precision + Recall} \tag{5}$$

Percentages of incorrectly classified instances are calculated according to Eq. 2. Sequentially, precision, recall and F-Measure calculations are shown in Eqs. 3, 4 and 5, respectively.

Table 2. Confusion matrix legend.

		Predicted	
		Malicious	Regular
Actual	Malicious	TP	FN
	Regular	FP	TN

Table 3. Classifiers' result without resource access sequence data [14].

	Random forest	Bagging	AdaBoost
Misclassified %	0.888	0.9111	0.986
Precision	0.6204	0.6164	0.5133
Recall	0.299	0.242	0.291
F-Measure	0.4011	0.3457	0.3690

Table 3 shows used classifiers' results without resource access sequence enrichment with N-Gram algorithm. Operation sequence feature is not evaluated in these experiments. This feature set has processor usage, resource usage duration and operation types of the user's execution. However, these operations of user's are not sequenced. Therefore, classifiers cannot reason about their order, but only if they appear in a malicious act or not. Random Forest classification results on this dataset have a large number of incorrectly classified instances. In addition, Bagging and AdaBoost algorithms with J48 decision tree base classifier do not obtain better accuracy than Random Forest algorithm.

Table 5 shows classification results with N-Gram feature extraction. Operation sequence features are filtered with the values $N_{min} = 1$ and $N_{max} = 5$

and feature extraction process in framework is shown in Fig. 2. After enriched feature extraction, the new feature vector includes the processor usage, resource usage duration, operation types of the user's execution and generated N-Gram features that includes the sequence of executed operations.

It is clear that Table 5 includes more accurate results than Table 3 for all classifiers as expected for the same classification instances. The number of misclassified instances drop off to 162 from 888 after the operation sequence feature is added.

Table 4. Confusion matrix of the proposed framework. The proposed framework runs Random Forest classifier with N-Gram feature extraction into feature set [14].

		Predicted	
		Malicious	Regular
Actual	Malicious	876	124
	Regular	38	98962

Table 5. Classifiers' results enhanced with N-Gram feature extraction [14].

	Random forest	Bagging	AdaBoost
Misclassified %	0.162	0.192	0.2
Precision	0.9584	0.9646	0.9381
Recall	0.876	0.839	0.857
F-Measure	0.9153	0.8968	0.8954

Among the classifiers, Random Forest algorithm gets the most accurate and promising results as presented in Table 5. Only 162 instances are labeled incorrectly out of 100 000. 38 of regular instances out of 99 000 are classified as malicious. This means, only 38 valid requests among 100 000 requests will be stopped as a result of suspicion. This is a low false-alarm rate for cloud providers and it is hoped to be enhanced further in the future. 124 malicious instances out of 1000 are classified as regular request. This accuracy rate is not stellar; but promising for future studies. It is foreseen that better approaches to detect malicious behavior may help to decrease false negative rate. Table 4 shows the overall confusion matrix of Random Forest algorithm with enriched N-Gram feature extraction. Precision result given in Table 5 indicates that, a malicious predicted instance is classified correctly with the probability of 0.95 by the proposed framework. This result could be misleading as most of the requests are benign and the experimented data is unbalanced. The recall value, which may indicate this unbalanced classification, shows that a malicious request is detected by the proposed framework with the probability of 0.87. Since classes are unbalanced F-Measure is evaluated as the main success criteria of the framework to inspect if it is close to its best value at 1. F-Measure value, being 0.91, indicates that proposed framework is unbalanced, yet accurate on both malicious and regular classes.

7   Discussion and Conclusion

A malicious behavior detection framework to be used in PaaS clouds by the cloud providers is proposed in this study. This presented approach utilizes machine learning techniques and especially beneficial in the concurrent multitenant PaaS ecosystem. Cloud customers share the resources of the cloud providers within the same process scope in the current ecosystem. This multitenant approach may lead to possible security flaws that may be rooted from cloud customers that share the same cloud provider or from cloud customers' users. Therefore, misbehavior must be detected efficiently. The proposed framework obtains a pseudo-isolation by monitoring threads' flow detecting malicious behavior. This has the benefit for all stakeholders in the cloud ecosystem. The cloud providers can protect their resources. The cloud customers can rely on the providers. The cloud users can trust that their privacy will not be violated. The proposed framework is deployed in the web application level and it can be integrated into any web application server in the PaaS cloud. The proof of concept implementation is realized in a standard JVM with an open source web application server with no source code modifications.

Many machine learning techniques that are good candidates for behavioral calassification are tested and combined in the proposed framework. N-Gram algorithm is utilized as it is helpful to filter the operation sequence to enrich and extract additional sequence features. Measured features are extended with the additional extracted features. Then, the proposed framework classifies the requests as benign or malicious using the combined measured metrics. This structure builds the classification module of the framework and it is built based on the training data. It is observed that, the Random Forest classifier is capable of detecting a malicious request with a probability of 0.87 in this setup.

One of the main flaws of the proposed framework may be the precision of measurements. More precise measurements may lead to better results. Moreover, it could be foreseen that features may be enriched better with better reasoning of the underlying nature of the problem. Then, better classifiers could be found based on selected feature vector. In the near future improved malicious behavior detection frameworks may appear based on more precise measurements and better enriched feature sets. Furthermore, under different configurations of cloud deployments machine learning algorithms or parameters may require to be polished.

References

1. Arshad, J., Townend, P., Xu, J.: An abstract model for integrated intrusion detection and severity analysis for clouds. In: Cloud Computing Advancements in Design, Implementation, and Technologies, vol. 1 (2012)
2. Banerjee, C., Kundu, A., Basu, M., Deb, P., Nag, D., Dattagupta, R.: A service based trust management classifier approach for cloud security. In: 2013 15th International Conference on Advanced Computing Technologies (ICACT), pp. 1–5. IEEE (2013)

3. Bazm, M.M., Lacoste, M., Südholt, M., Menaud, J.M.: Side Channels in the Cloud: Isolation Challenges, Attacks, and Countermeasures, March 2017. https://hal.inria.fr/hal-01591808. Working paper or preprint
4. Bazrafshan, Z., Hashemi, H., Fard, S.M.H., Hamzeh, A.: A survey on heuristic malware detection techniques. In: 2013 5th Conference on Information and Knowledge Technology (IKT), pp. 113–120. IEEE (2013)
5. Breiman, L.: Random forests. Mach. Learn. **45**(1), 5–32 (2001)
6. Fan, Y., Ye, Y., Chen, L.: Malicious sequential pattern mining for automatic malware detection. Expert Syst. Appl. **52**, 16–25 (2016)
7. Garfinkel, T., Rosenblum, M., et al.: A virtual machine introspection based architecture for intrusion detection. In: NDSS, vol. 3, pp. 191–206 (2003)
8. Hamad, H., Al-Hoby, M.: Managing intrusion detection as a service in cloud networks. Int. J. Comput. Appl. **41**(1), 35–40 (2012)
9. Hu, W., Hu, W., Maybank, S.: Adaboost-based algorithm for network intrusion detection. IEEE Trans. Syst. Man Cybern. Part B (Cybern.) **38**(2), 577–583 (2008)
10. Kiczales, G., et al.: Aspect-oriented programming. In: Akşit, M., Matsuoka, S. (eds.) ECOOP 1997. LNCS, vol. 1241, pp. 220–242. Springer, Heidelberg (1997). https://doi.org/10.1007/BFb0053381
11. Mamitsuka, N.A.H., et al.: Query learning strategies using boosting and bagging. In: Machine Learning: Proceedings of the Fifteenth International Conference (ICML 1998), vol. 1 (1998)
12. Modi, C., Patel, D., Borisaniya, B., Patel, H., Patel, A., Rajarajan, M.: A survey of intrusion detection techniques in cloud. J. Netw. Comput. Appl. **36**(1), 42–57 (2013)
13. Networking, C.V.: Ciscoglobal cloud index: forecast and methodology, 2015–2020. White paper (2017)
14. Özdemir, C.D., Sandıkkaya, M.T., Yaslan, Y.: Classifying malicious thread behavior in PaaS web services. In: Proceedings of the 8th International Conference on Cloud Computing and Services Science - vol. 1: CLOSER, pp. 418–425. INSTICC, SciTePress (2018). https://doi.org/10.5220/0006688204180425
15. Pirscoveanu, R.S., Hansen, S.S., Larsen, T.M., Stevanovic, M., Pedersen, J.M., Czech, A.: Analysis of malware behavior: type classification using machine learning. In: 2015 International Conference on Cyber Situational Awareness, Data Analytics and Assessment (CyberSA), pp. 1–7. IEEE (2015)
16. Sandikkaya, M.T., Harmanci, A.E.: A security paradigm for paas clouds. Proc. Rom. Acad. Ser. A Math. Phys. Tech. Sci. Inf. Sci. **16**(2), 345–356 (2015)
17. Sandıkkaya, M.T., Ödevci, B., Ovatman, T.: Practical runtime security mechanisms for an aPaaS cloud. In: Globecom Workshops (GC Wkshps), pp. 53–58. IEEE (2014)
18. Sanjay Ram, M.: Secure cloud computing based on mutual intrusion detection system. Int. J. Comput. Appl. **1**(2), 57–67 (2012)
19. Shabtai, A., Moskovitch, R., Feher, C., Dolev, S., Elovici, Y.: Detecting unknown malicious code by applying classification techniques on opcode patterns. Secur. Inf. **1**(1), 1 (2012)
20. Su, Z., Yang, Q., Lu, Y., Zhang, H.: Whatnext: a prediction system for web requests using n-gram sequence models. In: Proceedings of the First International Conference on Web Information Systems Engineering, vol. 1, pp. 214–221. IEEE (2000)
21. Uppal, D., Sinha, R., Mehra, V., Jain, V.: Malware detection and classification based on extraction of API sequences. In: 2014 International Conference on Advances in Computing, Communications and Informatics (ICACCI), pp. 2337–2342. IEEE (2014)

22. Wu, S.X., Banzhaf, W.: The use of computational intelligence in intrusion detection systems: a review. Appl. Soft Comput. **10**(1), 1–35 (2010)
23. Zhang, Y., Juels, A., Reiter, M.K., Ristenpart, T.: Cross-tenant side-channel attacks in PaaS clouds. In: Proceedings of the 2014 ACM SIGSAC Conference on Computer and Communications Security, pp. 990–1003. ACM (2014)

Author Index

Printed in the United States
By Bookmasters